Understanding Your Teen

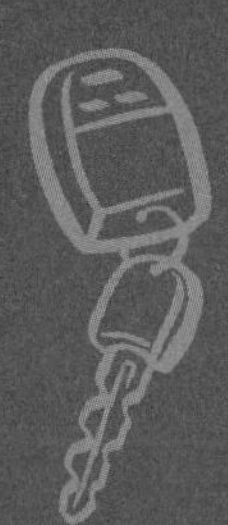

Understanding Your Teen:
Parenting Strategies That Work

EDITOR: CHRISTINE LANGLOIS

CANADIAN LIVING'S HEALTH AND FAMILY EDITOR

In collaboration with the Canadian Paediatric Society and

The College of Family Physicians of Canada

A **Canadian Living** Family Book

Ballantine Books

A Division of Random House of Canada Limited

We are grateful to the following for permission to adapt their material.
Canadian Paediatric Society: page 23
Health Canada: pages 17, 233-35
The College of Family Physicians of Canada: pages 65–69

PROJECT TEAM
Project Editor: Jean Stinson
Assistant Editor: Jaishree Drepaul
Preliminary Research: Quinn Ross
Fact-checking: Laurel Aziz
Cover and book design: Hambly & Woolley Inc.
Cover photograph: Chris Gordaneer, Westside Studios
Brush drawings: Bob Hambly
Photos: Courtesy of generous teens and parents; page 95, Joss Barrett/Masterfile Corporation; page 172, Dick Makin/Masterfile Corporation; page 195, Larry Bray/Masterfile Corporation; page 206, Ian Sanderson/Masterfile Corporation

Publisher: Caren King
Editorial Director: Bonnie Baker Cowan

CANADIAN CATALOGUING IN PUBLICATION DATA
Main entry under title:
Understanding your teen: parenting strategies that work

"A Canadian Living family book"
"In collaboration with the Canadian Paediatric Society and the College of Family Physicians of Canada."
On cover: Complete guide to teen development.
Includes index.
ISBN 0-345-39880-7

1. Teenagers. 2. Parent and teenager. 3. Adolescence.   I. Langlois, Christine (Christine Anne).

HQ769.U52 1999 649'.125 C98-932365-X

Ballantine Books
A Division of
Random House of Canada Limited
2775 Matheson Boulevard East
Mississauga, ON L4W 4P7
Canada

Canadian Living
Telemedia Communications Inc.
25 Sheppard Avenue West
Suite 100
Toronto, ON M2N 6S7
Canada

1999 2000 01 02 03 FP 5 4 3 2 1
Printed and bound in Canada by Friesens

Writers

LYNNE AINSWORTH
CINDY BARRETT
MARCIA KAYE
JOHN KEATING
SUSAN NOAKES
SUSAN PEDWELL
LAURA PRATT
MARK WITTEN

Expert Advisors

CANADIAN PAEDIATRIC SOCIETY
Danielle Grenier MD, FRCPC
Medical Affairs Officer, Canadian Paediatric Society
Diane Sacks MD, FRCPC, FAAP
Assistant Professor, Paediatrics, University of Toronto
    Liaison: Elizabeth Moreau

THE COLLEGE OF FAMILY PHYSICIANS OF CANADA
Carol P. Herbert MD, CCFP, FCFP
Professor and Head, Family Practice, University of British Columbia
Alan Pavilanis AB, MD, CM, CCFP, FCFP
Clinical Assistant Professor, Department of Family Medicine, University of Montreal,
Centre Hospitalier de l'Université de Montréal
    Liaison: Monica Proudler

Meg Hickling RN, *Sexual Health Educator*
Rena Mendelson MS, DSC, RD, *Professor of Nutrition, Ryerson Polytechnic University*
Penny Milton, *Executive Director, Canadian Education Association*
Anne Lindsay, *Nutrition Editor, Canadian Living*
Roger S. Tonkin, MD, CM, FRCPC, OBC
Professor Emeritus, Pediatrics, University of British Columbia
Executive Director, McCreary Centre Society

Contents

Foreword

The teen years are a time of developmental changes as profound as the changes in the first five years of life. Teens are on a physical, emotional, and social roller coaster that their families, especially their parents, ride with them. *Understanding Your Teen: Parenting Strategies That Work* is designed as a guide for parents and young people themselves as they move through puberty and toward adulthood and independent living.

When does adolescence begin? Some say it begins at age thirteen when a child officially enters the teen years; others say that puberty, which can begin some years before, is the gateway to adolescence. My advice to those parents trying to decide if this book will be useful is to start gathering information early so that you can be prepared for the changes in your child, so that you can be proactive rather than reactive. If your child's body is beginning to show the changes of puberty, her emotions are not likely to be far behind.

The team at *Canadian Living* has taken a broad view of health, considering body, mind, heart and soul as the aspects that collectively define a healthy person. This is true at all ages, but especially true in adolescence. Those of us in family medicine, pediatrics, and the other health professions have often failed to meet the health needs of adolescents in the most effective manner because we don't think holistically. More recent improvements in medical tracking of illness and death have increased our awareness of the preventable nature of the major causes of death and disability in young people. In 1994, for example, 128 of 201 teenage deaths in British Columbia resulted from the trauma of accidents and violence. Such findings underline the impact on health of the lifestyle choices that teenagers make. Parents can influence those choices, as can doctors, teachers, and other professionals.

Recent reports about the health needs of adolescents have also told us that young people need educational approaches geared to their developmental stage, and they need open communication not only with their parents but also with the other adults charged with their health care and education. We have learned that when they have a health concern, they are more likely to turn to family, to friends, and to the people with whom they feel comfortable. Young people want to be accorded privacy and confidentiality. They want these confidants to listen to them, to understand them, and to treat them and their concerns with respect. The more knowledge these people have about the issues that face adolescents and about practical approaches to resolving these issues, the more likely they will be able to help.

The Joint Action Committee on Child and Adolescent Health (JACCAH), a joint venture of The College of Family Physicians and the Canadian Paediatric Society, was established in 1997 as a vehicle for physicians to work effectively together to improve the health care of Canada's children and adolescents. We believe that young people are best served when they have a regular source for "first-line" medical care from either a family physician or a pediatrician, or perhaps in a less traditional setting such as a youth clinic. It's important that this first-line health-care professional know the adolescent as a person and know about adolescent health issues. Our committee is pleased to have provided consultation to the talented writers at *Canadian Living* magazine to ensure that the information in this book is accurate and useful. Both The College of Family Physicians of Canada and the Canadian Paediatric Society encourage parents and adolescents to use *Understanding Your Teen* as a resource to partner effectively with your health-care providers in making decisions about health and illness. This resource can help young people obtain the preventive and curative health care that is their right, according to the UN Convention on the Rights of the Child, and that, as Canadian citizens, they deserve.

Carol P. Herbert MD CCFP FCFP
Chair, Joint Action Committee on Child and Adolescent Health

Introduction

I remember that my teenage years sped by with a jumble of emotions, an exquisite balance of anticipation and fear—anticipation of all the possibilities opening up before me and fear about not measuring up to the expectations of my family, my friends, or myself. These are the same emotions I see in my own two teens as they morph into adulthood. Below their all-knowing exterior, teens are fragile creatures. They are hurt easily by a sharp remark, by a friend who stops calling, by a parent or teacher who brushes off their questions. They're so often unsure of themselves. Does she really like me? Do I look attractive? Can I pull off that interview?

If being a teenager has its tough days, parenting a teenager can be tough, too. Although your relationship with your teen is still pivotal in his life, much of his energy is directed toward moving beyond the family to claim his emerging adult self. You won't always be the first person he turns to for advice or comfort or companionship. Sometimes as the parent, you feel uncertain how to break through and let your child know you're there for him. Life with teenagers isn't all angst and mood swings, however. It's also a time of exuberance, high energy, and laughs. Lots of laughs, in fact. One thing many parents notice emerging is a wicked sense of humour that their teens didn't display as children. You can expect much more witty repartee than you ever had with an eight-year-old.

Understanding Your Teen is all about really understanding the developmental needs of teenagers so that you can parent them appropriately. It helps to know that teens sleep late because their circadian clock shifts, not because they're lazy; that teens delight in sarcasm and argument because their ability to think abstractly is developing, not because they're trying to make you crazy; teens need to spend hours and hours with their friends because they're building supports for independent living, not because they don't love you anymore. In fact, your child loves and needs you very much, even when he barely speaks at dinner or appears not to have heard a single word you've said for days.

Understanding Your Teen is also a reality check for us, as parents. We need to know that most teens are sexually active before they graduate from high school; that 80 per cent of kids in grade eleven drink alcohol; that many kids say they don't really like school but go anyway because that's where their friends are. Understanding the world of teenagers helps us respond to them with the information they need. It also gives us a chance to communicate our own views and values, although we realize that our teen may not always choose the path we would choose for her. During the teen years, we need to adopt a parenting style that involves negotiating, not dictating, that gradually loosens the limits so that our child emerges from her teen years as a self-disciplined, independent adult able to make responsible choices for herself.

In editing *Understanding Your Teen,* I was fortunate to work with a team of talented writers and expert advisors who helped ensure that the book is a synthesis of the latest information on adolescent needs at home, at school, and in the community. *Understanding Your Teen* is the third book in the **Canadian Living Family Book** series, following on from *Raising Great Kids* and *Growing with Your Child.* The collaboration of the Canadian Paediatric Society and The College of Family Physicians of Canada on this series has meant that the health and development information is current and consistent with what you'll hear when you visit your family doctor. The information in Family Resources will give you the Canadian organizations and specialized resources you can turn to.

The teen years are turbulent because kids do half their physical growing during adolescence. They experience much emotional, cognitive, and social growth during this time, too, and as a parent it's a wonder to behold. Your awkward, moody thirteen-year-old will quickly become a focused, self-possessed nineteen-year-old with plans for further education or work or travel that may need your support but definitely reflect her personal goals and dreams. So your job during adolescence is to do yourself out of a job. But don't worry. There's a reward in store for you after all your hard work and late nights. Although you will always be her parent, your years of active parenting will be over. Soon you will catch yourself grinning at your all-grown-up child, and you'll know that you've made a friend for life.

Christine Langlois
Toronto, November 1998

Body

1

Your teenager's body is experiencing a rapid metamorphosis from child to adult. Explosive growth fuels a voracious appetite. Your teenage daughter may have already grown to her full height, begun her period, and developed a more womanly shape; your teenage son may just be starting his major growth spurts and showing other signs of puberty. With your support, your teen is learning to take responsibility for all of his physical needs—how best to nourish himself, how much sleep and exercise to get, and how to explore his emerging sexuality.

Adolescence is the time when your child experiences almost half of his physical growth. At the onset of puberty, the central nervous system triggers the release of growth hormones that influence both height and weight. For most thirteen-year-old girls, their growth spurt may be ending, but for many thirteen-year-old boys, their growth spurt may just be beginning.

Girls can start puberty anywhere between the ages of seven and seventeen; some girls might begin their growth spurt at the age of eight, but most experience it at ten or eleven. At whatever age they start, most girls take three to five years to experience all the changes of puberty. Boys start puberty between the ages of eight and thirteen; most begin their growth spurt about age thirteen. Boys take four to six years to pass through all the stages of puberty.

Growth Patterns

The key factor in determining your teen's adult height and weight is her genetic inheritance from her two families of origin. A teen who wonders what she will look like as an adult need only look at her relatives for clues. Nutrition and physical exercise are also factors in growth, and some research has linked children's growth rates to their emotional environments.

It's during adolescence that your teen's body type is revealed. He may be an endomorph, a mesomorph, or an ectomorph. Endomorphs tend to be rounder and have softer curves. Mesomorphs are muscular. Ectomorphs tend to be naturally thin and angular. Kids need to know that these three distinct forms are all normal body types. An endomorph at her ideal weight may look heavier, for example, than an ectomorph friend at her ideal weight.

Nearly all your son's muscles and the bones in his skeleton grow bigger during pubertal growth. The bones of his skull become 15 per cent thicker. The forehead becomes more prominent, the jaw bones grow forward, and facial muscles develop. All these changes are more marked in boys than in girls. During puberty, most of the height gain is achieved through torso growth. This growth occurs after the hands, legs, and feet have grown to full size. Until they are full grown, some young people appear to have large hands and feet for their height. The shoulders and chest are the last body area to reach full size.

By the mid-teen years (about fifteen), boys catch up and surpass girls in physical growth. Before puberty, boys are only slightly taller than girls. After puberty, the average height difference between the sexes is 12.5 cm (5 in.). Aside from height, the most obvious physical distinction between the sexes is the broadening of the shoulders in boys, and the broadening of the hips in girls. These normal differences are caused by the action of sex hormones on the growth of the skeleton.

Girls' physical growth

Over the five or so years of puberty, girls add almost 25 cm (10 in.) and 18 kg (40 lb.) to their physique. When they are growing most quickly, girls add about 9 cm (3.5 in.) and as many as 9 kg (20 lb.) in a single year. Most girls reach 95 per cent of their mature height by the age of thirteen.

Most girls reach 95 per cent of their mature height by the age of thirteen.

During the last phase of puberty, a girl's weight and height continue to increase, but not in spurts, and her weight may increase even after she has reached her full height. A girl's body becomes more curved; her hips and thighs continue to broaden; fat tissue is laid down on the arms, legs, trunk, and buttocks; the bony hollows of the torso fill out. All of this growth means that girls will have the fat stores necessary to carry a baby during pregnancy. At the same time, their faces, necks, and shoulders become slimmer. Girls also gain muscle strength during puberty, but not to the same extent as boys.

Boys' physical growth

Most boys start their puberty growth spurt by the age of thirteen, and over the four- to six-year course of puberty, most boys add 25 cm (10 in.) and 49 kg (107 lb.) to their body. As boys go through puberty, their muscles enlarge and thicken, making their accumulated fat tissue appear to decrease. About age fifteen, the increased muscle strength reaches its peak. When they've finished growing, boys tend to be larger than girls, and most have proportionally longer legs because boys have two extra years of preadolescent growth, a time at which the legs grow the fastest.

Because children can experience stages of puberty both before and after becoming teenagers, the following two sections are repeated from *Raising Great Kids: Ages 6 to 12*, the earlier volume in the **Canadian Living Family Book** series.

Body

Puberty in Boys

Puberty begins for boys as early as the age of eight or as late as age thirteen; it usually takes a boy four to six years to pass through all five stages of pubertal development.

Stage One Internally, male hormones are beginning to flow. Outwardly, you may not notice any growth in height yet.

Stage Two Your son's body shape begins to change as new layers of muscle tissue and fat are formed. His physique starts to become that of a young man, rather than a child. Some boys may gain weight before they grow taller, which might cause them embarrassment. Let your son know that midline plumpness at this age is normal for lots of boys.

Another source of concern and embarrassment may be breast development. Let your son know that men have mammary tissue, too, and that about one-third of boys can expect some swelling under their nipples. This swelling will disappear spontaneously. Some boys worry that they're growing breasts or that they have breast cancer. The areolae of their breasts will also darken and increase in size.

Pubic hair first appears at this stage. A boy's testicles and scrotum begin to grow, and they grow to full size in about three years. His penis begins to grow later and takes several years to reach full adult size. Let your son know about the time difference so that he doesn't worry that his penis will never grow.

Stage Three The penis begins growing, more in length than in width, during this stage. His pubic hair becomes thicker and coarser. His testicles and scrotum continue to develop. Sometimes one testicle grows faster than the other. Assure your son that the difference in growth is normal. Because his testicles produce sperm and his prostate produces semen, your son may experience wet dreams (erotic dreams accompanied by ejaculation). Some boys may be frightened when they first awaken to feel the wet, sticky fluid in their bed, and most keep the news of their nocturnal emissions a secret. During this stage, too, your son will experience spontaneous erections more frequently, not all of them for sexual reasons. He may awake with an erection every morning, but they can also happen at other times, which may cause him embarrassment.

Some boys may begin to show a light sprinkling of facial hair on their upper lip. As his larynx enlarges, a boy's voice also begins to

Boys take four to six years to pass through all five stages of puberty.

change. His muscle tissue increases, his shoulders broaden, and he becomes taller and stronger. He has his most significant growth in height during this period.

Stage Four During Stage Four, a boy's penis begins to broaden, and the testicles and scrotum may continue to grow. Underarm and facial hair increase, and a boy's skin may become oilier. His sweat glands will increase their production of sweat, and body odour may begin to increase.

Stage Five Your son's testicles and penis will have grown to their full size. For most boys, physical growth in height slows, then stops. Some boys develop more body hair, and many begin shaving off facial hair at this stage.

Feelings

Most boys welcome the pubertal changes they're experiencing. They're happy to display bigger muscles, to show off their height and larger sex organs, if only in the locker room. Parents, too, are pleased to see their boys transform into young men. Our society is kinder to boys than to girls during puberty, and parents are less ambivalent toward changes in their sons than they are to the changes in their daughters.

However, parents don't always do a good job of explaining puberty to their boys or of discussing the physical and emotional changes as they occur. Penis growth and wet dreams are much less discussed than breast growth and menstruation. Mothers tend to do most of the talking with kids about pubertal changes, but mothers don't have personal knowledge about how boys change at puberty. Just as fathers may feel awkward discussing menstruation with their daughters, some mothers find themselves uncomfortable talking about wet dreams with their sons. Both of you should find ways to let your son know how his body will change. He needs to know that he can ask either of you any of the questions that concern him.

Boys who begin puberty later than their peers may find the experience very difficult. Assure your son that a late start has no bearing on how he will eventually develop. Also let him know that once he begins puberty, it may unfold more quickly; he may reach full size and maturity about the same time as his friends, even though they started sooner. Late-maturing boys may develop a poor body image and develop negative self-esteem, since they are usually shorter than their peers. Early-maturing boys tend to develop a more positive body image, and both adults and peers may regard them as relaxed and self-confident.

While preparing your son for the physical changes of puberty, prepare him as well for the emotional changes. Boys have mood swings, too, although our society doesn't always acknowledge that. Let him know that he won't always feel such intense emotions. Find ways to show him that you care when he's feeling low. Some kids appreciate a shoulder massage even when they won't let you hug them anymore.

Body

Puberty in Girls

Most thirteen-year-old girls have already gone through their major pubertal changes. The changes that puberty brings occur normally between the ages of seven and seventeen. The journey takes three to five years as your daughter passes through predictable stages of physical development.

Stage One The first outward sign you may notice is a slight growth spurt that could start when your daughter is about eight. Her hips and thighs begin to get wider. She will develop a rounded belly that is her energy store for puberty. The increased growth has been triggered by an increase in hormone production, which is also causing her ovaries to enlarge.

Stage Two Breast development begins. Called "budding," this breast growth begins with "buds" of enlarged tissue underneath the nipples. These buds are often tender to the touch and easily irritated by rough clothing or by jumping up and down. It's common for the two breasts to grow unevenly. One might begin to grow before the other or one might grow faster than the other. Let your daughter know that this may happen so that she's not alarmed. She may also worry that breast swelling is a sign of breast cancer. Reassure her.

"I was one of the first ones to go through puberty. I remember it because it was kind of embarrassing. I was one of only three girls in my class to have breasts. I started to get breasts in grade five, and then I got my period when I was in grade six. When I was one of only three, I kind of felt abnormal. I used to wear baggy clothing to try and hide them. But it's fine now. Right after grade six, right when I went into grade seven, I felt like everyone evened out. That was a great relief."

CATHY, AGE 12

Also during this stage, your child will start to grow more quickly in height, and her weight will increase. Fat deposits will continue to round out the hips and give the appearance of a smaller waist. She will begin to grow pubic hair. Her sweat glands will increase their production of sweat, and she will begin to produce body odour.

Stage Three Breasts grow larger. Pubic hair growth continues and the hair becomes curlier. Armpit hair starts to grow, and the hair on legs and arms gets darker and thicker. She begins to discharge a clear or white fluid from her vagina.

Stage Four Your daughter will likely have her first period during this stage, although it could occur earlier. Often a thick white vaginal discharge precedes her period. Also, her nipples become raised and separated from the areolae of her breasts. The growth pattern of her pubic hair takes on its distinct triangular shape. Her skin and hair may become oilier.

Stage Five At this stage, a girl's breasts have reached full development, and her pubic hair growth is complete. Her growth in height slows, then stops. This stage indicates that your daughter has probably attained her full height and that her menstrual periods probably occur in a regular pattern.

Menstruation

Although her breasts may have begun to develop, her first period may still be a year or more away. The range of normal for girls to begin their periods is between ten and fifteen years of age. Help your daughter get ready for her first period by explaining to her exactly what will happen. She needs to know that her period may start at any time during the day or at night, that it will usually start with a spotting of blood, but that it might start with a heavier flow. You don't want her to be totally surprised when she first sees the reddish or brownish menstrual blood on her underwear.

Make sure she has all the supplies she needs. Buy her a variety of tampons and sanitary pads well before you expect that her period might start. Show her the instructions on how to attach sanitary pads or how to insert a tampon. Suggest that she experiment to find which is most comfortable so that she knows what she's doing before her period starts. She should keep a couple of pads or tampons in her school bag or purse and take supplies with her when she goes away overnight. Let her know that if she chooses tampons, she should usually replace one at least every four hours. Health Canada suggests that a girl not use a tampon overnight. 

Her first periods may be irregular—she may have one period and then not have another for a few months, or she may get them more frequently until her body adapts to the hormonal changes. For most girls, a monthly period lasts four days, but a normal range is from two to eight days. It's common for a girl to have painless cycles (without ovulation) for one or two years after her first period. But some girls experience abdominal cramps before or during their periods; some might even have experienced minor abdominal discomfort before their first period.

Painful menstruation

Dysmenorrhea is the medical term for the painful menstruation that affects every woman at some point in her life and that can sometimes interfere with work or school. The symptoms, which include severe abdominal cramping, headaches, nausea, and vomiting, usually begin just before the menstrual period and last for up to two days. Some women experience a dull abdominal pain extending to the lower back and legs.

If your daughter experiences these symptoms, ensure that she visits her doctor in order to rule out a serious underlying condition such as endometriosis. Most often, fortunately, there is no underlying cause, but her doctor can help find an effective treatment to reduce or eliminate the pain.

He may prescribe medication (to reduce inflammation and ease aches and pains) to take before her period starts and for two days after. Or he may prescribe low-dose oral contraceptives to suppress ovulation and thereby eliminate the symptoms. Some women find that improved nutrition and adequate sleep and exercise help reduce painful menstrual periods.

Premenstrual syndrome

Premenstrual syndrome (PMS) encompasses symptoms (such as bloating, cramps, mood swings, irritability, acne, and breast tenderness) that begin seven to fourteen days before a girl's menstrual period. These symptoms are not very common in teens, but they have been linked to fluctuating hormones; if your daughter experiences them, she should consult her doctor. Managing stress, exercising, and changing one's diet can ease the severity of PMS. Reducing caffeine can ease breast soreness and irritability. Reducing salt can ease bloating.

Let your daughter know that she may also experience mood swings. Her feelings—both positive and negative—may be more intense than earlier in her life. She may cry or laugh more easily or have more difficulty controlling her anger. She may find it harder to concentrate. Suggest she record some of the emotional and physical experiences of her period so that she gets to know what to expect of her own body's menstrual cycle.

Feelings

Much has been written in recent years about girls in early adolescence. Because our society tends to value a very limited and mostly unattainable ideal of female attractiveness, the pubertal changes that turn girls into women can frighten some girls, and they may not welcome the changes at all. Others may find that their self-esteem is shaken, and they may be prone to eating disorders, addictions, depression, even suicide. Parents may find that they need to help their daughters talk through their volatile emotions during this time so that they not only accept the inevitable changes of puberty but also welcome and celebrate them.

A girl and her parents may all have mixed feelings about the beginning of her period. Your daughter will be curious and a little excited about this mysterious new level of physical maturity. At the same time, she may not be happy about the physical discomfort and inconveniences. She may feel irritated or even intensely embarrassed by the necessity of changing pads or tampons regularly and making sure she has everything she needs with her all the time. These feelings may increase if she's an early bloomer whose period starts at age nine or ten, or just earlier than her friends start theirs. Let her know that you understand her feelings.

A girl's reactions to her first period depend largely on what she learns about it beforehand and on the support she receives from family members. You may feel sad that your child is no longer "a little girl," but your daughter's first period is an important rite of passage. She will likely

Your daughter will become more emotionally independent as well as physically mature.

become more emotionally independent as well as physically mature. Some mothers find they have a strong emotional reaction to their daughter's first period. If, as a teenager, you had difficult menstrual periods yourself, you may worry that your daughter may experience the same discomfort. You should be aware that your own menses history is not any prediction of your daughter's experiences.

Dads may feel unsure about how to relate to their daughters. In some families, menstruation may be a taboo topic between the females and males. But daughters need to know at least that their fathers know about menses, and that they can help. If your daughter wants to tell her mother when her period starts but Mom's not available, Dad needs to be prepared to support his daughter, even to go out and buy pads if she needs them.

"Did I talk to my daughters about their periods when they got them? Are you kidding? When my daughters got their periods, there was no way I would say anything to them at all. I wouldn't even acknowledge it. My wife told me about it. It's a fact of life, sure. But I think they would have been incredibly embarrassed for me to say anything to them about it. And I know I would have been. I couldn't imagine a family where the father and daughters talked openly about that kind of stuff. Of course, a few years have passed now, and there's not the awkwardness around the subject anymore. Today, it's like, 'Dad, will you pick me up some pads?' and no one blinks an eye."

BOB, FATHER OF TWO

Personal Care

Some young teens avoid the commonly accepted routines of personal care: regular showers, twice-a-day teeth brushing, clean socks and underwear. Although your child's body is maturing (she menstruates, she sweats, and her skin is oilier), she may decide that she doesn't want to shower more than twice a week. In fact, twice a week is the average for early teens. Some shower less often, particularly boys.

What are parents to do? As with most everything else during this phase of your child's life, accept that she can make more decisions on her own, and negotiate, don't demand. It's her changing body, after all. Offer to pick up a favourite shampoo. Stock up on deodorizing insoles, and when the TV room takes on the odour of smelly feet, suggest that your teen use them.

> The aversion to soap and water is of relatively short duration in a teen's life.

The aversion to soap and water is of relatively short duration in a teen's life. By the time they're fourteen or so, most girls would no more go out of the house with greasy hair than they would go to school with a bag over their head. Boys may avoid soap and water a little longer, but by about age sixteen, they no longer fight the daily shower. Share the following information with them.

Sweat glands

Sweat glands are activated during puberty, producing a substance that interacts with bacteria to cause body odour. Body odour occurs mostly in the underarms, around the genitals, and in the feet. Physical exertion and psychological stress can cause sweating. Lots of teenagers get clammy hands or break out in a sweat when they're nervous. Deodorants (designed to mask odour) and antiperspirants (designed to mask odour and prevent wetness) can help, although they're not a replacement for regular bathing, as some teens seem to think. Letting the body cool down after a hot shower before applying deodorant or antiperspirant will make either more effective.

Shaving

Most teenage boys start showing facial hair between the ages of fourteen and sixteen. The first growth is usually on the outer edges of the upper lip. Moustaches fill in toward the centre. Soft hair on the upper cheeks and just below the centre of the lower lip appears next. Sideburns may also grow at this time. Chin hair grows in last. With your teen's maturation, his facial hair grows thicker and darker.

Some young men show the full extent of their potential beard by the time they're eighteen. Others don't develop their full facial beard until ten years after puberty. A young man's first razor is an important rite of passage that acknowledges his transition to a new stage of maturity. Some teens have to shave every day; others rarely need to pick up a razor. Both are normal.

For girls, shaving is also a rite of passage. Girls often begin shaving their legs and underarms as soon as the hair grows in during puberty. Since shaving does not affect the rate of hair growth or how thick it becomes, you might just respect your daughter's choice.

Dental hygiene

When they take on responsibility for remembering to brush and floss their teeth, teens can sometimes get lax about dental hygiene—which can lead to bad breath and cavities. Between the ages of thirteen and sixteen, a teen's teeth are particularly prone to cavities.

You may have to continue to remind your teen to brush and floss his teeth, but beware—too much nagging can be counterproductive. But one measure you can take is to keep making regular appointments for him; your dentist and dental hygienist can reinforce the advantages of regular daily brushing and flossing as a means of avoiding other treatments on either teeth or gums in later years.

Your child will be very conscious of any acne that develops because of hormonal changes.

Acne

The hormonal changes of puberty increase production from the oil glands in the skin of the face, scalp, neck, chest, and back, which means that many teens develop acne. The glands of the hair follicles in the skin produce an oily substance (sebum) that combines with dead cells and tiny hair remnants to plug the follicle. Under the skin surface, the plug forms a bump, a *whitehead*. If the plug opens to the skin surface, it darkens to form a *blackhead*. If the wall of the plugged follicle ruptures, the area becomes a red and swollen bump. If the follicle wall breaks near the skin surface, it may become a *pimple*. If the follicle wall breaks beneath the skin, *cysts* can form, which may cause scarring.

Acne tends to run in families, and occurs most commonly between the ages of fourteen and seventeen. For some teens, it may last for a year or two. For others, acne persists throughout their teenage years. Acne is common in both genders, but boys may suffer more severely because

they have more skin oils. Girls often find that their acne flares at certain points in their menstrual cycle because of hormone activity. Although some people believe that chocolate, greasy snacks, and salty foods can aggravate acne, there is no scientific evidence to support the belief. However, if you notice that certain foods aggravate your teen's acne, then eliminating them might help.

There are no foolproof cures for acne, but every case can be treated and improved. It's important to seek medical help early to avoid scarring. If your teen has acne, consult your family doctor, who may refer you to a dermatologist. Topical treatments are effective for a lot of teens, as are systemic antibiotics for others. For milder cases, washing all the areas affected by acne no more than twice a day with a special soap can help. Washing too often can irritate the skin, causing more outbreaks. Girls with acne should avoid perfumed and oil- or alcohol-based makeup and facial lotions.

Treatments

There are different treatments available that bring improvement within a few weeks or months. Be prepared to stay with a treatment for at least two months before deciding it doesn't work. Acne treatments are meant to prevent future outbreaks rather than clear up the pimples that have already occurred.

Benzoyl peroxide is available as a cream, gel, lotion, or soap, and can be bought without a prescription, but your doctor should recommend the most suitable strength and frequency for your teen's type of acne.

Antibiotics: Your doctor may prescribe an oral antibiotic, or one available in cream (least drying), lotion (less drying), or gel (most drying) form. For them to be effective, your teen must follow closely the directions for use.

Tretinoin (Retin-A, Stieva-A) is applied to the skin once daily. With this treatment, the skin may appear to get worse before it gets better, usually in several weeks. The teen must avoid the sun or use a strong sunscreen during treatment.

Isotretinoin (Accutane) is usually prescribed to treat severe cases of acne, particularly cystic acne. Although this treatment is very effective, a young woman should know that if she becomes pregnant while under treatment, the drug can cause a miscarriage or birth defects.

Tattoos and Body Piercing

A glance around most high-school cafeterias will confirm that tattooing and body piercing are popular features of teen culture. If your teen wants to undergo one of these procedures, ensure that the decision she makes is an informed one because all body piercing and tattoos involve some risk to health and require regular maintenance.

In their teens, most kids begin to take responsibility for their own health care.

Your teen must consider whether or not she'll be able to deal with any lifestyle changes that may result. During the healing time for a bellybutton pierce, for example, she may not be able to sleep in certain positions or wear certain clothes. If she chooses to have lip or tongue piercing, she may find it painful to eat or speak until it's healed. A piercing could also affect her participation in her favourite sports: Some kinds of piercing will be snagged during contact sports; during the healing period, she won't be able to remove a bellybutton ring to go swimming. If she gets an eyebrow ring or a visible tattoo, will it affect her chances of getting a job?

You might suggest that your teen first try a removable tattoo or a clip-on ring for nose, lip, or bellybutton. These are less expensive, pose few health risks, and are widely available in many fashion accessory stores. If your teen decides to proceed, make sure that he chooses a reputable tattoo or piercing parlour. If he is under eighteen, most parlours will refuse to serve him without your written permission or without speaking to you in person.

You or your teen should make sure that the technician is qualified and that the parlour is clean. Inquire about safety procedures: All needles, forceps, and similar equipment should come from a sealed, sterile package and not be re-used. Inquire about the kind of jewellery to be inserted

in the opening; to reduce infection, all body jewellery for new piercing should be 316L or LVM surgical stainless steel, solid gold (14K or higher), niobium, or titanium. The technician should also provide written instructions about any after-care required to avoid infections. The healing time for most piercing ranges from several weeks to a year or longer.

Solo Health Care

Your children are ready to take charge of their own health care when they're mature enough to ask questions of all health-care providers and to comprehend and deal in a responsible fashion with the information provided. In order to build a trusting relationship with your adolescent, the doctor will usually make a point to mention that their discussions will remain confidential.

In most Canadian provinces and territories, children as young as twelve can choose not to have their parents accompany them either when they go to their doctor or when they go into the doctor's examining room. They may also consent to a treatment if doctors believe them capable of understanding the implications of the treatment. In Quebec, the age is fourteen years and older, and parents have to be informed if the youth is admitted to hospital for more than twelve hours.

At the Children's & Women's Health Centre of British Columbia in Vancouver, health-care professionals say that children aged twelve and older are capable of deciding whether they want to pursue a recommended treatment. This policy grew out of the efforts of health professionals to deal with sexually transmitted diseases (STDs). If the matter is debatable, the case may go to the hospital's Ethics Committee.

Parents should have begun talking with their children at an early age about all aspects of bodily health so that nothing develops into a taboo subject between them. Single parents need to inform themselves about the health concerns of their opposite-sex child. Most kids want to talk to their parents about personal health issues that concern them; they just don't want to get a lecture. When it seems to you that your children are mature enough to handle a visit to the family doctor on their own, discuss with them whether they would like you to accompany them or to remain in the waiting room. Let them know that you respect their privacy, and that you'll understand if they want their discussion with the doctor to be private. You may still talk separately with the doctor about your own concerns after the examination.

A teenage girl by age eighteen or earlier if sexually active should include a Pap smear in her annual physical. This is a short and simple test to detect possible cancerous cells in the cervix. Because cells undergo a series of changes before they become cancerous, the analysis of the Pap smear will reveal any pre-cancer cell changes. To ensure greater accuracy of test results, a woman should not douche, should not use birth control creams or feminine deodorants for 48 hours before the appointment, and should not have sexual intercourse for 24 hours before her physical.

Ensure your daughter understands how her doctor will obtain the sample of cervical cells for the test. She will insert the instrument called a speculum into her vagina to open it wide enough to touch the cervix with the tip of a cotton swab, transfer the sample to a glass slide, and send it to a laboratory to be analyzed for abnormalities.

Although Pap smears are not 100 per cent accurate, the procedure has greatly reduced the number of deaths from cervical cancer detected too late for treatment. When the Pap test results are positive, it means that abnormal cells are present 95 per cent of the time. If the results are positive, your doctor will want to discuss the implications of the cell changes and the necessary treatment. Abnormal cells on the cervix indicate not only cervical cancer but also infections such as herpes and human papilloma virus (HPV).

> **Ensure your daughter understands how her doctor will obtain a Pap smear.**

Self-examinations

Some teens may want to establish a routine of monthly self-examinations for signs of problems. Although breast cancer is very rare among women under twenty, teenage girls who perform regular exams of their own breasts will become familiar with the exercise and the feel of a normal healthy breast. Your daughter should do this while sitting or standing, and use a circular, massaging motion with one hand over the breast and her other arm raised above her head. If she has any concerns, she should discuss them with her doctor.

Boys in their late teenage years might also learn to do a regular check for testicular cancer, which is very rare at this age. They should check each of their testicles individually for the presence of a lump, soreness, or tenderness, and discuss any concerns (abnormal lumps, discharge from the penis) with their doctor.

Daily Nutritional Requirements

The eating habits of teenagers are often rather strange, and teens take nutritional risks. They may miss family meals and fill up on fast food; they may skip breakfast and experiment with supplements. Some girls cut calories to lose weight; some boys pack in calories to gain weight. In brief, they've turned a corner and realized that they can do whatever they want with their bodies. But don't point out to your son that he's living on grease. A parent's direct criticism of what a teen eats is not usually effective. Your job is to provide a variety of nutritious foods and then back off. Teens should be allowed to decide what and how much to eat.

Lay out wholesome breakfast foods, provide nutritious snacks that they can tuck into a backpack, and set regular dinner times. Teens may act savvy, but they still rely on their parents for meeting their nutritional needs. They also look to parents for nutritional guidance. Look for the "teachable moment." When you're both sitting at the breakfast table gazing at the cereal boxes, point out the nutrition information. Compare and see which cereal scores highest in iron, fibre, and the B vitamins. If, after a night of bingeing on snack foods, she feels nauseous, help her make the connection between the food she eats and her physical and mental well-being.

Teens need to aim for the maximum number of servings suggested in Canada's Food Guide to Healthy Eating to get the basic nutrients they need. However, the diets of many Canadian teens are low in both calcium and iron. Growing teenagers, male and female, need the maximum number of servings of milk products for calcium and the maximum of meat products for iron.

The importance of calcium

During adolescence, kids grow faster than at any time except infancy; in fact, half of their growth occurs in this period. They need calcium-rich foods, such as dairy products, to help build strong, healthy bones. A calcium deficit during childhood and adolescence might never be fully overcome in later years. Reducing or eliminating milk products during this all-important growth spurt could mean that your child will fail to reach her growth potential, and may contribute to her developing osteoporosis in later life.

Canada's Food Guide to Healthy Eating recommends that youths aged ten through sixteen have 3 to 4 servings of milk products a day. After age sixteen, it's 2 to 4 servings. Examples of one serving are: 250 mL (one cup) of milk, 50 g (2 slices) of processed cheese, 50 g (1 in. x 1 in. x 3 in.) cube of cheese, or 175 mL (¾ cup) of yogurt or ice cream. A single serving of milk packs a big nutritional punch: as much protein as a large Grade A egg, almost as much potassium as a banana, 45 per

Canada's Food Guide to Healthy Eating

Enjoy a variety of foods from each group every day. Choose lower-fat foods more often.

	Daily Servings	
Grain Products	5–12	Choose whole grain and enriched products more often.
Vegetables & Fruit	5–10	Choose dark green and orange vegetables and orange fruit more often.
Milk Products		Choose lower-fat milk products more often.
Ages 4–9	2–3	
Ages 10–16	3–4	
Adults	2–4	
Meat & Alternatives	2–3	Choose leaner meats, poultry, and fish, dried peas, beans, and lentils more often.

Note: Taste and enjoyment can also come from other foods and beverages that are not part of the four food groups. This category includes higher-fat, higher-calorie foods like soft drinks and chocolate bars that add little more than energy to a diet, so use these foods in moderation.

Different People Need Different Amounts of Food

The amount of food you need every day from the four food groups depends on your age, body size, activity level, growth rate, appetite, and whether you are male or female. For example, young children can choose the lower number of servings, while male teenagers can go to the higher number.

Examples of one serving:

Grain Products
1 slice of bread
30 g cold cereal
175 mL (¾ cup) hot cereal
½ bagel, pita, or bun
125 mL (½ cup) pasta or rice

Milk Products
250 mL (1 cup) milk
50 g (2 oz. or 2 slices) cheese
175 g (¾ cup) yogurt

Vegetables & Fruit
1 medium-size vegetable or fruit
125 mL (½ cup) fresh, frozen, or canned
250 mL (1 cup) salad
125 mL (½ cup) juice

Meat & Alternatives
50–100 g (2–4 oz.) meat, fish or poultry
1–2 eggs
125–250 mL (½–1 cup) beans
100 g (⅓ cup) tofu
30 mL (2 tbsp.) peanut butter

Adapted from Canada's Food Guide to Healthy Eating, Health Canada, 1992. With permission of the Minister of Public Works and Government Services Canada, 1998.

Body

cent of the daily requirement for vitamin D—a total of 25 nutrients in all. Vitamin D is essential to the proper absorption and utilization of calcium, which is why milk is fortified with vitamin D.

But in spite of this, many teens start to snub milk and substitute cola for the milk they used to drink. Some teens drink 2 L a day, as if addicted to cola. Caffeine—whether it's in cola, coffee, or tea—may increase one's excretion of calcium. If your teen drinks cola instead of milk, his store of calcium is reduced both by not consuming milk products and possibly by leaching the calcium out of his body. Don't challenge the cola-crazy teen, but don't put cola on your shopping list either. Pour a glass of milk for him at dinner. If he doesn't drink it, try chocolate milk the next day; the nutrients from milk are still there.

> **During adolescence, kids grow faster than at any time except infancy; in fact, half of their growth occurs in this period.**

Stock your fridge with tubs of yogurt and your freezer with frozen yogurt and ice cream, ready for teens to grab when hunger strikes. Tuck individual servings of cheese, pudding, yogurt, or yogurt beverages into your teen's lunch bag. Try the following ideas to increase your whole family's calcium intake:

> Begin the day with a fruit frappé or milkshake. Make it "to go" if your teen is running late for school.
> Add a slice of cheese to a lunch sandwich.
> For an after-school snack, have fruit and a yogurt dip.
> Make hot chocolate (with milk) on frosty days. Make milkshakes on hot days.
> Dilute condensed soups with milk, not water.
> Crown casseroles with a bubbly cheese topping.
> Grate cheese over salads.

> Pour cheese sauce over steamed broccoli or cauliflower.
> Serve quiche, cheese soufflé, and cheesy pasta dishes often.
> Add skim-milk powder to meat loaf, mashed potatoes, casseroles, and baked goods. Just 15 mL (1 tbsp.) of skim-milk powder contains 70 mg of calcium.
> Serve a cheese tray with crackers and apple and pear slices as dessert.

> Make a milk dessert—pudding, tapioca, rice pudding, or baked custard.
> Use evaporated milk when baking. It has double the calcium of regular fresh milk.

Ironing out the differences

A diet that's low in iron can lead to decreased immune function, loss of energy, and a reduced capacity for learning. It can also lead to iron-

You may find it hard to keep enough milk in the house during your kid's peak growing years.

deficiency anemia, which is characterized by a pale complexion, list-lessness, and irritability. During adolescence, the incidence of iron deficiency decreases in boys but increases in girls. Girls can be low in iron because of dieting; eating inadequate amounts of meat, poultry, and fish; and increased iron losses due to menstruation. Experts offer widely different estimates on the percentage (from 29 to 84 per cent) of young Canadian women who don't meet the recommended nutrient intake (RNI) for iron.

Meat, fish, and poultry contain heme iron (from animal blood), which is more easily absorbed and used by the body than the iron in vegetables and grains. However, heme iron and vitamin C enhance the body's ability to absorb the iron in grains and vegetables. To increase your family's iron intake:

➤ Pick whole-grain cereals and iron-fortified cereals. Read the nutrition panel on the label, and check the amount of iron (sometimes identified as *ferrous sulfate*) listed; choose ones that also have fibre—oatmeal is among the best.

➤ Choose whole-wheat breads to make school lunches.

➤ For an after-school snack, bake bran muffins chock full of raisins and dried apricots.

➤ Serve meat, fish, and poultry often.

➤ Add red kidney beans to casseroles.

Body

Now is the time for your child to gradually reduce the amount of fat in her diet.

Gradually reducing fat

Adolescence is a step-down period from the higher-fat diet of childhood to the lower-fat diet of adults. Reduce the fat component of your meals gradually so that by the time your teens achieve their full growth potential, their fat intake includes the same lower-fat foods appropriate for the adults in the family.

During their growth phases, many teens need the calories of higher-fat foods. As a concentrated source of calories, nutritious higher-fat foods such as peanut butter and cheese are particularly important to vegetarians, kids involved in sports, and teens who can't seem to find the time to eat. The Canadian Paediatric Society (CPS) has concluded that people should not eliminate or restrict foods that are nutritious just because of their fat content. This message from the CPS differs from that of the Committee of Nutrition of the American Academy of Pediatrics (AAP), which suggests that parents start cutting back on fat, saturated fat, and cholesterol for their children after the age of two. The CPS, however, cites cases of parents, overzealous in their reduction of fat intake, whose children have suffered delayed growth and delayed puberty because of the misapplication of dietary advice meant for adults, not children.

Vitamin and Mineral Supplements

A study of over 200 kids aged eight to fifteen in Saskatoon revealed that 36 per cent take vitamin or mineral supplements. However, only 14 per cent consistently use the same supplement throughout the year. Beta-carotene may have been the rage last month. Now zinc's hot. Adolescence is a time to experiment, and the multi-billion-dollar supplement industry is ready to supply their desires.

> **A daily supplement won't substitute for the hundreds of nutrients supplied by a balanced diet.**

Teens who eat the number of servings recommended in Canada's Food Guide don't need vitamin and mineral supplements. But a daily supplement containing 100 per cent or less of the RNI of vitamins and minerals is usually safe. If your teen's meals are particularly erratic, it may even do a little good, but it won't substitute for the hundreds of nutrients supplied by a balanced diet of real foods.

It's when kids self-prescribe individual vitamins that they can get into trouble. Supplements of a single nutrient may interfere with the absorption of other nutrients. For example, if he takes large doses of zinc over a prolonged period of time, your son could become deficient in iron and copper. As a general rule, the water-soluble vitamins B and C can be taken without major health hazards because you excrete the excess in your urine. But no vitamins, even the water-soluble ones, are safe in excess.

If your teen takes various supplements, help her to determine safe amounts.

Help your teen determine if the dosage she's taking is within healthy limits. Ask her to consider consulting your doctor or a dietitian at the public health department. Diet books and infomercials offer a lot of contradictory and inaccurate information, so she needs help in selecting information from reputable sources. If your daughter has thrown caution to the wind and is consuming a cocktail of supplements, it's time to intervene—her health is at risk. Of particular concern are mega-doses (more than five times the recommended adult dose) of the following nutrients:

Vitamin A At 25,000 International Units (IU) a day, vitamin A can cause serious liver damage, hair loss, and bone and joint pain. If there's a chance your daughter may be or could become pregnant, more than 10,000 IU increases the risk of birth defects.

If your teen drinks only unfluoridated bottled water, she may need a fluoride supplement to ensure strong teeth.

Vitamin D Prolonged use of 2,000 IU of vitamin D a day can cause nausea, high blood pressure, and kidney damage.

Niacin At 2,000 mg a day, niacin can cause an irregular heartbeat and liver damage. However, some people experience headaches, flushing, cramps, and nausea with just 50 mg a day.

Selenium Over 150 mcg a day of this antioxidant mineral may cause baldness and nail and tooth loss.

The fluoride question

Health Canada, the Canadian Paediatric Society (CPS), and the Canadian Dental Association (CDA) all agree that a fluoridated water supply is the most effective, cost-efficient means of preventing dental caries. The CPS recommends that children be given fluoride supplements if they live in an area where there is little or no fluoride in the water supply.

If you're unsure whether your tap water is fluoridated, contact your municipal office. The level of fluoride will be identified in parts per million (ppm). Bottled water generally has very low fluoride content.

If you use bottled water, read the labels. Also take into account the proportion of tap water to bottled water that your child uses. The chart below shows the CPS's recommended dosages.

Canadian Paediatric Society Fluoride Guide for Children Ages 6 to 16			
Fluoride concentration in principal source of drinking water	<0.3 ppm	0.3–0.6 ppm	>0.6 ppm
Amount of fluoride supplement needed, per day.	1.0 mg/day	0.5 mg/day	0 mg/day

In contrast, dentists through the CDA recommend fluoride supplements for children aged six to thirteen only when the fluoride in the water supply is less than 0.3 ppm. For them, it recommends 1.0 mg a day, as does the CPS. But the CDA is wary of recommending fluoride supplements when the fluoride concentration in drinking water is at the higher levels. Too much fluoride causes dental fluorosis, which in its mildest form causes white flecking on the teeth. In its severest form, fluorosis causes pitting and brown staining of the teeth. The CDA believes that children may be getting more fluoridated water from other sources than home, such as at school or in bottled water. The CPS recommends that teens continue to limit the amount of toothpaste with fluoride per brushing to the size of a pea; that they spit it out, not swallow it; and that they rinse thoroughly after brushing.

> **If you use bottled water, check the labels for fluoride concentration.**

The fluoride supplements are available in drops, chewable tablets, and lozenges. Chewable tablets or lozenges are recommended because the primary action of fluoride is topical. Regular dental checkups usually include a fluoride application to the teeth after a cleaning by the dental hygienist. Be sure to keep fluoride supplements in a locked cabinet away from younger children, because swallowing 230 to 500 mg of fluoride can be fatal.

Eating Vegetarian

The vegetarian movement is sweeping across Canada, and teenage girls are leading the way. Most often, they're drawn to vegetarianism because of animal rights issues. They object to the way agribusiness enterprises treat animals in farm factories. They don't want to eat anything that involves killing an animal.

Be alert to an interest in vegetarianism that may mask an eating disorder. If your teen shows a persistent preoccupation with her weight and shape and is unwilling to eat foods like nuts, seeds, and legumes (chickpeas, beans, lentils) because they are higher in fat, consider whether she may be developing an eating disorder. If her vegetarianism is philosophical or political, she will not exclude high-protein, high-fat nutritious foods like nuts and seeds. Vegetarian foods usually offer more fibre and less fat and are also more economical than meats. Compared with meat-eaters, vegetarians are more likely to have healthy weights, and they have a reduced risk of heart disease, Type II diabetes, osteoporosis, hypertension, and some types of cancer. But if your "vegetarian" is eating erratically and nibbling only on lettuce leaves and carrot sticks, she's not a vegetarian—she may be developing an aversion to food.

> **Teenage girls are the main players in the vegetarian movement sweeping across the country.**

What's Your Type?

Your teen will likely experiment with various forms of vegetarianism before committing to one. The following are common types of vegetarianism:

Partial or semi-vegetarian Consumes limited amounts of meat, fish, poultry, dairy products, and eggs.

Lacto-ovo vegetarian Consumes dairy products and eggs, but no other animal products.

Lacto vegetarian Consumes dairy products, but no eggs or other animal products.

Ovo vegetarian Consumes eggs, but no dairy products or other animal products.

Vegan Consumes no animal products of any kind, including the eggs from poultry, the milk from mammals, and the gelatine from bone marrow.

Nutrition check for lacto-ovo vegetarians

If your daughter is a lacto-ovo vegetarian, she usually won't have a problem getting enough protein. However, she must take care to obtain adequate calories, iron, and zinc.

Calories Vegetarian diets tend to be high in fibre, so a teen might feel full before she has enough calories to meet her energy needs. The adolescent years are important ones for their physical and mental growth and development, so choose lots of energy-dense foods such as nuts, cheese, peanut butter, dried fruits, and tahini (a paste made from ground sesame seeds).

Iron Vegetarians can get sufficient iron in their diet if it includes iron-rich foods like seeds and nuts, legumes, egg yolks, iron-enriched breakfast cereals, tofu, dried fruit like raisins, dark green vegetables like broccoli, enriched pasta, brown rice, wheat germ, and blackstrap molasses. To increase your intake of iron from these sources, eat them with foods rich in vitamin C: citrus fruits, broccoli, cauliflower, potatoes, green peppers, tomatoes, or cantaloupe. Pace your beverages. Avoid drinking cola, coffee, tea, or hot chocolate at mealtime, because the caffeine in them decreases your body's ability to absorb the iron from other foods.

Zinc Good sources of zinc for the vegetarian teen include sprouts, legumes, roasted nuts, eggs, and dairy products.

Integrating Vegetarian Choices

Your family may already enjoy some vegetarian dishes, such as split-pea soup, baked beans, macaroni and cheese, pancakes, omelettes, meatless chili, and quiche. One way to accommodate a vegetarian in the family is to prepare more vegetarian meals.

- Make tacos with refried beans instead of ground beef.
- Add chickpeas instead of ham to rice dishes.
- Order vegetarian pizza instead of pepperoni pizza.
- Replace the nutrients your family would get from meat with the nutrients from legumes, seeds, nuts, eggs, and dairy products.
- When you make a stir-fry, remove some vegetables for your teen and mix them with tofu in a separate dish, before adding chicken for the rest of the family.
- When you're barbecuing burgers, toss on a veggie burger for your teen.
- When you bake potatoes, make your vegetarian teen's potato a main course. Pile on the cheese, sour cream, and green onions. She might even have "bacon bits," which don't contain a speck of real bacon but do contain TVP (textured vegetable protein).
- When you prepare a casserole, divide it into portions before adding the tuna or chicken. In your teen's casserole, add kidney beans or a couple of sliced tofu wieners.
- Offer all the possible variations of pasta or noodle dishes.

Turning Vegan

Just when you've mastered integrating the needs of a lacto-ovo vegetarian into your family meals, your teen announces that she has turned vegan. She explains that although people who drink milk and eat eggs don't kill animals, they do exploit them, and she just doesn't want to be part of it. Vegans eat no meat, eggs, milk or milk products, honey, or gelatine (which comes from the skin, bone marrow, and connective tissue of animals). Purist vegans also avoid using other animal products. They don't wear or use products made from leather, wool, or down. Some will not use glycerine soap (from animal fat) or moisturizing lotion containing lanolin (from sheep's wool), and they won't wear silk (made by silk worms).

"The hardest thing about being vegan is arguing with people who think it's an unnatural way to live. I had to change doctors because my doctor was giving me such a hard time about it. A few of my friends are the worst. They're carnivores and eat hamburgers all the time. It doesn't bother me that they eat meat, but they get mad because I refuse to go inside a McDonald's."

DENISE, AGE 18

Dining out with a vegan can get complicated. At some fast-food restaurants, the only thing a vegan can order is a tossed salad. But she can have fries if they're deep-fried in vegetable oil. If you know your daughter and her friends are heading for the local fast-food hangout, suggest she eat before "going out to dinner." But take her vegan commitment as an opportunity for the family to explore different restaurants. Indian restaurants serve many curried vegetable-only dishes, and Chinese restaurants excel at tofu stir-fries and other vegetable-only dishes.

Nutrition check for vegans

As a vegan, your teen faces even more concerns about adequate nutrition. Not only does she need your help to ensure she receives sufficient energy, iron, and zinc, but also sufficient calcium, protein, and vitamins B_{12} and D.

Calcium Good vegan sources of calcium include tofu made with a calcium compound such as calcium sulphate, broccoli, kale, sesame butter, and almonds. Soy milk is now calcium-fortified.

Protein Choose whole-grain breads, nuts, nut butters, chickpeas, hummus (made from chickpeas), lentils, and soybean products like tofu. It was once believed that only by combining specific plant foods in the same meal would you consume a complete protein. Now dietitians know that if you eat different plant foods over the course of the day, you absorb all the amino acids needed for a complete protein.

Vitamin B_{12} Because plants contain no vitamin B_{12}, a vegan will need a daily supplement of 1.0 mcg of B_{12} to prevent a deficiency. (This dosage is available in most multivitamins.) Another way a vegan can get B_{12} is by choosing soy milk for breakfast cereals or simulated meat products fortified with B_{12}.

Vitamin D Chemicals in the skin form this vitamin when your body is exposed to the sun. The climate from November to March or April in most of Canada doesn't guarantee enough sunshine for people to produce adequate vitamin D, so Health Canada regulations ensure that milk and margarine are fortified with vitamin D. If your vegan child spends less than 15 minutes per day outdoors (without sunscreen) or lives in the Far North, where sunlight is limited, he needs a supplement containing 2.5 mcg of vitamin D daily.

Transferring responsibility

If your thirteen-year-old has become a vegetarian, it's up to you to ensure that she receives adequate nutrition. But it's up to her to decide whether or not it's OK to eat marshmallows, which contain gelatine. Encourage an older teen to learn all she can about vegetarianism through a local vegetarian association (some have youth groups) or by taking vegetarian cooking classes. If she does a school project on vegetarianism, she'll also have to get down to the details.

If your teen has become a vegan or if you're concerned about her nutrition, consult a dietitian. Contact Dietitians of Canada for the name and number of a dietitian working in your area. Their usual rate is about $60 an hour. If your daughter's doctor refers you to a dietitian who works in a hospital or a community clinic, there is usually no charge.

Encourage your vegetarian to learn as much as possible about balanced nutrients in meal preparation.

Filling the Bottomless Pit

With many teens, you don't have to worry that snacking will ruin their appetite for dinner. Teenagers have a knack for constantly snacking yet being constantly hungry. No matter how many bags of groceries you lug into the house, they still groan, "There's nothing to eat."

The key is to plan snacks that are as nutritious as the meals you plan. After you've helped them make their school lunches, don't stop. Before you head off to work, consider what your kids will eat after school. If you don't plan wholesome snacks, they'll head to the variety store for a bag of potato chips or grab a stack of chocolate chip cookies at home to fend off hunger. You may think that's OK because your teens are still a healthy weight, but eating a lot of chips and cookies in their teen years forms poor eating habits that are hard to change and could lead to weight gain after their growth period.

The average teen will eat whatever you bring home, so avoid buying snack foods that aren't nutritious. Many teens won't go to the trouble of taking a fruit or vegetable out of the fridge and washing and cutting it, but they're delighted to eat them if you prepare them. A fruit or vegetable tray with a yogurt dip makes a welcome after-school snack. If you're not going to be home, cut up veggies in the morning and bag them, or buy bags of ready-to-eat carrots and other nibblies, and leave your kids a note. Teens tend to eat whatever they can see, so make sure that the note or snack is in clear sight.

Other good snack foods that also satisfy hunger include applesauce, bread sticks, pizza, cheese, cottage cheese, yogurt, devilled or hard-cooked eggs, peanuts, sunflower seeds, oatmeal cookies, whole-grain muffins, hummus and pita bread, breakfast cereals, fig bars, and bagels or rice cakes spread with cream cheese or peanut butter.

Even teens who don't cook anything else will microwave popcorn to snack on—buy the low-fat variety. Or teach them to make popcorn on top of the stove with just a little oil, or to use a hot-air popper and drizzle a small amount of melted butter or margarine over the top. For variety, suggest tossing popcorn with garlic powder, Parmesan cheese, or curry powder.

Soft, sticky sweets such as raisins, fruit leathers, and granola bars are poor choices because they stick to the teeth and may encourage cavities. If your teen likes granola bars, those made with oats, nuts, and seeds are high in both protein and fibre. Unfortunately, they're also high in fat. Choose granola bars marked "low fat." Treat the family to an angel food cake at dinner. It's loaded with protein and has only a trace of fat. Served with fresh fruit and a yogurt sauce, it makes a great snack.

To quench thirst, stock the fridge with ice water, both plain and flavoured milks, frozen fruit-juice-on-a-stick, yogurt beverages, and fruit and vegetable juices.

A kid's diet is influenced by whatever his peers are eating.

Food on the Fly

When just hanging out with other kids, most teens eat whatever's going down: potato chips flavoured to burst the taste buds; candy so sour that it makes their lips pucker; fries in a cardboard box that's dripping with grease.

You may find these fast foods repulsive, but they aren't likely to hurt teenagers as long as you still serve nutritious foods at home. Because teenagers have such a high calorie requirement, they can eat between 500 and 1,800 calories a day of foods that are nutritionally empty and still get the nutrients they need from the rest of their daily intake. Girls have the lower calorie needs, and boys aged nineteen to twenty-two have the highest. All kids who are active in sports or other physically demanding activities have higher energy needs.

So don't worry if they eat candy. You probably can't stop them anyway. The 1992 study *Health of Canada's Youth* revealed that about 29 per cent of boys and 21 per cent of girls aged eleven through fifteen eat candy or a chocolate bar at least once a day.

What kids do risk from eating sweet foods is cavities. You could suggest that your daughter brush her teeth in the school washroom after eating candy, but her response is likely to be "Yeah, right, Mom." A more workable solution might be to pack an apple or celery sticks in her backpack for her to eat after she eats candy. Since these foods help clean

the teeth, they're sometimes called "detergent foods." Eating a slice of Cheddar or mozzarella cheese can also help counteract some of the negative effects of oral bacteria. Another solution is to hand him a pack of sugarless gum. Chewing sugarless gum actually does help reduce dental decay.

Fortunately, your teen's consumption of fast food and candy is self-limiting. It's an expensive habit that quickly wipes out a kid's allowance. When she can eat at home for free, your daughter isn't likely to use her own money to feed herself.

"At school, I'll buy a chocolate bar. I like Hershey's Cookies 'n Cream, or a box of Smarties, or a bag of chips. But only if I have the money. I used to buy candy two or three times a week, but I kept running out of money. For the summer I'm baby-sitting five children in one family. Then it'll be better. I'll have lots of money."

ANDREA, AGE 15

Begin with Breakfast

Breakfast is essential for everyone, and even more so for teens. If your teen skips breakfast, the reason may be related to your own breakfast habits—about 18 per cent of adults have only coffee or tea for breakfast. If your kids are on their own in the morning, they might steal a few more minutes for sleep rather than make and eat breakfast. If your daughter is having a bad-hair day and needs extra time for styling, she'll be tempted to skip eating. And left to his own devices, your teenage son's day might start in the corner store. What you don't want is for your children to eat chocolate bars for breakfast.

Breakfast should include a protein food such as eggs, milk, peanut butter, and cheese. Protein helps sustain energy throughout the morning by maintaining blood glucose levels. The body's level of blood sugar (glucose), the sole energy source for the brain, runs low without regular nourishment. And without breakfast, your teens (and you) will have difficulty concentrating. Some kids experience nausea, headache, and fatigue, and many feel apathetic and irritable. Kids may make up the calories, but not the nutrients, throughout the day.

It's best to eat breakfast shortly after rising, and eating a real breakfast at home probably provides more vitamins, minerals, and fibre than eating out. Try setting out cereal and fresh fruit. Rice cakes spread with peanut butter are another breakfast option for the teen too tired to make toast. Wrap up a slice of leftover pizza or, as they tear out the door, hand them a juice box, yogurt, or bag of dried fruit and nuts or cereal to have on the way to school or between classes.

High-Energy Eating for Athletes

If you're the parent of a teen athlete, you're busy. When you're not driving your sports enthusiast to or from practices, you're at the grocery store stocking up on enough food to keep your teen's hunger at bay. To meet the body's nutrient demands for growth plus the requirements of high energy for training, teen athletes may need over 4,000 calories a day.

Encourage a teen who is involved in strenuous activities or sports to choose more servings from the food groups of grain products and vegetables and fruit than the number suggested in Canada's Food Guide to Healthy Eating. Endurance athletes such as marathon runners, cyclists, and tri-athletes need 15 or more servings daily from these food groups, which provide carbohydrates, the main source of energy for exercise. The National Institute of Nutrition in Ottawa recommends that adolescents participating in high-intensity long-duration training consume a diet that provides about 60 per cent of total energy intake from carbohydrates. Offer your teen lots of whole-grain bread, potatoes, legumes (beans, peas, chickpeas, lentils), corn, pasta, rice, cereal, and fruit.

SEE PAGE 17

Teen athletes may need over 4,000 calories a day.

If he comes home talking about carbohydrate-loading before the big meet, talk to his coach. Carbohydrate-loading is a strict regime that involves consuming a very high carbohydrate diet and tapering activity for the two or three days before an event. It may be harmful to growing teens.

Pumping iron

SEE PAGE 19

All athletes need plenty of iron-containing foods such as meat, legumes, vegetables, and grains. But dietary iron deficiency is even more prevalent in adolescents who are athletic, particularly female high-endurance athletes. Iron is the component in red blood cells that delivers oxygen to working muscles. A simple blood test at the doctor's office is all it takes to diagnose whether your daughter does have an iron deficiency. If she does, her doctor may suggest iron supplements. But ensure she takes no more than prescribed, since too much iron can cause abdominal pain, nausea, and vomiting.

Drink up

The athletic teen needs to drink extra fluids to regulate her body temperature. Active muscles generate heat, and fluids help remove that heat. Without adequate fluids, your teen may become dehydrated, which causes fatigue and increases the risk of cramps and heat exhaustion. An adolescent's sweat losses are similar to those of an adult.

To prevent dehydration, your teen should drink before, during, and after exercise. Quenching one's thirst alone does not satisfy the body's need for water, especially during exercise when thirst is blunted. You need to make sure that your teen leaves the house with a filled water bottle and that the coach insists that she drink.

> To prevent dehydration, your teen should drink before, during, and after exercise.

For training that lasts one hour or less, water is the preferred beverage. Avoid coffee, iced tea, and colas. The caffeine in these drinks acts as a diuretic and may increase urine output and fluid loss. When the level of training or competition and heat or humidity are extreme, your teen may benefit from a sports drink. If you're tired of paying big money for little bottles of sports drinks, mix up a huge jug of your own for a fraction of the cost. Simply combine 2 mL (½ tsp.) of salt, 375 mL (1½ cups) of granulated sugar, 500 mL (2 cups) of unsweetened orange juice, and 4.5 L (18 cups) of water.

Resisting Puberty

Girls who are active in gymnastics, figure skating, diving, or dancing may feel pressured to stay the size and shape of a little girl. The stars in these fields, whom your daughter wants to emulate, have prepubescent body builds. Young girls in these sports may restrict eating to delay puberty, even though they may not be conscious of doing so. They may balk at eating even the minimum requirements set out in Canada's Food Guide to Healthy Eating.

If your daughter starts to develop womanly curves, her coach may wrongly ask her to go on a diet. Or there may be more subtle suggestions that she's no longer the right size. A comment like "That costume doesn't work—it's way too tight now" is enough to make any young girl question her shape. Talk to the coach or trainers to be clear about their attitudes to body shape and health. If they are inappropriate, consider another club.

Or maybe the criticism comes from within your daughter. Standing in front of a floor-length mirror during ballet practice places an exaggerated emphasis on the body. You can count on her to compare her body shape with the bodies of the other girls in her class. You can also be sure that she'll want to be more like the thinner girls.

Your daughter should feel proud of her new womanly shape.

Limiting food in adolescence can jeopardize your daughter's health by stunting her growth. It can also delay or stop menstruation, which may weaken her bones and increase the risk of fractures. Worse yet, dieting can evolve into an eating disorder. If your daughter is developing large breasts, her balance will change, too, and she may not be able to do triple pirouettes the way she used to.

Your attitude is pivotal. Your daughter needs to know that her body hasn't betrayed her. She needs to be reassured that the world is still filled with opportunities for her. She needs to feel valued as a person, not just for her abilities on the parallel bars. If she decides to participate less in the sport, she may need your help and guidance filling the time she once spent in the gym. If your family has basked in the reflected glow of your child's talent, helping her change direction can be a difficult task. You, too, may have a hard time letting go of your child's dream of being an Olympic gymnast.

For more information on sport nutrition and sport-related eating disorders, contact the Sport Medicine and Science Council of Canada. SEE PAGE 228

Cooking for Fun and Survival

By the time your child turns thirteen, you might expect that she would occasionally have dinner prepared for you when you arrive home late from work. Unlikely. Teens love to be fed. They may reject your advice, they definitely don't want you to fix their hair, but they do want you to feed them. If you're the one who does all the cooking, how will your child ever learn to plan and prepare meals? He'll be on his own before you know it, but you're still making the sandwiches he takes to school for lunch.

In adolescence, the focus shifts away from the home and into the larger community. Your daughter no longer wants to spend Saturday afternoon baking cookies with you. However, she may want to learn about cooking—just not from her parents. If she wants to take a cooking course with her friends, tell her it's a great idea. Give her a cookbook for Christmas.

If your son mentions that he would like to bake a birthday cake for his girlfriend, hand over the recipe but don't go far away. He may need to ask you what vanilla extract is or how to crack an egg. Think twice about what you say, and don't let a quick quip from you end his culinary education. Take a deep breath and say something encouraging like "Yeah, breaking an egg can be tricky. Let's practise with a couple of eggs. We can use them up in an omelette tomorrow."

When your teen complains there's no food in the house, give him some cash and send him to the grocery store.

When your teens complain that there's no food in the house, open your wallet and send them to the grocery store. If your son last entered a grocery store when he sat in the little seat in the shopping cart, it's time he ventured back in. Make the most of his interest in food by having him do the family grocery shopping or make a meal. Even with your list, the groceries he buys may be unusual; even with your advice, the meal he makes could be burnt. Help isn't really what you're after. You want your child to develop some idea of grocery costs and to be able to put a meal on the table. With that knowledge tucked under his belt, you'll feel a lot more comfortable sending him out into the world.

Ten Facts about Nutrition for Teens

1. Food is one of life's joys. Eating is a pleasure for everyone to enjoy.
2. What you eat today affects your health not only now but in years to come. For example, if you consume a sufficient amount of calcium now, you can reduce your chances of osteoporosis in later life. Milk is not just for children.
3. If you focus on lower-fat foods, you can reduce your risk of many diseases, from heart disease to cancer.
4. There is no one perfect food. You need to eat a variety of foods for peak nutrition.
5. Business people, not nutritionists, plan fast-food meals. If you heavily entrust your nutritional needs to food chains, your diet will have too much meat, salt, and fat. You'll need to add dairy products, whole grains, fruits and vegetables to your diet.
6. When you're hot and sweaty, there's nothing quite like water to drink. Drinking adequate water throughout the day is essential to good health.
7. Food in its original form beats processed food. A handful of ripe cherries is more nutritious than cherry chews. A bowl of oatmeal is nutritionally superior to processed oatmeal cookies.
8. Go with whole wheat and other whole-grain breads, which offer a multitude of nutrients that white bread doesn't.
9. Make a habit of choosing the lower-fat alternative.
10. Cooking is a grand adventure when you're ready to embark.

The Family Meal

Dinner is a ritual that can keep the family in touch. But in the teen's quest for independence, he may frequently miss family meals. It's not just that having dinner with his family doesn't top his priority list. He has competing responsibilities with homework, a part-time job, the basketball team, not to mention a dozen or so friends.

So don't have lofty expectations that the evening meal will bond the family together. Your teen may not even make it to special dinners. How can he if they fall during his shift as a lifeguard at the pool? If you want to continue enjoying the companionship of a meal with your son, you'll need to be flexible and work around his schedule. If he's having a warmed-up dinner at 10:00 p.m. when he's back from the pool, make yourself a cup of tea and sit down beside him. He doesn't want to eat alone in the kitchen. And he won't even know what he's eating if he eats in front of the TV.

As much as possible, encourage your adolescent to eat at home. Research shows that when a teenager eats one of the day's meals away from home, it significantly decreases his intake of calcium, iron, vitamin C, and thiamine. What's missing from fast-food meals are fruits, vegetables, whole grains, and milk.

Since teens tend to move in a pack, when dinner time rolls around you could find that your daughter has three of her friends lounging in your living room. It's perfectly within your rights to tell them that you're going to have dinner now and that you'll see them later. But occasionally, why not invite them to join you? It will nourish the friendships, and enjoying a meal with your teen's friends is a good way to get to know them.

"Dinner at our house lasts only about twenty minutes, but I can't imagine not having one meal together as a family every day. Everyone appreciates being part of it all, even though some kids are more vocal at dinner than others. If there are candles in the house, the kids always ask if they can light them. Candlelight dinners with the lights dimmed makes dinner feel like a celebration, a celebration of being together."

BETH, MOTHER OF FOUR

On the spur of the moment, can you transform a dinner for four into a dinner for seven? Adding a pasta dish is quick, especially if it's frozen and all you have to do is pop it into the microwave. Don't overburden yourself. Make the most of the extra hands, and have them set the table and help with cleanup. Feeding the neighbourhood kids can be costly. If your son is always having dinner at his friend's, drop off a lasagna to let the friend's parents know you acknowledge the cost as well as their effort.

When your kids reach adolescence, you can take manners a few steps beyond "no elbows on the table." Discuss how to politely refuse a food you detest, and how and when to use the full range of utensils in a place setting. Try not to correct your teen at the table, since teens are ultra-sensitive to criticism. Instead, catch her doing something right.

Make conversation the focus of your family meal, not eating. But parents have so much advice to give their children that it can be tempting to turn family dinners into a lecture series. Advice and reprimands are bad for digestion. They squelch the possibility of meaningful dialogue. Give it a break at dinner.

If your teen doesn't have to be on the defensive, she might tell you more than you really want to know. "Pass the salt, and did you know that Sally got her navel pierced in a tattoo parlour?" Most parents can't listen for sixty seconds without giving advice or trying to fix the problem, as they perceive it. Set a goal of listening intently for one full minute to what your child has to say. No need to ask questions or interrogate as she goes along in her story.

Teens can offer a fresh, exciting perspective on the world. If you disagree with her views on global warming, don't cut her off. Try saying "I'd like to think that one over" or "I see how you could feel that way" or "That certainly is a unique way of looking at the problem." Yes, you can make it all the way through to dessert without a blowup.

Socializing, including sharing meals, cements teen bonds.

Body Image

Body image problems are on the increase for both teenage girls and boys. Role models on TV, on billboards, and in magazines set impossible standards that kids feel they should measure up to. Boys can get caught up in wanting muscles that ripple. Girls stand in front of the mirror poking at their tiny waists, which they perceive as blubbery.

Health Canada's 1992 survey *The Health of Canada's Youth* found that 42 per cent of thirteen-year-old girls and 48 per cent of fifteen-year-old girls say they need to lose weight. When teenage girls compare their looks with those of the women they see in movies and on TV, it's not a level playing field. Adolescence is a time of voracious eating and rapid growth. It's common and perfectly normal for girls approaching puberty to look chubby. Girls need a relatively high percentage of body fat for menstruation to begin.

> **The current notion that you can have any body you want is more fantasy than fact.**

Between the ages of ten and fourteen, the average girl gains 18 to 22 kg (40 to 50 lb.). The steadily rising numbers on the bathroom scale can seem scary. This weight gain can be especially alarming to a girl growing up in North America, home of the multi-billion-dollar dieting business.

A study of girls aged fourteen to eighteen in Nova Scotia found that 44 per cent of them were dieting. If your teen tries out several diets, she faces the risk of developing an eating disorder as well as the risk of gaining weight instead of losing it. When she restricts her intake of food, her appetite increases. Soon, all she can think about are burgers and fries. Inevitably she'll satisfy her hunger with a bag of chips or, more likely, half the contents of your fridge. Then she'll feel ashamed and out of control.

The current notion that you can have any body you want is more fantasy than fact. Good eating habits and exercise help shape and condition the body, but some people are naturally petite, others naturally tall, some slender and others large. Larger teens do not necessarily eat more than their slender friends. There's increasing evidence that we all have an inherited set-point, a certain optimal weight that is genetically determined, like hair colour and height.

The body struggles to maintain the set-point, so it may crave foods in a desperate attempt to remain healthy. The only way to lower the set-point is through adequate eating and regular aerobic exercise. Aerobic exercise is continuous movement that makes the heart beat faster, but not to the point of puffing. In aerobic exercise, you should be able to speak comfortably. To reap the most benefit from aerobic exercise, one should maintain the activity for at least 20 continuous minutes. Exercising to lower the set-point, and not for the joy of physical activity, can be deadening. It's important to preach overall good health and acceptance. Body size is not a choice.

Ten Ways to Promote a Healthy Body Image

Follow these guidelines to help your teen feel secure about who he is.

1. As a parent, wear your own weight and shape with comfort and pride. Work through your own negative attitudes, and your kids will benefit, too.
2. Sell your bathroom scale at the next garage sale. It's too easy to let the numbers on the scale determine how you feel about yourself. Besides, no scale weighs what really counts—your child's intelligence, thoughtfulness, and zany sense of humour.
3. Take the time to help your teen find a style that looks good on her. No one looks good in everything. You may be at your wits' end standing outside the store changing room, but resist muttering "If you'd only lose a few pounds, buying clothes wouldn't be such a chore."
4. Challenge stereotypes. Ask whether the female star must always be wafer thin. Question whether the male lead could have developed those bulging muscles without steroids.
5. Discuss dieting. If your daughter knows that most diets fail, why would she start one? Educate your adolescent about the genetic basis of weight; discuss the concept of set-point.
6. Avoid fighting over food. Don't limit portions or ban certain types of foods. But do help your teens learn about nutrition so that they know what their bodies need to stay healthy.
7. Enjoy your food. Make sure your kids know that eating is one of life's great joys, that satisfying hunger is nothing to be ashamed of.
8. Encourage your teen to enjoy her body. Draw her a warm bath. Hug her often. After she's had a hard day at school, offer to massage her back.
9. Don't comment on a teen's weight. Instead comment on his explosive science project or the superb job he did cleaning his room. You can't have both good self-esteem and a poor body image.
10. Don't let family or friends comment on your teen's weight. Stand up for your teen.

Body

Be a good role model. Your daughter will be more likely to appreciate her body type and her personal attractiveness if you appreciate yours.

Parenting the larger teen

If your teenager is excessively overweight, you should, of course, consult her doctor and perhaps ask for a referral to a dietitian. With the help of a dietitian, she can analyze what she eats to see if her weekly consumption is too high in calories.

Also check whether she has opportunities to exercise. Teens can feel vulnerable and totally exposed in the high school gym. Joining the high-school intramural volleyball team is not likely the answer for the overweight teen. Cycling, walking, or working out to an exercise video are more realistic options.

If you're sure that your child is exercising and that her diet is good, then relax. Being plump is usually not a health issue. It's more dangerous to be 30 per cent underweight than 30 per cent overweight. The real danger is the social stigma that can go along with being overweight.

To spare your teen ridicule about her weight, you may find yourself becoming critical of her eating habits. Or you may be repulsed by the way her stomach sags over her jeans. If you don't feel comfortable with your teen's body shape, it could be time to look at your own attitudes about body shape.

If parents criticize their teen's body, who else will hold her steady through the storm of adolescence? Parents need to help their kids eat sensibly and adjust to whatever body nature has given them. It's worth pointing out that most of us manage to lead happy and satisfying lives despite having wide hips or a thick waistline.

"Daniel sees himself as obese, as the fat kid. He isn't fat—on the doctor's graph he's at the top end of normal. He's just bigger than his friends. In adolescence, conformity is so important. Any difference is considered wrong. I know Daniel is embarrassed by his weight. I can tell by the way he walks—he hunches his shoulders and lowers his head. When he goes swimming, he won't take off his shirt. He hides his body. In a way, body image problems are worse for boys. Girls say, 'Oh, I hate my thighs. Oh, my stomach is so fat.' Boys don't talk about how they feel about their bodies. The only time they talk about it is when they tease."

ANN, MOTHER OF 13-YEAR-OLD DANIEL

What's wrong with Johnny?

A growing number of boys feel pressured to achieve a hard, lean body. For some boys this pressure turns into an obsession with a particular body image. Getting hooked on a look can lead to excessive exercising, unhealthy eating patterns, and steroid use. A large-scale study by the Canadian Centre for Ethics in Sport found that almost half of the young men who use steroids do so to change their appearance.

Appearance is exceedingly important to young men. When they like how they look, they feel better about themselves, more accepted by their peers, and more sexually attractive. Parents shouldn't shirk off the pressures boys feel to get "the look." The message that teenage boys are bombarded with today is that if you have a "cut" body, you're cool. Watch the guys with rippling muscles running along the beach in your son's TV shows. Glance at the "abs" (abdominal muscles) in magazine ads. Take a close look at the undulating washboard stomachs in music videos. This focus on male physique didn't exist twenty years ago.

While many teenage girls say they want to lose weight, their male counterparts may want to gain weight. One Canadian study found that by age thirteen, about 21 per cent

The message that bombards teenage boys is that they should have a "cut" body.

of boys say they need to gain weight. The numbers on the bathroom scale are already going up at a phenomenal rate. Between age twelve and sixteen, a boy typically gains between 22 and 27 kg (50 and 60 lb.)

If your son feels he's too thin, you may find that cans of amino acid or protein powder supplements suddenly appear in the kitchen. Contrary to what your son may believe, these products do not lead to muscle development. They don't even promote health. Over time, they can affect his body's excretion of calcium and his kidney function, but fortunately their use is usually self-limiting. They don't have an appealing taste and they quickly wipe out a teen's savings.

Of male high-school students, 41 per cent said they would like to change how they look. Some boys may be trying to outgrow their feelings of being small or weak as children. The embarrassment of always being picked last for sports teams may still sting. Others are certain that girls look the other way when they walk down the hall. They believe that a more developed body will get them dates.

Eating Disorders

Helping a teen with an eating disorder is among the most difficult challenges that a family can face. Parents should know that, fortunately, there are specialists who can help them help their child, that treatment for eating disorders is available. As with many disorders, there's a better chance of recovery if you recognize the problem and treat it in the early stages.

Research is ongoing into the causes of eating disorders, and the results are a subject of debate. Most experts believe that an eating disorder is a strategy that young people use to cope with problems too painful to talk about. They use their bodies as vehicles to play out the issues they face, usually issues of control, sexuality, separation, and self-esteem.

Of the people with eating disorders, 90 to 95 per cent are female. People with eating disorders may have suffered a trauma such as psychological, physical, or sexual abuse, or be part of a family in which the caregivers are addicted to alcohol or drugs. However, many people with eating disorders have not experienced such traumas. An eating disorder may have no single cause. In someone who is vulnerable, a disorder can be triggered by an event she doesn't know how to handle, which can be as common as being teased or as devastating as rape or incest. An eating disorder often begins when the person is dealing with a difficult transition: puberty, a new school, the breakup of a relationship. Every person's experience is unique, but often the teen who develops an eating disorder feels shame, disgust, and anger about her body. Some feel a need to purify or even punish their bodies. They feel powerless to change anything else in their lives.

There are two main types of eating disorders: anorexia nervosa and bulimia nervosa. Both are characterized by excessive concern about one's weight and shape and a negative, distorted body image. Although a teen may weigh only 32 kg (70 lb.), when she looks in a mirror, she sees herself as obese. She thinks that others also consider her mammoth in size, even if you think she looks skeletal when you see her thin arms and legs.

Anorexia Nervosa

Of the women in Canada between the ages of fourteen and twenty-five, an estimated 2 per cent suffer from anorexia, a condition defined as a drastic weight loss caused by self-induced starvation. It can, however, begin earlier. The child may begin by eliminating desserts from her meals.

A study of girls between fourteen and eighteen in Nova Scotia found that 44 per cent were dieting.

Then she may also exclude bread. She could go on to deny herself more and more food until she's eating only celery sticks and water. Eventually she may try to exist on water alone. The anorexic may go to the extreme of counting the calories she consumes from the glue after licking a postage stamp.

Behind this potentially fatal illness is a girl's strong desire to control everything and to become thin. Some may already be painfully thin in their parents' eyes; others become anorexic because they were overweight children, were either ostracized or encouraged to diet, and were praised when they lost pounds. Anorexics believe their only problem is being too fat. They have a distorted body image and don't recognize how underweight they are, which makes it difficult for them to recognize that they need treatment.

Of Canadian women between the ages of fourteen and twenty-five, about 2 per cent suffer from anorexia.

Typically the anorexic makes up excuses to miss meals. Most adolescents have voracious appetites, but if your daughter often says that she had a huge lunch and doesn't want dinner, you might well be alert to other indicators of anorexia. The British Columbia Ministry of Health includes the following as signs of anorexia:

➤ She develops obsessions about food and recipes. An anorexic may eat vicariously by grocery shopping, by watching cooking shows, or by cooking food for others.

➤ She develops unusual eating habits. She may cut her food into tiny pieces or eat only the crumbs that others leave behind.

➤ She always feels cold.

➤ She shows a noticeable weight loss.

➤ She involves herself in excessive exercise. As a way of burning calories, an anorexic may spend hours in the gym or go on day-long walks.

> **An anorexic may eat vicariously by watching cooking shows or by cooking food for others.**

The athletic teen needs to drink extra fluids to regulate her body temperature.

Body

Bulimia Nervosa

Of the women between the ages of fourteen and twenty-five, an estimated 1 per cent have bulimia nervosa. This disorder is characterized by cycles of binge eating followed by purging or other inappropriate compensatory behaviour to rid the body of calories. Because young girls don't know about or can't execute the methods of purging, this disorder doesn't usually begin until the mid-teens.

For a bulimic, a binge is eating boxes of cookies or litres of ice cream in a short period of time. Methods of purging themselves include self-induced vomiting or using diuretics, diet pills, or laxatives. Teenagers with bulimia use stimulant laxatives such as Correctol or Ex-Lax most frequently because these cause diarrhea soon after eating. This leads to the loss of fluid, which may give a false sensation that she has lost weight. The abdominal pain, which is a common side effect, serves to make the teen's emotional pain real. The misuse of laxatives has serious complications, including dehydration and electrolyte imbalance. Many anorexics also suffer constipation from a combination of inadequate intake of food bulk and excessive vomiting, as well as the laxative habit, and may go days without having a bowel movement. Seek medical advice for your teen as soon as you become aware of the problem.

> **Teenagers with bulimia use stimulant laxatives to cause diarrhea soon after eating.**

To induce vomiting, some teens use syrup of ipecac, an over-the-counter drug intended to induce vomiting in someone who has accidentally swallowed a poison. If used repeatedly, the drug becomes toxic to the muscles and can destroy heart tissue irreversibly, weakening the heart. If your child is using ipecac, she needs immediate medical attention. Unlike anorexics, bulimics know they have a problem. However, they don't want to admit to what they consider shameful and disgusting behaviour.

Signs of Bulimia

The British Columbia Ministry of Health includes the following as signs of bulimia:
- She eats large amounts of food, but shows little weight gain.
- She becomes excessively sensitive, secretive, and irritable about food and eating.
- She goes to the bathroom after meals and vomits in secret.
- She has a chronic sore throat and hoarse voice.
- She leaves evidence of vomiting or laxative abuse.

How to Help

Parents may feel helpless watching a child struggle with an eating disorder. Because of their worry, they may vacillate between being too involved or not involved enough. In an attempt to gain control of the situation, some parents revert to parenting techniques they used when their teen was a young child. Trying to force or tempt a child into eating may perpetuate the eating disorder. You may simply want to have your daughter spend more time at home so that you can make sure she's eating regular meals and nutritious food. But if you no longer allow your teen to hang out with her friends or go to the mall, her symptoms may escalate. Support her by letting her continue to spend time with her friends, to do the things other teens her age are doing.

You can help best by maintaining good communication with her, by showing your interest in her activities and her feelings. She needs to know that she's not alone and that you care about her. Talk about things other than food and weight. Let her know that you're concerned about her health and seek help from your family doctor or from an eating-disorder clinic that can offer a multidisciplinary approach.

Your role is that of a parent or a concerned friend, not a therapist. If your child refuses help, negotiate with her, but don't demand. Offer to go with her to the doctor's. Promise a shopping trip after the appointment. Say "I know you don't think you have an eating disorder, but unless a doctor confirms that, we'll never know for sure." If she's adamant about not seeing a doctor, maybe she'll talk with a school counsellor or a therapist who can help her recognize that she does need medical help. The National Eating Disorder Information Centre in Toronto keeps a national registry of therapists and programs.

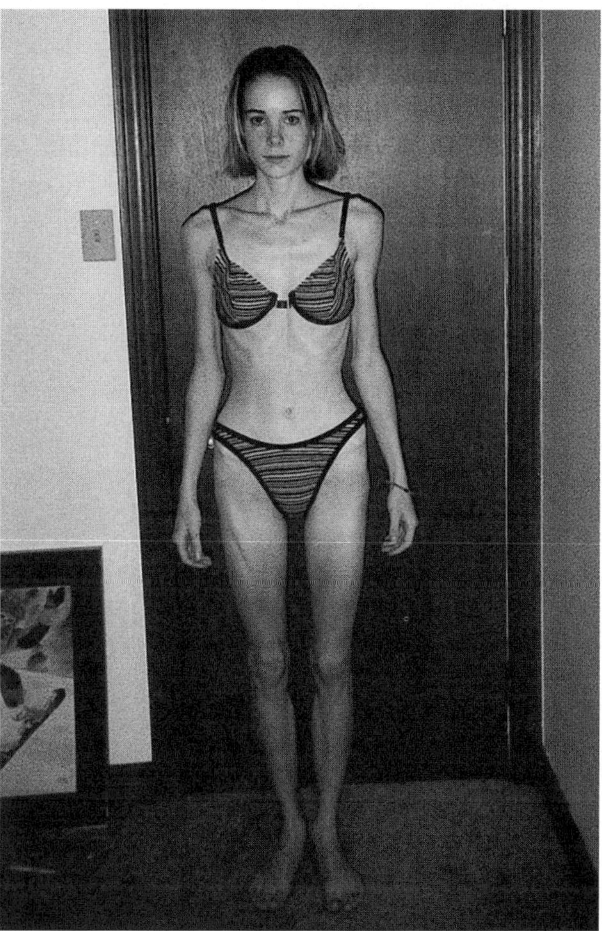

As part of her therapy, this teen had photos taken of her anorexic self for a reality check. She is now a healthy weight.

SEE PAGE 226

Steroids

Most parents are happy to encourage a teenager's involvement in sports. They see the sports environment as a healthy one, safe from the other pitfalls of the teen years. But even as early as age fourteen, teenage male athletes are more likely to try an anabolic steroid, a drug with serious health consequences. Anabolic steroids are a group of synthetic hormones similar to the male sex hormone, testosterone. Some teens believe that steroids will help them develop improved muscles, physical appearance, and performance in sport more quickly than through exercise.

High school steroid users typically come from white middle-class families. Most are boys. Few teenage girls use steroids because girls usually want to lose pounds, not gain them. Pressure to use steroids is particularly intense for members of health and fitness clubs, those involved in weight training, and members of provincial sport teams.

> **Steroids are being taken by fourteen-year-old boys in a hurry to mature.**

The 1993 *National School Survey on Drugs and Sport* suggests that 83,000 Canadians between the ages of eleven and eighteen have tried anabolic steroids. This large-scale study for the Canadian Centre for Ethics in Sport found that more than half of the guys who take steroids do so to improve their abilities in sports. That means almost as many boys use steroids for other reasons—for muscle definition and that "cut" body look. Steroids are being taken by fourteen-year-old boys in a hurry to mature, by seventeen-year-olds who hate being skinny, as well as by eighteen-year-olds desperate for a university sports scholarship.

Know the risks

For the growing boy, steroids pose the risk of stunting growth by accelerating puberty and prematurely closing the growth centres of long bones. Steroids increase acne and the growth of body hair. All users risk high blood pressure and liver and kidney damage. And although steroids may temporarily increase one's interest in sex, they shrink the testicles, cause sterility and impotence, and enlarge the breast tissue in males.

It's still controversial whether anabolic steroids are physically addictive, but dependence and depression from withdrawal have often been reported. They are a hard habit to break, nevertheless—users get hooked on the look that steroids give because when they discontinue steroids, they lose body mass and feel fat and weak.

Steroids can be taken orally or by injection. One of the risks of taking anabolic steroids is the risk of contracting HIV, the virus that leads to AIDS, or Hepatitis B by sharing needles or even the same vial of steroids.

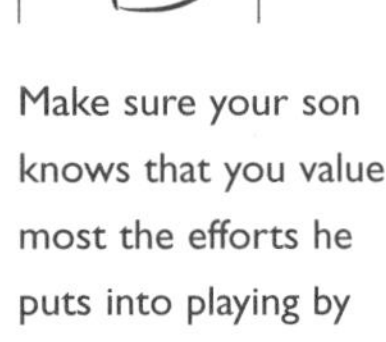

Make sure your son knows that you value most the efforts he puts into playing by the rules.

While young teens tend to value the camaraderie and excitement of playing sports, by the time they reach eighteen, winning may have become the only thing that matters. With this attitude shift, kids in sports are more likely to use drugs. As a parent, what values do you project? When your son crashes through the front door after a game, is the first question you ask "Did you win?" A better opener might be "How was the game?" or "How did you play tonight?" Make sure your son knows that you value most the efforts he puts into training, into playing by the rules, and into working toward a personal best.

Thirteen is not too young to talk about steroid use as a form of cheating. Discuss the importance of playing drug-free. As your child gets older, he'll take more responsibility for getting himself to practices and games, so you won't have as much contact with other team members and coaching staff. But keep your eyes open. Is there any indication that your son is subtly or overtly being pressured into taking steroids either by his teammates or his coach? If you suspect that steroids have infiltrated the team, it's time for you to intervene.

Finding pills or vials and syringes in your son's bedroom may make you paralyzed with anger and fear. But doing nothing is the worst thing you can do for your son. The Sport Medicine Council of Saskatchewan recommends the following:

➤ Take action. First-time users may not know what they're getting into and need the facts.

➤ Seek professional help from a physician who specializes in sports medicine.

➤ Show your support. Going off steroids can be physically and emotionally traumatic.

For more information, contact your local drug addiction centre, the Canadian Centre for Ethics in Sport, or the Drug Awareness Program of the Royal Canadian Mounted Police.

SEE PAGE 220
SEE PAGE 227

How Do I Know?

Almost all anabolic steroid users experience side effects. The Canadian Centre for Ethics in Sport offers these indications of steroid use.

Swollen or puffy face This common side effect, sometimes described as a round or "moon" face, is caused by water retention.

Severe acne Steroids can either cause acne (especially on the upper back, shoulders, arms, and face) or make existing acne worse.

Rapid weight gain Users can gain between 5 and 10 kg (11 to 22 lb.) during the first 6 to 12 weeks.

Personality changes Your child may experience extreme mood swings—from bursts of anger known as 'roid rage, to near euphoria.

Jaundice The eyes and skin become yellow, indicating liver disease.

Premature hair loss Certain steroids can cause hair thinning or even balding.

Obsessions Users may be preoccupied with their image, body, and the foods they eat.

Fitness for Life

During her teen years, your child starts making her own decisions about how physically active she wants to be. Your daughter may decide that she loves lunch-time intramural basketball at school, or aerobics classes at the local community centre, or jogging with her boyfriend. Or she may become less and less physically active as she focuses on other aspects of teen life—friends, schoolwork, a part-time job—so that her only exercise is walking to the bus stop in the morning. It's unfortunate, but if she chooses to be less active, she'll have lots of company. Almost two-thirds of Canadians under the age of nineteen aren't active enough to maintain cardiovascular health.

The interest that teenage girls show in physical activity decreases more drastically than does boys' interest. According to a 1994 study conducted by Sport Canada, only 64 per cent of girls between the ages of fifteen and eighteen participated regularly in sports compared with 89 per cent of boys the same age. Impress upon your teens, girls as well as boys, the benefits of exercise. It not only improves physical health, it improves mental well-being; it increases self-esteem and reduces depression; and team sports demonstrate the value of cooperation and team play as well as the competitive spirit. Young people who are physically active are more conscious of what they eat and drink, and are aware of the problems created by smoking and drinking. They develop friendships with other like-minded kids that revolve around healthy activities.

Playing sports increases self-esteem and reduces depression.

Talking about fitness with your kids isn't as powerful as modelling a healthy approach to fitness. In a Sport Canada study of Canadians between the ages of fifteen and twenty-four, the rate of the young people's participation in sports was about 12 per cent higher when one of their parents also participated regularly. A mother's participation in sport had a bigger impact on her kids' participation rate than a father's, but both made a noticeable difference in how involved the kids were.

"I do soccer and track and field. I was captain of the track and field team at school this year. I've always done sports. I did ballet when I was four, then quit and did riding. I run a lot on my own. I find that physical activity is very relaxing. You feel better about yourself. The girls who do sports have much higher self-esteem than girls who don't. And I think it makes you better at school. You get more energy. I find if I have a gym class in the morning, then my concentration in science class in the afternoon is better."

JEN, AGE 16

So if you want your fifteen-year-old to put down the TV remote control and go outside and toss a football with his brother, the best way to encourage him is to get into the physical activity yourself. If you can't handle a football, there are simpler ways to model an active lifestyle. Leave the car at home and walk to the store or to your job, if possible. Take the stairs instead of the escalator at the mall.

Another way to encourage teens to be active is to support their efforts in the same way you did when they were younger. Drive them to the gym, offer to coach their team, watch their dance performances. A study by the Canadian Fitness and Lifestyle Research Institute (CFLRI) showed that teenagers don't receive as much parental support for their physical activities as younger children do. Parents of teens were more likely to complain about the transportation hassles, the costs, and the inconveniences to other family members caused by their teen's participation

> Encourage your teens to be active in the same way you did when they were younger.

in sports. Parents of teens were also less likely to agree that their kids' participation had positive rewards, such as developing social skills and improving their capacity for learning.

If your teenager expresses an interest in joining a team or taking karate lessons or buying the hottest new exercise video, encourage her and show your interest in her achievements. Take part with your teenager occasionally, if that's appropriate. Offer to assist the team's coach or to coach the team, if you can, or show up in the stands for practices and games. When talking with your teen about her involvement, focus on the game rather than on the outcome. Tell her it was a great play she made in the first inning, and don't dwell on the fact that her team lost.

If your teen shows signs of waning interest, don't push. Let him move on to something new. Otherwise, he may be reluctant to commit to an activity again. What's important is that he's involved in physical activity, not that he plays a particular sport. He may be a dabbler who moves from activity to activity, always trying something new. Or he may be interested in a new activity because that's what his friends are doing. If his dabbling in various activities becomes a financial burden, make an agreement that your son will sign up or pay for lessons for short periods only.

> **If your teen loses interest in a sport, don't push. Let him move on to something new.**

At home, set the scene for physical activity. Fill your house with equipment to encourage physical activity: bikes in working order, ice skates, a basketball hoop on the side of the garage, a Ping-Pong table instead of a big-screen TV. And plan family vacations around physical activities. Choose hiking or cycling holidays over lazing-at-the-beach holidays.

Have realistic expectations. Being an energetic teenage athlete should be reward in itself.

When your teen is keen

For many kids, the teen years are a special time when sports and physical activity really dominate their lives. These kids are in their physical prime—strong, fast, and overflowing with energy. Organized athletics provide them with a positive learning experience. They learn the importance of dedication, discipline, practice, and cooperation with others. They learn to savour winning and accept losing. And often, they can bask in the admiration of their peers.

If you're the parent of a dedicated athlete, nurture this passion for athletic activity in a way that will sustain your child throughout his life. Some parents get caught up in the importance of winning or the slim chance of a future for their teen in professional sport. Having unrealistic expectations may end in disappointment for both you and your child. Being an energetic, passionate teenage athlete should be reward in itself. As a parent, you need to celebrate what your child is, rather than what she might become.

Sleep Needs

With the beginning of puberty, most young people go from being well-rested to being chronically sleep-deprived. Most teenagers simply don't sleep enough. Homework, TV, friends, extracurricular activities, and telephone conversations steadily push bedtime further and further back. Some studies of teens who also have a part-time job show that teenagers who work more than 20 hours a week experience very high levels of daytime sleepiness.

It's not just that teens don't set aside enough time for sleep. Their bodies tell them to stay up late. Beginning with puberty and continuing into their twenties, their sleep-wake cycle lengthens to 25 or 26 hours, which is why most teenagers are liveliest in the evening, stay up late and sleep late the next day. The absentee rates of university students for the first class of the morning have reached 40 per cent. Some education administrators have considered accommodating this circadian shift by changing the hours of high school and university so that the school day starts later and ends later.

Most teenagers don't sleep enough because they have so many activities on the go.

When your teen does get adequate sleep, he's more cheerful, more alert, less susceptible to colds and flu, and also less accident-prone. If your son is learning to drive and is obviously dead tired, you're well within your rights to hold on to the car keys. The immediate effects of sleep deprivation are poor concentration and judgment. Some researchers go as far as to suggest that some of the impulsive and irresponsible behaviour associated with "the crazy teens" may simply be a consequence of inadequate sleep.

> **You'll know your teen is getting enough sleep if he awakens refreshed.**

Teens need to learn that sleep is not wasted time. Virtually all dreaming that a person remembers occurs in the rapid eye movement (REM) segment of sleep. Dreaming may be one part of sleep that your teen appreciates, because many teen dreams are sex dreams. REM sleep is important for other reasons. Without adequate REM sleep, a person can't concentrate, makes frequent mistakes, and is more prone to depression. Your teen needs adequate REM sleep to remember for longer than a few days what she has been studying.

Your teen has probably discovered that cramming for exams actually works. She can memorize chemistry formulas at 2:00 a.m. and spew them out on an exam paper later that morning. But she may not realize that if she doesn't get adequate REM sleep, the formulas won't move on from her short-term memory to her long-term memory. That's why she flounders in chemistry class the following term.

How Much Is Enough?

As with adults, individual sleep needs vary. You'll know your teen is getting enough sleep if he awakens refreshed. But if he has to set three alarms to wake up in the morning, he's definitely not catching enough ZZZ's. The Canadian Sleep Society's recommendation is that teens should sleep one hour more of each twenty-four hours than they did in their pre-teen years. Their rapid body growth during adolescence requires between 9 and 11 hours of shuteye. To achieve this amount of sleep, your teen's bedtime should be somewhere between 8:30 and 10:30 p.m. If that fact surprises you, it confirms how deeply sleep deprivation is ingrained in our society, as Vancouver psychologist Stanley Coren points out in his book, *Sleep Thieves* (Free Press Paperbacks, 1997).

During adolescence, a teen must gradually take control of his own bedtime. For a young teen, emphasize that sleep is not a disposable commodity. Reach an agreement that the TV, computer, and CD player will be turned off at a set time; and restrict phone calls after that set hour. Although he may grumble at the restrictions, he may feel relieved, even grateful, that you're helping him get adequate rest.

Body

Several surveys of teenagers have found that more than half wish they had more time to sleep. Try to help your teens assess their time commitments. Listen attentively, but help them make the connection between lack of sleep and poor grades, between staying up all night and succumbing to a flu virus, between fatigue and too many commitments.

If your teen is a persistent night owl, take a look at your own sleep habits. Adolescents often fail at doing what we tell them, but always excel at imitating what we do. If you want your teen to go to bed at a reasonable hour, you need a bedtime that's not dictated by your workload or the TV listings. If you have the habit of staying up late to meet a pressing deadline, your teen is more likely to stay up past midnight to finish an assignment. If you stay up late to watch an old movie on TV, guess who'll be on the couch beside you?

"On a school night my bedtime is usually 10 p.m., but I'd rather go to bed at 11:30. On the weekends I stay up really late. Once we were having a party in the rec room in the basement, and I stayed up to 7 a.m.! We were having fun, and I didn't even know it was late."

ALEX, AGE 15

In our fast-paced society, going without sleep in order to achieve goals is often considered admirable. The executive assistant who works until midnight to prepare the minutes for the board meeting is rewarded with a bonus. The person who not only holds a full-time job but also obtains a diploma or degree through evening classes is admired. Make sure you don't inadvertently reward your child for staying up late by praising the subsequent achievements.

Sleep Problems

Adolescents have to cope with significant new conflicts and anxieties, which may affect their sleep. They might have more nightmares, a sleepless night, or occasional trouble falling asleep. However, a change in sleeping patterns can be a tip-off that something's not right. Adolescents going through depression typically sleep too much. They sleep deeply all night, take naps, or even spend the whole day in bed. They withdraw into sleep as a way of avoiding the problems that they find impossible to solve. If your child sleeps excessively or has problems with sleep, discuss them with your family doctor.

SEE PAGE 228

The organization Sleep/Wake Disorders Canada provides informative publications and information on self-help groups. Among the descriptions of over eighty disorders of sleeping and waking, you may find background information and suggestions that help you understand what's happening with your child and the avenues you can explore with your doctor.

Delayed sleep phase syndrome

If your teen complains that he can't fall asleep until 3 or 4 a.m. and can't get up for school in the morning, chances are that his sleep phase cycle has shifted. The remedy for this sleep disorder may actually be to go to bed later. Yes, later. Since a teen's natural circadian rhythm sends him to bed later, this approach, recommended by the Canadian Sleep Society, works to correct the phase shift. Your teen should move his bedtime forward three hours each night until he has moved entirely around the clock and reached the desired bedtime. The process takes a week to work. Once he has reached the ideal bedtime, he must maintain both bedtime and wake-up time even on weekends or he will knock the cycle quickly out of phase again.

Or he can try the "weekend crash treatment." Beginning on Friday, he doesn't sleep at all, day or night. On Saturday, he goes to bed around midnight. Then on Sunday morning, he should get up at the time he needs to wake for school. On Sunday night, his bedtime should be 9 or 10 p.m. By Monday, he will have achieved his goal of being awake during the day and able to sleep at night. These regimes are severe, so your teen has to be motivated to get back into sync with the rest of the world. If he wants to give either approach a try, help him out by waking him at the appropriate times.

> **If your child sleeps excessively or has problems sleeping, consult your family doctor.**

Night terrors

Night terrors usually occur within an hour or two of falling asleep. A younger child experiencing a night terror (or partial waking, as it's sometimes called) typically sits up, opens his eyes, and grinds his teeth. After a few minutes he lies back down and returns to sleep. But in adolescence, night terrors can be much more dramatic and frightening.

For a teen, a night terror might start with a bloodcurdling scream. Then she may jump out of bed, knock furniture over, even break a window or lamp. During a night terror, your teen risks physical injury. Don't try to restrain her or you, too, will risk injury. Instead, block her access to the stairway and other areas where she might hurt herself. Turn on the light in the hall. Push aside the clutter that covers her bedroom floor. Make a safe place for her to calm down.

One or two episodes of night terrors per year are nothing to be concerned about. But one or two night terrors a month may be cause for concern. The adolescent who guards her feelings during the day is the typical victim of night terrors. Perhaps she's unable, or too frightened, to express her anger about a move, a death in the family, or her difficulties at school. Arrange counselling to help her deal with the emotional blocks that bring on frequent night terrors.

Sexuality

The stats are clear. More than 80 per cent of North Americans have their first sexual intercourse as teenagers. It's a major step into adulthood and one that a teen should feel comfortable discussing with his parents. But few do feel comfortable. Many kids even say they're reluctant because their parents are too serious about sex or take too long to answer their questions. They also complain that parents don't talk about the associated feelings. Most parents do talk about all the frightening negatives—the dangers of contracting a sexually transmitted disease (STD), the possibility of an unwanted pregnancy, and the pain of being abandoned by someone you thought loved you.

For many parents, adolescent sexuality is a highly charged emotional issue. Despite the statistics, most parents have difficulty acknowledging the emerging sexuality that accompanies their teen's increasing independence of thought and action. As parents, you can't control your teen's behaviour and you can't preserve her from all the risks inherent in taking on more adult roles. Most parents know that the majority of teenagers move from kissing to more intimate sexual behaviours, then to intercourse. But if you don't talk about sexual behaviours, your teen may interpret the lack of acknowledgment as disinterest in her feelings and even disapproval of all sexual activity. That won't stop her from exploring her own sexuality, but she may explore under a blanket of guilt, fear, and misinformation. Rather than risk losing your respect by asking you questions about topics that make you uncomfortable, she risks disease and pregnancy.

It's true that the stakes are high. Your teen might become entangled in an emotional relationship that he is too immature to handle. Your son could make his girlfriend pregnant. Either son or daughter might contract an STD, which could cause illness or infertility, or they could become infected with HIV (human immunodeficiency virus), which most often leads to AIDS (acquired immune deficiency syndrome).

When parents do discuss sexuality and responsible sexual behaviour with their teens and answer questions or direct them to appropriate resources, the young people eventually gain enough self-confidence and information to behave responsibly in sexual situations. Teens certainly need the facts about the potential pleasures and pains of sexual relationships. But they also need the opportunity to talk with adults about what's most on their minds: How do you know at what point in a relationship the time is right? How do you tell your boyfriend No when the time isn't right? How do you become a good lover and have sex that's mutually pleasurable?

Sue McGarvie, an Ottawa sexual health educator, believes that parents don't talk to their kids about sex with enthusiasm because they're afraid their kids will want to have sex. "But what's wrong with that?" she asks.

Teens and Sex Now

Today's teenagers are more likely to have sexual intercourse on a date than were their parents at their age. Although it's important to know your own child, statistics from the Canadian Institute of Child Health suggest that the following is typical of adolescent sexual behaviour in the 1990s.

Early adolescence: ages twelve to fourteen

For the most part, sexual relationships occur only in the daydreams of early teens, although there is some experimentation. About 25 per cent have had sexual intercourse by age fourteen. The girls who engage in regular sexual activity are usually dating older boys or men, and sexual intercourse may not have been their idea. In one study, nearly three-quarters of the girls who had intercourse before age fourteen said they were having intercourse involuntarily. Engaging in sexual intercourse at this early age may originate from conflicts with the adults in their lives, including sexual abuse, or it may be a symptom of low self-esteem and lack of knowledge and support.

Middle adolescence: ages fifteen to seventeen

This is the stage at which teens tend to fall in love for the first time. Because teens at this age are still self-centred, the boyfriend or girlfriend may not be appreciated for his or her unique personality but rather for reassuring the partner that he or she is OK. The beloved may serve as a mirror to reflect that the teen is indeed sexy and attractive. Mid-adolescents are usually comfortable with and proud of their new bodies. They may choose to show them off with clothes that bare almost all. Even if you view muscle shirts or mini skirts as sexually provocative, your teen may see them as simply flattering or fashionable.

In Canada, about 40 per cent of teens have had sexual intercourse by age sixteen, and more than half by age seventeen—53 per cent. This sexual activity coincides, unfortunately, with a time when many teens feel almost invincible. They can't quite believe their sexual intercourse could lead to pregnancy or to STDs.

Late adolescence: ages eighteen to twenty-one

By the end of their teenage years, about 80 per cent of young people have had sexual intercourse. By this age, your teen usually feels more secure, so relationships with the opposite sex become less sexually exploitive. Each appreciates the partner not only for how they make one another feel but also for their unique combination of qualities and talents. Peer attachments lessen in importance as the couple relationship comes into stronger focus.

"After all, why do people have sex? Because it feels great." McGarvie suggests that parents should remember to include the positives about sex along with the negatives. At her talks with parents and kids, McGarvie raises the topic of orgasms, although parents are often shocked. "But if your kids are going to be having sex, you want them to be having orgasms," she says. This kind of discussion helps kids learn about positive sexuality as part of a real, loving relationship.

Some aspects of sexual relationships needn't always be treated as serious topics. After all, much of what our culture considers humorous has sexual connotations. Help your teen relax about the topic and view sex as a natural part of life, at the same time learning how to keep private intimacies private.

Parental silence about sexual behaviour may provide a fertile ground for a teen's curiosity: She might respond to older teens or adults who prey on the uninformed; or the silence may breed anxiety that interferes with her ability to eventually enjoy a sexual relationship. Teenagers who are unaccustomed to discussing their sexuality may also deny to themselves that they want to have sex and, as a result, won't take precautions against either STDs or pregnancy.

> **Help your teen relax about sex and view it as a natural part of life.**

The majority of sexually active teens use contraception on an ongoing basis, but about 20 per cent use no contraception; 19 per cent of the girls who do use the pill don't also use condoms for protection against STDs. Often the boy expects the girl to take sole responsibility for protection, but she may not be fully informed about the various methods. Information and openness are key: There's evidence that teens whose parents teach them or encourage them to learn the facts and myths about sexuality and discuss sexual health openly are more likely to delay involvement in sexual intercourse until they're older. They're also more likely to decide to use some method of protection against sexually transmitted diseases and a method of birth control if they do decide to engage in sexual intercourse.

Even if your own beliefs and values lead you to disapprove of birth control or of sexual intercourse before marriage, even if you prefer that your teen wait until she's older and is involved in a loving relationship, discuss the facts and implications of sexual intercourse because your teen may, as an independent thinker, choose to take her relationship that far. Make sure she has information not only to prevent an unwanted pregnancy but also to avoid contracting STDs that might prevent a future wanted pregnancy.

When and how?

Meg Hickling, a registered nurse and sexual health educator in Vancouver, believes that parents don't talk to teens about sexuality nearly as often as they could or should. Most kids don't want to talk about it when there's intense, eye-to-eye contact with their parents, and they don't want to answer direct questions about their own behaviour. But they would like to have more general discussions with their parents. Hickling suggests that parents use situations in which their kids are a captive audience. Long car rides often give parents and teens the chance to do their best talking. Teens will also talk more openly with parents when everyone's busy together, making dinner, tidying the kitchen, cleaning out the garage. Approach the subject from a sidelong direction. Develop a conversation from an item you watched on the news together. Certainly there are ample references to sexuality and sexual behaviours on television and in movies to serve as lead-ins to frank and open conversations between parents and teens.

Answering your teen's questions

"When am I ready?" Your son isn't likely to look up from his breakfast cereal and ask you this question, but you can bet it's on his mind. As his parent, your role is to be a wise influence and provide information; when to become sexually active is your teen's choice. If you would like to influence his decision, here are some topics you might think about so that you can offer your own version at an appropriate time.

➤ Sexual intercourse should be part of a loving relationship, and each partner should feel both sensitive to and protective of the other. Some people believe you're ready to have sex if you're comfortable telling your partner what feels good to you. Others feel you're ready to have sex when you can go to the drugstore and buy condoms with your own money, or when you can make an appointment with your doctor to get backup birth control.

> **Long car rides often give parents and teens the chance to do their best talking.**

➤ If teens put off having sexual intercourse until they feel confident about discussing these topics, it may ultimately make their first experience better. But they may feel they're abnormal or may fear rejection by others if sexual intercourse isn't part of their relationship. Both males and females might use variations of the line "You'd do it, if you loved me" on each other. Give your teen a possible response: "If you loved me, you wouldn't pressure me." Or suggest helpful relationship books that reveal favourite "lines" and responses that can deflect unwanted attention with humour or with compassion.

> Remind your teen that she is in charge of her own body and can set limits on sexual behaviour. If your daughter doesn't know how to raise the topic with her partner, suggest some openers: "I really like the kissing, but I don't want to go any further." She might also add, "If I have to worry about stopping you from going further, it keeps me from the fun of kissing you."

> Let your teen know that he can enjoy sexual feelings and give and receive sexual pleasure without having intercourse. And he needs to know that abstinence from sexual intercourse is the most effective method of preventing both pregnancy and sexually transmitted diseases.

> Teach your teen that when one partner says No, the other partner must stop whatever sexual activity he's doing; teach her not to put herself in vulnerable situations, in any place, with any person or group that makes her uncomfortable or uneasy; teach him not to make himself vulnerable by using alcohol or other drugs that decrease his inhibitions or cause him to act irresponsibly.

Birth Control

The basic information every teen needs to know before having intercourse should include birth control. Be sure your teen knows that every time a man and a woman have sex, there is the possibility that they might make a baby. Despite lines to the contrary, a girl can get pregnant the first time, during her period, using withdrawal, standing up, or while on drugs.

The 1995 Canadian Contraception Study revealed that almost all Canadian women between fifteen and forty-four knew about oral contraceptives and condoms. Why some teenagers choose not to use birth control isn't clear. Some girls may fear that discussing contraception makes them appear too easy or rather sex-crazed. Some teens just conclude that pregnancy happens to others—not to them.

Some research shows that teenagers who are accustomed to talking openly with their parents about sexual matters are not less sexually active, but they are more likely to use birth control. Supply your teen with the information she needs in case she's considering having sexual intercourse with her boyfriend. Saying "Use precautions" isn't enough. You wouldn't teach her to drive with such vague instructions, but sexual intercourse can have enormous consequences on her health and well-being.

Give her all the details she needs through discussions, pamphlets, books, as well as access to medical counselling. If you feel awkward about opening the discussion, try, "I understand that a lot of people your age get involved in sexual intercourse, so it's really important to me that you learn about protecting yourself from disease and pregnancy."

Your teen has a wide range of birth control options. But none, except abstinence from sexual intercourse, is 100 per cent effective.

The pill The birth control method used most frequently is the pill. The pill stops ovulation and alters the pH of the vagina, making it inhospitable for sperm; it also thins the endometrium so that eggs can't implant. Most birth control pills are very effective; the failure rate of less than 1 per cent includes those women who sometimes forget to take the daily pill. The pill has several positive side effects along with some negative ones. It reduces the severity of menstrual cramps and headaches; it reduces acne and anemia. But it may cause some nausea, breast tenderness, irritability, and spotting between periods. It's also advisable for women who smoke not to use the pill.

"Lack of knowledge about sex is often a problem. It's sometimes surprising how little people know. One time there was a girl, I think she was thirteen, who phoned. She was having oral sex with her boyfriend and swallowed his semen. She was worried that she could get pregnant."

DENISE, AGE 18, A VOLUNTEER WITH A SEX HELP LINE

The condom In addition to providing birth control, the latex condom is the only protection against STDs. Girls should not be shy about asking a partner to wear one. When fitted snugly to the penis, a condom contains the male's ejaculate and prevents the sperm from entering the woman's vagina. The user and his partner must learn how to put on a condom and how to squeeze out any air bubbles to prevent pressure that might result in breakage. Condoms have an expiration date, and teens should know to check the date on the package and open it carefully to prevent tearing. They should also know that condoms can sometimes fail. An oil-based lubricant like lotion, oil, or petroleum jelly weakens a latex condom, possibly causing it to break. Using a spermicide such as nonoxynol-9 improves protection from pregnancy. Although many condoms are lubricated with nonoxynol-9, it is more effective when applied in the vagina.

Other birth control Teens should know: that a spermicide protects against STDs while it also kills sperm; that a woman must be "fitted" for a diaphragm or cervical cap, which provides a barrier between the sperm and the uterus; that the contraceptive sponge absorbs sperm and inactivates it with a spermicide.

Emergency contraception pill (ECP) Parents and teens should know that their family doctor can prescribe this "morning-after" pill and that it is effective not just the morning after but up to 72 hours after intercourse. Some clinics and rape crisis centres also keep it on hand. It cannot be used by women with heart disease, a blood-clotting disorder, or severe migraines.

More birth control information is available from a variety of sources. Direct your teen to her doctor, to Planned Parenthood, telephone talk lines, teen clinics, and the library. If she seems unsure or unwilling, pick up some brochures for her, and leave them in her room.

Unwanted Pregnancy

Although any sexually active teen couple can make a baby, some teen couples are at higher risk. Parents who don't discuss sex at all or who talk only about abstinence from sexual activity leave their children without important knowledge that might prevent their daughter from becoming pregnant or their son from impregnating his partner. The teens in these families may not know enough about the sexual acts their bodies want to perform and the consequences of those acts, let alone about protection. A teenage girl with little sexual knowledge is more likely to be coerced into sexual intercourse by an aggressive older partner. The statistics from a Toronto public health office show that 26 per cent of teen mothers age fifteen to seventeen and 31 per cent of teen mothers age eighteen to nineteen had partners who were twenty-five or older.

If your daughter does get pregnant, she needs your support. Accidents happen—his condom breaks, her diaphragm doesn't fit properly, or she forgets to take the birth control pill regularly. Teens are about as consistent about birth control as adults are. Two-thirds use contraceptives the first time they have sexual intercourse; more than three-quarters use contraception on an ongoing basis. Trying to assign blame won't change your daughter's situation.

Discuss the choices she has: abortion, or taking the pregnancy to term and either raising the child or giving the baby up for adoption. Help your daughter find realistic information and counselling, if she wants it, about the positives and negatives of each choice. It may be very difficult for you not to impose your own beliefs. Let her know how you feel about the choices, but ultimately it is her decision.

If your son impregnates his partner, fight the feeling of panic and concentrate on his needs. The decision about what to do about the pregnancy will be primarily his partner's, but the situation is also painful for the young man involved—although his trauma is not usually acknowledged. Avoid laying blame, and help him get the information he needs to deal with his questions and his fears. Let him know you support him, and help him get counselling, if he wishes.

Sexually Transmitted Diseases

Sexually transmitted diseases (STDs) are acquired during sexual intercourse (vaginal, oral, or anal) with an infected person. Adolescents have the highest rate of STDs of any age group—one in six sexually active teenagers contracts an STD each year. The infections are caused by different organisms, usually bacteria or viruses. Even a person who doesn't look or feel sick can be infected, so partners should always take precautions before sexual intercourse. All teenagers should learn the signs and symptoms of STDs.

The most common symptoms are warts, lumps, and sores in the genital region; discharge from the vagina or the penis or from the anus; a burning sensation when urinating; a sore throat; itching in the genital or anal region; and lower abdominal pain or pain in the groin. Some STDs are totally without symptoms but can still lead to internal complications when not detected and treated. Until she is eighteen or twenty, a young woman's cervix has immature cells that are more susceptible to diseases such as chlamydia and the papilloma virus (which can cause cervical cancer). If left untreated, some STDs are life-threatening.

Prevention

The most successful way to prevent acquiring or transmitting STDs is to not engage in sexual intercourse. However, those who choose to have sex can lower the risk of infection by always using a condom, even while engaging in oral or anal sex. Using the spermicide nonoxynol-9 along with a condom kills some STD-causing germs. It also reduces the risk to limit the number of different partners, to not have sex with an infected person, and to abstain from sexual intercourse if you have and are being treated for an STD.

> **The most successful way to prevent STDs is to not engage in sexual intercourse.**

Washing the genitals with soap and water and urinating right after sexual intercourse might eliminate some STD-causing germs before they cause infection. Women should not douche—most odours come from outside the vulva, so douching is not necessary for cleanliness, and it may actually spread infections. The chemicals in douches may also irritate a teen's vagina, upset the balance of healthy bacteria, and increase the risk of getting pelvic inflammatory disease.

Diagnosis and treatment

Most STDs can be diagnosed during a doctor's physical examination. He may test a culture of the secretions from vagina or penis, or perform a blood test. STDs caused by bacteria can be treated with antibiotics, but those caused by viruses have no definitive cure. However, early detection of STDs can limit how far and how fast they spread and progress.

STDs caused by bacteria

Chlamydia has relatively few symptoms, especially in women. If there are symptoms, they usually include itching around the vagina, pain during sex, painful or frequent urination, or an odourless, yellow vaginal discharge. Other symptoms are a dull pain in the pelvic area and bleeding between menstrual periods. Chlamydia can also cause pelvic inflammatory disease which causes infertility in women. Symptoms in males include painful urination and a watery, milky-coloured discharge from the penis.

Gonorrhea (the clap or the drip), like chlamydia, has few symptoms in women, but when present they include white, green, or yellow vaginal discharge and painful urination. Men may experience a thick, yellow penal discharge and painful urination. Gonorrhea has been linked to pelvic inflammatory disease and arthritis.

Syphilis shows the same symptoms in both sexes. The early signs include chancres (painless red sores) that appear on the areas of sexual contact—the genitals, anus, tongue, and throat. The glands near the chancre might swell. A few months later, a sore throat, fever, lack of appetite, or joint pain may occur. The sufferer may develop a scaly rash on the soles of the feet or the palms of the hands. After these symptoms have disappeared, there may be no signs for a few years. When the symptoms recur, the tertiary stage of syphylis affects the brain, the spinal cord, and the skin and bones. Syphilis also causes heart damage, blindness, and death.

> **Adolescents have the highest rate of STDs of any age group.**

STDs caused by viruses

AIDS (acquired immune deficiency syndrome) results from infection with HIV (human immunodeficiency virus), which lives in an infected person's blood and other body fluids. HIV attacks the immune system which protects against bacteria and infections. With a compromised immune system, people with HIV become susceptible to every infection and cannot easily recover from even a minor illness.

Most people who contract HIV have become infected in one of the following ways: from the blood, semen, vaginal secretions, and open sores of an infected person; from sharing a needle previously used by an infected person to inject drugs or to pierce or tattoo the body; from a transfusion of the untested blood of an infected person; by getting the blood of an infected person in an open, bleeding sore. Contracting HIV through exchanging saliva while kissing has never been known to happen. Because the virus can't survive long outside the body, it isn't transmitted through casual contact such as touching, shaking hands, or hugging. The virus also cannot be transmitted just by swimming in a public pool, using public telephones, water fountains, or toilets, nor from insects such as mosquitoes.

> **Early detection of STDs can limit how far and how fast they spread.**

Anyone who thinks he is at risk should consider getting tested for HIV. A woman who is or suspects she became pregnant during unprotected sexual intercourse should get tested. An HIV-infected mother may transmit the virus to her fetus or through breast-feeding the baby, but treatment during pregnancy can decrease the effects on the baby.

Most tests for the HIV antibody are accurate if done three to six months or longer after the time a person might possibly have been infected. Anyone who is reluctant to reveal his concern to his family doctor can go to a clinic that provides anonymous testing. If, however, the test result is positive for HIV, the affected person must consult his doctor immediately to discuss the options for treatment. If the test result is negative for HIV, the person concerned must still take into account that the symptoms of AIDS can develop up to eight years after infection by HIV.

Hepatitis B has the same symptoms for both sexes. They are fever, tiredness, loss of appetite, muscle pain, headaches, and dizziness. As the disease progresses, symptoms include loose, light-coloured stools, yellow skin and eyes, dark urine, and tenderness in the liver area. Hepatitis B may lead to liver cancer or liver failure.

Herpes shows the same symptoms in men and women. The first signs are itching or tingling around the genitals. Small blisters may form in this area and burst, causing a burning feeling, especially during urination. Eventually, these sores turn into scabs. Other symptoms include fever, body aches, and swollen glands. Although herpes outbreaks may occur for many years, even a lifetime, they become less frequent and less painful with time.

Human Papilloma Virus (HPV) may cause the growth of painless, soft, flesh-coloured warts around the genital area or on the cervix. Sometimes the virus causes warts that cannot be seen by the naked eye. HPV has

also been linked to cervical cancer and cancer of the penis. Common treatments include burning the warts off with liquid nitrogen or laser surgery.

Mononucleosis, caused by the Epstein-Barr virus, is a type of herpes virus. Although "mono" can affect anyone of any age, it is more common in teenagers and young adults and is usually spread by sharing beverages, by kissing, or by any activity that results in direct contact with infected saliva. Mono has a 30- to 50-day incubation period. Not everyone who is infected experiences the symptoms: a very sore throat, fever, fatigue, chills, enlarged lymph glands, and usually an enlarged spleen or liver. Less common are jaundice, rashes, and bleeding gums.

Your family doctor can request a blood test to detect the antibodies to the Epstein-Barr virus, which will confirm infection. She might also request other tests to rule out strep throat and meningitis which resemble mono. Because antibiotics are ineffective against a virus, the usual prescription for mono is lots of rest and plenty of fluids. Acetaminophen or ibuprofen can ease any pain and headaches. Mono goes through an acute stage lasting two weeks, but the fatigue may last for several months. Most people can resume normal activities after the acute stage, but should avoid strenuous activity until their doctor says they've recovered. Heavy lifting or contact sports could cause the spleen to rupture even if it isn't visibly enlarged.

> **Mononucleosis is usually spread by sharing beverages or by kissing.**

Trichomoniasis (trich)

Caused by an organism called *Trichomonas vaginalis*, trich is acquired during unprotected sexual intercourse with an infected person. If left untreated, trich can cause a urinary tract infection. Men rarely have symptoms, and women can be infected for a long time before they experience any signs. Symptoms include a watery, yellowish or greenish, bubbly vaginal discharge, an unpleasant odour, and pain and itching during urination. Trichomoniasis can be treated with antibiotics.

Sexual Orientation

Many teens question their sexual preference during adolescence, and homosexual crushes are quite common. Some teens worry about the implications of being approached sexually by a person of the same gender. They fear this might indicate that they themselves are homosexual. Statistics show that about 18 per cent of boys and 6 per cent of girls have participated in at least one homosexual act by the age of nineteen. Your teen needs to know that questioning one's sexuality is normal during the teen years and not always an indication of his sexual orientation. Just knowing that other kids have the same questions and that about 1 in 10 people is gay or lesbian can be very reassuring to a teen.

Some teens may be reluctant to discuss sexual orientation, but if you want to maintain open communication with them, don't avoid the topic. If there's a news report about the progress being made regarding gay people's rights, you might comment, "Isn't it too bad that we can't just let people be who they are?" By conveying your own willingness to accept people as they are, you may release your teen, who's wondering about her own sexuality, to talk with you. As a parent, you should be prepared for the possibility that your child's sexual orientation may be homosexual.

"It would have been better if I had been told as a youngster that love can occur between men and men as well as between men and women. I remember thinking that it was an alien concept, so pursuing women was an easier route to take.

I think if my parents had been more enlightened about homosexuality and could have said that it wasn't a disease or anything crazy, that would probably have erased a lot of the confusion. I would have learned as a teenager that homosexuality was acceptable. Instead, it was just like a distant planet that no one knew about. So why visit it? If it's unknown, it could be dangerous."

FRANK, AGE 32

If you sense that your teen is struggling with this question, give him every opportunity to discuss it with you, even if you find it difficult and painful. Many adults have strong beliefs about homosexuality, and if your child suspects that he is gay, he may be afraid to talk with you. As a result, he may suffer a profound sense of isolation and loneliness, which may even lead to suicidal behaviour. Don't let your unwillingness to talk set him up for a life of pain and secrecy. Reassure your child that he is loved, no matter what his sexual orientation. A sympathetic professional with experience in the issues of gender orientation may be able to help both of you deal with your teen's sexual preference. Contact a support group such as Parents, Families and Friends of Lesbians and Gays (P-FLAG). Check your phone book for a local chapter.

SEE PAGE 227

Body

A Teen's Point of View: My Body

My body is changing so rapidly that it can scare me. If I'm a late developer, I may worry about being left behind. I need your help to accept what's happening to me.

Age Thirteen

All Kids

- My bones grow faster than my muscles, so I'll start looking awkward and uncoordinated.

- I get jumpy when I have to sit for a long time.

- I may not be at my best first thing in the morning on a school day. I like to go to bed late and sleep in the next morning.

- I may mumble in my sleep.

- My nose may stick out until the rest of my face grows to catch up with it.

- I have a very healthy appetite. Please don't tease me or make an issue out of how much food I need to eat.

Girls Only

- I could be well on my way to physical and sexual maturity, while most of the boys are just beginning puberty.

- If my periods haven't started yet, they likely will this year, although they could start anytime up to age seventeen. And if I'm like most girls, the onset of my periods won't mark the first stage of my sexual development, but one of the last stages.

- One breast may be bigger than the other. It may always stay bigger, just as I have one hand or foot bigger than the other.

- From so much rapid growing, I might get red-purple stretch marks on my hips or breasts. They'll fade with time.

- The hair on my legs gets darker. I get more hair under my arms and in my pubic area.

- My oil and sweat glands become more active. I may have acne.

- Very gradually, my voice continues to get lower.

Boys Only

- I'll grow taller this year, but I probably won't have my big growth spurt until next year.

- My penis gets longer but won't necessarily get thicker yet, so it may look thin in proportion. The skin of my scrotum gets darker. One testicle will probably hang lower than the other.

- I get more pubic hair and more underarm hair. If I haven't used deodorant yet, I'll probably need to start.

- I get erections more and more often. They happen spontaneously, sometimes when I least expect them—for example, in the middle of class. This can cause me a lot of embarrassment.

- I get wet dreams, which cause me to ejaculate involuntarily in my sleep.

- The hair at the corners of my upper lip—what will ultimately be my moustache—gets a little darker, but I don't need to shave yet.

- My voice may start to change, getting deeper and maybe cracking a little.

Age Fourteen

All Kids

- I have a lot of energy and enthusiasm. I'm usually up for anything.

- I like to be busy all the time. If I have too much time on my hands and not enough activity, I get bored and restless.

- I'm less likely to need reminders to go to bed on school nights. I recognize when I'm tired and I don't fight it. If I push myself too hard during the day, I might need the occasional nap after school.

- I talk in a loud voice, even when you're sitting right beside me. I'm not doing it on purpose: As my body grows and changes, I'm not always aware of the strength of my own voice.

- I continue to have a good appetite. I may still wolf down everything that's put in front of me, or I may become a little more discriminating.

- I'm developing my own style in clothes. I'm less influenced by fads than I used to be.

- My face, neck, and shoulders look bigger and stronger.

- If I've been wearing glasses, I may be ready to try contact lenses.

- I'm more likely to act on my sexual urges, especially through masturbation. I may go through some confusion about my sexual orientation.

14

Girls Only

- I look more like a young woman than a girl. My hips are rounded, and my breasts continue to become fuller.

- My pubic hair is becoming thick and full. I may have some downy growth on my lower abdomen or upper thighs.

- I'm careful about my appearance. I shower regularly and I use sanitary pads quite lavishly. I may not feel ready to try tampons.

- I'm close to my adult height, especially if I've started menstruating. (Bones usually don't grow much in length once menstruation has begun.) But if I haven't had my first period yet, I could do a lot more growing in the interim.

Boys Only

- This is the year when I'm likely to have the most rapid growth in height. But even if I don't grow much now, I still have lots of time. I may not reach my full height for another five years.

- My "fat stage," if I had one, is over. My body is looking more muscular.

- I look ungainly because of the way my bones grow. First my hands and feet get bigger, then my forearms and lower legs, then my upper arms and thighs, and finally my hips and chest.

- My lower jaw gets bigger, changing the contours of my face.

- My voice continues to deepen. It may happen gradually, or my voice may crack and sound hoarse as my larynx and vocal cords grow.

- My Adam's apple becomes more prominent.

- My penis gets a little longer and a lot thicker.

- My pubic hair becomes darker and denser. It may start growing up toward my belly button.

- If I haven't had wet dreams before, I'll have them now.

- I'll get a little more hair on my upper lip and chin, and my sideburns grow longer. If my facial hair is especially dark and dense, I may need to shave, although probably only a couple of times a week. If the hair is fair and sparse, I may not need to shave for another few years.

- The hair on my arms and legs gets darker.

- I could start getting acne.

Age Fifteen and Up

All Young Adults

- I'm definitely looking more like an adult than a child. My features become sharper and more defined.

- My posture may still look a little awkward. I may hunch over when I'm standing, or lumber when I walk. But gradually my stance will look relaxed, and I'll slowly develop a new sense of poise.

- My appearance matters to me, although I don't agonize over it so much anymore. I spend a lot of time on my hair. My room, though, may still be a mess.

- My sexual orientation becomes more firmly established. I'm more likely to act on my sexual desires.

Young Women Only

- My physical and sexual development is almost complete. I'll continue to gain some weight, and my breasts and hips may get fuller.

- My reproductive organs are fully developed. But the tissue around my cervix may continue to undergo changes for a few years, making me particularly vulnerable to long-term problems from sexually transmitted diseases.

- I may or may not masturbate regularly and have involuntary orgasms in my sleep.

- If my periods have been light and sporadic, they'll gradually become more regular. But my cycle may be longer than 28 days, possibly 40 days or even longer, and may go on that way for several years.

- My appetite settles down now that my phase of rapid growth is over, but it's still vital that I eat well-balanced meals.

- The way I eat now will affect my future long-term health. I need you to make sure that I don't skip breakfast or eat only fries for lunch.

Young Men Only

- I'm still growing. I need to eat a lot of food in order to fuel these changes, and I will for another few years. I might need a huge snack only an hour after dinner.

- My shoulders broaden and my muscles continue to develop, sometimes appearing to bulge beneath my skin. My veins, especially in my arms, become more prominent.

- By sixteen, I'll likely need to shave, but probably not every day yet.

- I may get hair on my chest and abdomen.

- My sperm are fully mature.

Mind

2

As your teen's brain approaches maturity, she becomes more capable of abstract thought, more adept at using logic, more inclined to speculate about the future. At the same time, she has difficulty understanding risk, which can sometimes lead to dangerous behaviour. Your teen's intellectual life revolves around school and her choices for her future education and eventual work life. Yours is a supporting role—helping her choose her unique path based on all her strengths and interests.

Throughout the teen years and beyond, the human brain continues to be refined. Neurons, the electro-chemical impulse-transmitting cells in the brain, fire off the impulses that create neural pathways. These pathways enable the brain development that allows the human child to learn language, understand feelings, or develop hand-eye coordination. While neuron cells are busy connecting with each other, connective brain cells, called glia cells, nourish the neurons, and fatty, insulating sheaths of myelin are formed around the nerve fibres. This process of myelinization protects the connections and allows nerve impulses to travel through the brain more quickly and more efficiently.

The Adolescent Brain

As their brains approach maturity, teens are poised for tremendous cognitive development. Experts speculate that as the myelinization of neural connections increases and strengthens, the learning processes of teens mature and their ability to think abstractly improves. There is as yet little research linking myelinization with the development of

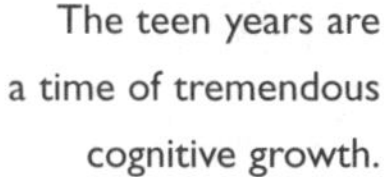

The teen years are a time of tremendous cognitive growth.

abstract thought, but parents and teachers watch this development unfold throughout the teen years.

You may not have realized that your teen's ability to be sarcastic signals a greater capacity to handle more abstract thought, but that's exactly what's happening. Along with an appreciation of sarcasm, she can also appreciate and use metaphor, satire, and irony—all evidence that she's thinking more abstractly. Teens also find some television programs more entertaining as their ability develops to appreciate different levels of humour.

Teens become more capable of handling advanced concepts in mathematics and the sciences and can handle a more complex curriculum. Algebra appears as a separate topic or course on the mathematics curriculum, because teens have a greater capacity to comprehend letters standing in for unknown numbers in an equation. They also handle better the process of hypothesizing (setting up a tentative explanation or theory) and testing the hypothesis through investigation of the facts.

"About two years ago, when our son Leigh was fifteen, we realized he was in a real funk about something. It took a lot of talking for us to figure out that he was suddenly carrying the weight of the world on his shoulders. He was seeing all the hunger and war and disaster in the world, and for the first time it hit him that these were real people who were suffering.

My husband, Tom, had told me a similar story about himself; how he was baby-sitting his siblings one evening when he was about fourteen, and his parents came home to find him sobbing. He'd been watching the news and was suddenly struck with an awareness of all the problems of the world.

Later that year, Leigh watched the movie *Schindler's List* with his twelve-year-old brother, Carey. I could clearly see that the portrayal of the Jewish Holocaust really struck Leigh, while the same wasn't true of his brother. But Carey is fifteen now and studying World War Two in history, and he wants to see that movie again. At this age, he's ready to relate to something that he can't actually touch or feel or see, something that happened fifty years ago, and yet I know this time there will be the connection."

JEANNE, MOTHER OF FOUR

These developments in cognition also turn teens into delightful conversationalists. For some parents, adolescence is their favourite phase of childhood, because they enjoy the stimulating conversation, the quick humour, and the verbal sparring their children are now capable of after years of communicating on a much simpler level.

These cognitive changes support teens as they begin to go through the phases of separation from their parents and the rest of the family to develop individual identities. Kim Schonert-Reichl, who teaches adolescent psychology at the University of British Columbia, points

out that adolescents comprehend the concept of friendship in the abstract. They understand their own feelings and the importance of empathizing with others' feelings, of sharing thoughts, feelings, and secrets, of trusting someone close.

Teens show a tremendous variation in the age at which their thought processes begin to mature, and unlike their physical growth and development, their emotional and cognitive developments are not in constant progression—there is a kind of ebb and flow of mature and immature thought. Kids don't all show their capacity for abstract thought at the same age. Nor are they able to apply abstract thought in other areas of their lives despite having acquired the capacity in academic subjects. A grade eight teacher who uses sarcasm to make a point in class may make half the students laugh with her but leave the others wondering why she would say such a thing. And some of those who understood the sarcasm might still not be able to grasp algebraic concepts.

Have you ever wondered why you and your teen spend so much time arguing? One result of their cognitive growth and development is that teens become more adept at using logic. They're better at teasing out the inconsistencies in all that you say and do. You may be in the middle of lecturing your teen about her messy room when she turns the tables on you: "What about all your paperwork that's been spread over the dining room table for over a week? At least I keep my mess in my own bedroom!"

"A year ago Jen, who's now sixteen, was saying that she was going to grow up and become a model and live in California, marry a movie star, and have twins—one boy and one girl. Today she laughs in wonder that she ever thought that way, and while she hasn't informed us of a new plan, we can see that her thoughts on the future have become a little more realistic."

TRISHA, MOTHER OF THREE

Try convincing your immortal teen about the perils of smoking if you smoked when you were a teenager: "Why shouldn't I make my own mistakes?" If you refuse permission for an evening out on a school night, you may be met with: "When has going to work in the morning ever stopped you from going out at night? So what if I'm a little tired tomorrow morning? I'll make it up tomorrow night." Verbal combat with a teen can be hard on your own self-esteem, but try to step back from the arguments rather than take them personally. Consider your teen's need to have his say part of his brain development.

Another result of thought maturity is that teens can speculate about the future, not only their own but the future of their environment. This is a time when they take hold of a social cause with a passion and devote a lot of time and energy to it. Be prepared to have every slip of yours

thrown back at you. You might view bringing some desk supplies home from the office for your "home work" as justifiable, but a teen on the lookout for a parent who doesn't practise what she preaches may consider it inexcusable. Choosing to be the designated driver and drinking soda at an event at which your teen notes the number of glasses of wine everyone drank is a more powerful message than all the verbal instruction you give on the dangers of drinking and driving. Modelling the kind of behaviour you expect your kids to demonstrate remains important as they move through adolescence.

Unfortunately, many teens have difficulty understanding risk in the abstract, and they have an unshakable belief in their own invincibility. Car crashes, lost limbs, unwanted pregnancy, and sexually transmitted diseases happen to other people; they are cloaked in an invisible, protective force field. Dr. Schonert-Reichl suggests that a belief in their own infallibility, their "personal fable," may help protect teens at a time when they're feeling a lot of stress from the many changes they experience in a short time span. One study Schonert-Reichl conducted among 75 twelve- to fifteen-year-olds in Vancouver showed that the stronger a kid's personal fable, the less likely the teen was to experience symptoms of depression in response to stress.

Mind

Adults take risks every day when they drive cars, speak up at a public meeting, or apply for a new job. Adolescence is the time to learn that healthy risk taking is a good and necessary part of adult life. But, as a parent, you have to help your teen learn about unnecessary and foolish risks. Parents and educators have much better success piercing the teens' force field of invincibility by using concrete examples.

➤ One principal had the car wreck from a teen's drunk-driving fatality towed to the front of the school before the graduation dance to impress upon other teens the danger of drinking and driving after their prom parties.

➤ An effective presentation on water safety could be made by a teen who had to be confined to a wheelchair after damaging his spinal cord diving into unknown water that proved to be too shallow.

➤ A talk about safe sexual practices by a teen who developed AIDS (acquired immune deficiency syndrome) after becoming infected by HIV (human immunodeficiency virus) during unprotected sex makes a much stronger impression than a talk by a health-care professional.

You can help your teen move from concrete examples or experiences to abstract thought in other areas of his life. When he's trying to solve a problem or understand what went wrong in a situation, don't impose your own view. Instead, help him to see other possibilities for himself. Ask, "What were you thinking when you decided this was the best approach to that problem?" Get him thinking about what went wrong and what he would do differently next time.

In her late teens, your teen will once again be more willing to show her affection for you.

Your teen's teachers will be important role models and sources of support as she navigates high school and her future career choices.

Look for opportunities to involve your teen meaningfully in family decisions. When you and your partner are discussing where to go on the annual family holiday, ask your son for input. If he suggests a trip to the Yukon in February, resist the urge to make a sarcastic remark about the chances of total body frostbite. Instead, deal with the idea in a straightforward manner. Ask, "Why the Yukon?" Discuss what appeals to him. Ask him, "How cold do you think it might be then? How could we check on the temperatures?" Take his choice seriously, but help him figure out when would be the best time for him—and the rest of the family—to experience what you all like doing on vacation. Although a winter holiday in the Far North might not be appealing for your whole family, listen carefully to his thinking; perhaps he's looking for an adventure vacation or a chance to experience nature in the raw.

> **Look for opportunities to involve your teen meaningfully in family decisions.**

Negotiating the Transition to High School

High school is exciting and scary all at the same time, and many a student loses some sleep over the biggest change he's had to deal with since kindergarten. Even though you won't be there to hold his hand and show him where to go, you can help prepare him for the changes ahead.

Both classmates and teachers in elementary school talk about the big move; rumours abound about initiation rites and the intimidation of new students. To ease your teen's mind, check out the rumours with older kids and their parents. A word or two from a responsible older teen about what to expect in the first year of high school can help calm the fears.

New students and their parents usually have an opportunity to tour the school building and see all the facilities during an orientation session, so be sure to attend. If possible, get an outline of the courses offered and the names of the staff members. If it's a large school, you can get to know the layout a bit during the orientation, but ask for a school map that includes service areas such as the main offices, the cafeteria, the library or resource centre, and the guidance offices. Study the map together at home, so your teen knows ahead of time how to negotiate the hallways.

"Jake is in grade eight, and making the transition from elementary to high school has been a real struggle. His first semester was pretty bad; he failed one course, got a C minus in another, and so-so marks in the other two courses. So when the second semester started in February, I called all four teachers and asked them to phone me when even the smallest incident arose, rather than waiting till it built up. They all appreciated this pro-active approach and began phoning me about once a week with little stories to tell: Jake was fooling around; Jake was late; Jake didn't show up for a detention. Each time I thanked them for keeping me up-to-date, and each time I talked to Jake about the minor infraction and had him deal with it the next day at school. He caught on real quick that I knew everything that was going on, and pretty quickly settled in.

We're halfway through the second term, the teachers are hardly calling at all now, and Jake is doing noticeably better than last time around. This is the parent-teacher-student combination working at a tangible level. I recommend it."

JOHN, FATHER OF JAKE

Don't forget that something as basic as a combination lock for his locker can be a stumbling block for a nervous new student. Show your teen how to set the combination, record it in a safe place (a notebook or backpack), and use it for his locker. Try also to find out about what extracurricular activities are available at the school. A teenager's social life is almost as important as his academic life during high school, and in the first weeks of school, a new student might find himself painfully isolated. More friendships are formed in a club or on a sports team than in the homeroom, so talk about which activities interest him enough to try out for them or join them.

"I was dreading the day I would have to go to high school. I really thought I'd just be a nobody. What I found is that people really accepted me and let me be who I was. Even the geekiest people here have friends."

JENNIFER, AGE 14

Choosing a School

Transitions from one school to another vary across the country. Some provinces have organized middle schools after grade five or six. Others call them senior public or junior high schools. But almost all provinces call grades ten to twelve secondary school or high school. If your community supports more than one high school, this may be your teen's first opportunity to choose which school she attends. Most kids want to go to the same school as their friends, but encourage your daughter to check out all her options.

Some secondary schools specialize in programs such as technical subjects, including graphics arts, business programs, or arts and music courses that are not available at other schools. Many schools also develop their own culture and traditions: One high school may be a sports powerhouse; another might have links to local business and industry and offer a strong co-op program through which students spend part of their school year in the workplace; some schools have a stronger focus on and reputation for academic achievement. Talk to other parents and older students in your community about the different secondary schools available. The one your teen attends can help or hinder his achievement.

Each spring, some Nova Scotia secondary schools open their doors to the parents of new students. Over a cup of coffee with teachers and administrators, parents learn about the variety of courses offered at the school and what courses their teen should take to be eligible for admission to the next level of education or training. It's such a popular event that at larger schools the open house must be extended over two nights to give all parents a chance to visit their teen's new school.

Academic Survival

Most classroom teachers in the last grades of elementary school talk to students about the demands of high-school courses and the hard work that lies ahead; they talk about the importance of having good work habits and of doing homework—in fact, they hand out major assignments themselves. You can also help prepare your teens by talking about the following Ten Steps to High School Success.

1. Use a calendar agenda or diary, so as not to miss an assignment or test because you forgot to write it down.

2. Be prepared for class by doing the reading assignments the night before. This makes it possible to follow the class discussion.

3. Listen actively in class. Focusing on what the teacher and other students say and participating in the discussion contribute to overall marks and reduce or help with follow-up homework.

4. Take notes. Concentrate on key concepts and key facts. Don't try to write down everything the teacher says. Listen to the point she's making; if it's an interesting variation on what you've read or a tip that helps you understand, jot it down. But for the basics, you can usually check the textbook for details.

5. Organize your notes. Date them; use a highlighter to emphasize definitions or important concepts; write down any questions you have about the subject so that you can ask them in class.

For lots of teens, the highlight of the school day is time with friends.

6.   Ask questions if you don't understand. It's too easy to let a question go and miss an important concept. Asking questions as well as answering them demonstrate your interest and give your teachers opportunities to expand on topics that may also puzzle other students.

7.   Learn to manage your time. Set aside enough time to get your homework done or to study for a big test. Tell friends not to phone during your "study period." When you've finished your work, reward yourself with a phone call or a game.

8.   Set up a study space. Don't waste time hunting down a calculator or searching for an eraser. Gather up all the supplies you need and keep them in an easy-to-reach box. If you can't create any other space and the kitchen table becomes your work table, choose a study time that doesn't bump into meal preparation.

9.   Make a friend in every class. If you're sick and miss a class, call your buddy in English class and find out what the teacher covered while you were away.

10. Never pull an all-nighter for a test. No one is at his best when he works through the night and tries to write a test or exam without adequate sleep. Be fair to yourself and set aside enough time to study or write that essay.

The best study space is wherever your teen studies best.

Mind

Parents in the High Schools

Opportunities for parent involvement in school decrease at the high-school level, and maybe that's as it should be. Teens need a place to call their own and high school is as good a place as any. Although parents aren't needed as often to volunteer in the classroom or to help with fundraising, you may find that the parents' council requires your services, or that your contributions to career day may be solicited.

To get to know your teen's high school and to signal your interest, attend several of the events that the school sponsors or that your teen participates in. Buy tickets for the school play or a musical event. Even if your teen isn't a member of the cast, all classes likely have a certain number of tickets to sell. Your own child may want to sit with his friends rather than his parents, but at least you'll have shared the event and be able to talk about it at home. Don't miss open house or meet-the-teacher night. Showing your own school spirit sends a clear message to your teen about how important his school and his education are to you.

When you do visit the school, make an effort to meet the school principal and other key staff, even if it's only a brief introduction. You'll be glad you can put faces to names. Talk to your teen's teachers to get to know who they are and to make connections beyond the fifteen-minute parent-teacher interview.

"High schools aren't designed for parents. They're large institutions that society uses as launching pads for kids to leave the nest. Parents pretty much have to stick with the parent groups and whatever other extracurricular activities they can worm their way into."

JOHN, PARENT OF ONE

Parents have made themselves more welcome in some high schools than in others.

Parents, Welcome!

Parents have made themselves more welcome in some schools than in others. At Cumberland Junior Secondary School on Vancouver Island, each sports team has a parent rep who serves as a link between the team coach and the parents of team members. The school also has nine other parent volunteer committees. Parents are a common sight in the hallways as they make their way to the Parent Office, the school's unofficial headquarters for them, several days each week. It has a meeting room, a resource library, and the planning centre of their school lunch program. Parents who can't attend a meeting can check the council's Web site, which is chock full of the information kids always seem to forget to tell parents.

Evaluating Student Progress

At the beginning of classes in September, most teachers provide students with an outline of their courses, either for the semester or for the full school year. The outline usually includes plans for evaluating student achievement throughout, showing the allocation of percentages of the final mark to class participation and homework, to major projects or essays, to short tests, and to full-length exams. It's good for parents to become familiar with this information so that they can help their kids balance the emphasis on different phases of each subject in which they enroll. The teacher usually writes comments on the student projects or assignments throughout the semester. Report cards at the end of the semester and of the course usually include the mark or the letter achieved and a general comment.

Beyond the Report Card

For a fuller assessment of how your teen is coping in high school, make a point of attending parent-teacher nights so that you can talk individually with each teacher. You may have to make the rounds of from four to eight different subject teachers. If it's not possible to schedule time to see each teacher in one night, talk with your teen to choose which teachers to meet and which ones to talk with by phone or to meet another day. Each subject teacher keeps a record of student attendance, assignments, and tests. In your meeting with each teacher, ask basic questions.

➤ Is my teen attending your class?

➤ Is my teen behaving in your class?

➤ Does my teen complete homework assignments and hand them in on time?

➤ How is my teen doing in tests?

Most highschool teachers return essays and assignments with a mark and any comments to the students. If you have concerns about these assignments, bring a marked one to the interview and ask the teacher to discuss what problems your teen's work shows. If the teacher suggests that your teen needs additional help with general study skills, inquire about programs the school offers—for example, a tutorial on study or work habits or remedial classes. Many high schools offer workshops designed to boost academic skills.

When you suspect there's a problem, always call the school; don't wait for a teacher to call you. At the high-school level, teachers are responsible for many more students, so the system for reporting back to parents can sometimes break down. If you wait, you may lose valuable time that could have been spent helping your teen. To make an appointment with a teacher, call the school and leave a message with your home or work telephone number. The school secretary will be able to tell you what unassigned periods the teacher has and when you might expect a return call.

Many of the activities your teen takes part in at high school can't be graded and won't show up on his report card but are, nevertheless, very important. Clubs, teams, student government, and community service are all part of the high-school experience. Encourage your teens to get involved and applaud their efforts. Sometimes when a student is going through a bad patch at school—classes are boring, he's struggling with math—it's the drama club or basketball practice that keeps him going. The friendships they make and the experiences they gain make high school a place they want to be. Kids who participate in activities outside of class have greater motivation, and do better academically.

What Do Low Marks Signify?

Marks typically take a nosedive when a young person changes schools, and the change to high school also occurs for most students during puberty. Just as your teens are coping with a changing body, possibly with attendant mood swings or new sexual thoughts and feelings, they face a more challenging curriculum and the new experience of being low man on the social totem pole in a much wider society. Within the first year or two, most students adapt and their marks return to what's normal for them.

But it's important to be able to read your own child. The poor marks your teen receives, whether on assignments, tests, or end-of-semester report cards, might signal any number of other issues. Do they signify

Having outside interests can help a teen do better academically.

academic problems, a psychological problem like depression, societal pressures to conform to preconceived notions of what a girl should do or want, or peer pressures to reject parental values or participate in drug use? Of course, the quality of the school, your family life, your teen's personal motivation, her friendships, and her intellectual ability all play a role in her school success. A teen whose parents are divorcing, or one who is the target of a bully, or one who has broken up with her boyfriend may not be able to focus in class and may get lower marks than usual. If the personal situation is temporary, time and the academic boost that comes from working smarter, not harder, will help restore the student to her or his previous level of achievement.

SEE PAGE 84

A teen who continues to struggle with particular subjects in school, even though he appears to be working hard at them, may already be living up to his academic potential. Some people don't have the intellectual or memory skills needed to handle successfully the courses necessary for admission to college or university. But if you're unsure whether it's your teen's performance or potential that's in question, suggest that he take aptitude tests.

Most high-school guidance departments can offer the kind of aptitude tests and interest inventories that help a student learn about himself. If not, you might contact a psychologist and inquire about the tests available and the related fees. Check your health-care plan to see if a psychologist's fees and aptitude tests are covered. Most people like to see an objective analysis of their capabilities and interests, and students may be relieved to find that the test reveals what they already knew— for example, that they learn best from hands-on experience and don't learn easily from reading and writing. Such an official analysis might end months of miserable conflict between parent and child about their academic achievement. Parents should not impose the goal of a university degree if their child gives no immediate evidence of interest in or ability to pursue that goal.

You can both consider other options for his future and be prepared to accept that your teen may not be best served by what the school system has to offer at this time. Be aware of your teen's strengths and his interests. Set an achievement target that your teen supports. If he's getting 50s and you want 80s, compromise and set a target for the mid-60s as a first step. The worst thing a parent can do is to assume the child is lazy or unmotivated, warns psychologist Harvey Mandel, author of *Could Do Better: Why Children Underachieve and What to Do about It* (HarperCollins, 1995), a step-by-step guide to helping parents help their kids who are underachieving. "Too many parents make the assumption that, if my child fails now, his life is over. Parents need to know that teens can survive most of the difficulties they will ever encounter.... Don't give up hope."

When Your Teen Is Unhappy at School

Most teens understand the importance of getting an education, but less than half say they enjoy going to school, according to Alberta sociologist Reginald Bibby and youth worker Donald Posterski, coauthors of the book *Teen Trends, A Nation in Motion* (Stoddart, 1992). In their survey of 4,000 Canadian high-school students, Bibby and Posterski found that more than 75 per cent identified school as a source of considerable strain. And when asked what they liked about school, the answer was "friends." What they disliked most were classes and homework.

Your teen may not share with you how unhappy he is at school. And even when his behaviour suggests that he isn't happy, he may not admit it. He may tell you that failing a test is nothing, or that everybody skips math. But underneath the macho bravado is a kid who's worried that he's not making the grade. Try to assess what's at the root of his dissatisfaction, then help him to get the most out of his high-school career.

I hate school because it's too difficult for me.

She may be right, or at least she may be right about the particular program she's enrolled in. But your teen may be able to overcome this feeling with a little extra attention from one or more of her subject teachers. It's possible they are unaware that your daughter is having problems with their subject. Find out which subject or topics within the subject pose the greatest difficulty for her; then ask her guidance counsellor for advice. The counsellor may be able to match up your daughter with a tutor who can help her get back on track in a subject.

Don't rule out a learning disability. It's possible that your teen has managed to compensate for a learning disability throughout elementary school, but the more demanding curriculum of junior high or high school overcomes her coping strategies. You might consult your family doctor first and arrange for an examination to determine if there's any medical problem. Talk with the teachers and principal concerned or a counsellor at the school or the board to begin an assessment process. If the assessment reveals a learning disability, follow up to get help for her.

> **A guidance counsellor may be able to match up your teen with a tutor who can help her get back on track.**

SEE PAGE 94

I hate school because I have no friends.

A friendless teen feels like a lost soul. Joining clubs or school teams can provide an immediate source of like-minded people to befriend, but even taking the step of joining may be difficult for a teen who has low self-esteem or is shy or anxious. Talk to a guidance counsellor and let her know

how your teen feels. She may suggest that one of his teachers nudge, prod, or pull your teen into an activity or club that will introduce him to a new group of people.

I hate school because it's so boring.
It's true that most students find some school classes boring and others exciting and challenging. But if your square peg won't or can't fit into the round hole called school, try to find ways to convince her that the end result—a job, a choice of college or university—makes "the torture" worthwhile. Your teen needs to know that not everyone who graduates looks back on their high-school years as a wonderful experience. Many people stuck it out because they had long-term goals that would have been unattainable without a high-school diploma.

Help your teen focus on what needs to be done now to reach long-term goals. Talk about her passions and her interests and what she wants in her future. Help her establish short-term goals that will lead toward her current long-term objective. When you have an idea what future work she envisions for herself, help her find ways to meet with people who work in her "dream" fields, and to interview them about the kinds of courses they took to prepare for the work they do. Once she has a clearer sense of the academic background and skills or training she'll need to be successful at the work, she will be more motivated to complete the relevant high-school courses to qualify for advanced courses.

Skipping Class

A bored or unhappy student skips classes as often as he can get away with it—a sunny day may be all the reason he needs. Skipping too many classes reduces a student's level of performance since contribution in class counts for a significant portion of his mark in many subjects. Above all, habitually skipping classes may lead to dropping out of school altogether.

"You're not a teenager if you can't come up with a good excuse. And I've heard them all. My favourites are: 'I know all the material anyway, so it's not necessary for me to be in class.' 'I skipped because the teacher doesn't like me.' 'Oh no, Sir, I was in class. The teacher just didn't see me.'"

CHRIS, PARENT OF TWO AND GUIDANCE COUNSELLOR

The challenge for teachers and parents is to find a subject or program that can re-ignite the interest of the student who has given up on school. But before you can help, you need to know when your teen is not in class. In a high school where 20 per cent of students may be absent or late every day, keeping track of students can be an administrative nightmare. In some very large schools, it's too easy for students to be marked absent and to disappear for days without follow-up from the school to the home. Find out what your high school's policy is on absenteeism, whether there's a system in place for tracking student attendance at school and in individual classes, and whether there's a system for informing parents of lateness or absence. If you suspect that your teen is skipping one or more classes, call the teachers concerned. You can also be part of the solution rather than the problem by informing the school when your teen will be absent. That's one less phone call for a school secretary to make.

For some teens, the skipping may begin after a failed mid-term test. Finding out early enough to help get the extra help she needs to be successful in the subject can make a world of difference. Educators agree it's important that all students, regardless of their reasons, pay the consequence of skipping a class. The consequence is usually a detention.

To combat poor attendance, one Montreal high school has developed an automated system to track students. Teachers fill out an attendance card for each class. The cards are read by a scanner and a computer calls the parents of all absent students in the evening, asking the adult to record a reply explaining the student's lateness or absence. Four times a year, a list of absences is attached to the student's report card and delivered to parents.

Another school in Quebec got skipping under control by making teens who were chronically late or who skipped school attend a special Saturday school. Setting up the Saturday school required a lot of teacher time and board expense, but the technique worked, and very few students skip school now.

Find out what your high school's policy is on absenteeism.

Learning Disabilities and ADHD

The transition to high school from elementary school can be stressful for any youngster, but it's even more so for the young teen who's coping with a learning disability (LD). It's difficult for his parents, too. If your child's disability was diagnosed early and is being dealt with at his public school, you both might fear the effects of his entering the unfamiliar environment of high school with new teachers and different expectations. Discuss your concerns and questions with the professional staff at the current school or at the school board during his final year. Go with him to the orientation evening for new students at the local high school and check out the resources available. Find out how classes are adapted to respond to the needs of students with particular learning disabilities and what resources will be available for your teen.

A child's learning disability is usually identified in kindergarten and the primary grades, but some disabilities become more obvious in junior high and high school—particularly in mathematics and problem solving which require the ability to remember and apply the memorized material. In high school, teens face an increased amount of written work, and the demand on their capacity to remember or memorize in several different subjects increases. Although problems may have first appeared when your child was in grades five and six, they might not have been as severe. Students with this disability have a history of poor handwriting, some difficulty learning to spell, and messy or incomplete notebooks. Or they may find science classes fascinating and have no trouble understanding scientific concepts, but they falter when faced with memorizing the vocabulary of biology or the formulas in chemistry. Difficulty learning a second language can also be an indication of a learning disability.

"When I was about eight years old, people started testing me because I was having so many problems in school, specially with reading. They said I have dyslexia. For a while in grade eight, a teacher sat with me through some classes, like math, science and English. But that was a problem for me because other kids would bug me about it. I got kicked out of that program because I was skipping so many classes.

In grade nine, I went to a regular secondary class and that was better. I made it better because I knew then it was either sink or swim. I tried to pay more attention and concentrate harder. One of the teachers at my school has helped me with some study skills and my parents help me with my homework. Grade ten is going pretty good."

MATTHEW, AGE 16

If you are concerned that your teen may have a learning disability, check with your family doctor to rule out any physical health problems. She may also be familiar with the assessment process used within the local school boards. The assessment usually involves educators in the student's school, a counsellor from the school, and an educational psychologist with the board. If the school board has a waiting list of two or three months, your doctor might know whether the child development clinic at a nearby hospital or university conducts these assessments. Weigh the costs and time involved against time lost until your child's turn on the school board's waiting list.

The advantage of the formal assessment through the school or school board is that the identification of a learning disability usually entitles the student to special education help. Your teen's teachers and guidance counsellor and others in the school or board can provide the remedial and tutoring options needed. They can also suggest what coping and learning strategies might benefit your child. Some high schools accommodate learning disabled students by allowing students to tape-record classes, by offering extended time for completing tests or exams, and by providing different, less-crowded rooms for writing them.

Kids with learning disabilities need not have lower expectations than their peers. They can still achieve their academic goals, although they may require a longer time; for example, taking a smaller class load each year and spending an extra year to get their high-school diploma. In some provinces, colleges and universities also offer special services and resources to these students. A learning disability doesn't fade with time, but a person who develops strategies for offsetting the disability will improve his learning abilities as he matures.

Attention deficit hyperactivity disorder (ADHD) is the expanded term that encompasses what was once called attention deficit disorder (ADD), one of whose characteristics was hyperactivity. It is rare for it to be diagnosed as late as adolescence, but it's fairly common for the disorder to continue throughout adolescence and into adulthood. How it manifests itself may change during adolescence—what once appeared as hyperactivity may evolve into a constant need to be busy and a feeling of restlessness. In about 60 per cent of cases, the original characteristics of the disorder continue, causing difficulty both for the teens and for those around them. But a child who responded well to Ritalin, the most common medication, may continue with this medication as a high-school student.

Whether your child has been dealing with a learning disability for several years or the diagnosis is new,

One-on-one tutoring can help focus a teen who has a learning disability.

as a teen he must learn gradually to shoulder responsibility for requesting help when needed, for recognizing his personal responsibility for learning and implementing the life skills and learning strategies that will carry him into adulthood. It's still important for you to develop and support your teen's strengths. If he has an aptitude for sports or music or art, the pleasure he gains from successes in these fields will boost his self-esteem and give him added strength to surmount other obstacles.

Learning Strategies

Students with learning disabilities will find that these tips help them cope. All students who are in transition from integrated studies in one classroom with one or few teachers to distinct subject classes with several teachers will find these suggestions helpful.

- ➤ Use an agenda book or a small lined calendar book to organize your time and list your homework and assignments.
- ➤ Sit near the front, close to the teacher and away from the distractions out the windows.
- ➤ Use an expanding file folder or one large binder with dividers and a three-hole punch to organize handouts and homework papers in subject categories.
- ➤ Enroll in classes to acquire skills in computer use, particularly keyboarding and word processing. Computer programs offer real help for students with learning disabilities in writing and mathematics.
- ➤ Consider acquiring a home computer and word processing software for use in writing and research. A laptop computer would allow a teen with a learning disability to take notes during classes or at the library.
- ➤ Learn to use the spell checker in the word-processing program on the computer; if you don't have a computer, check out the usefulness of a hand-held spell checker or dictionary.
- ➤ If handwriting is a problem and you don't have a computer, ask a friend who takes good notes if you can photocopy them.
- ➤ Use a highlighting pen to emphasize the main ideas in photocopies of materials or in the textbooks that you own.
- ➤ Tape-record classes or dictate your notes about the research you've been doing so that you can input them later.
- ➤ Try to enroll in classes with teachers who adapt their instructional style to the needs of their students.
- ➤ Focus on developing skills in self-evaluation and self-editing.
- ➤ Write information in notebooks in a way that reflects your personal learning style. Arrange material in hierarchical format with headings and subheadings, using ruled note paper; use blank note paper to sketch out some kinds of information graphically.

- ➤ Colour-code your notebooks to help you organize them and to find them quickly in your locker.
- ➤ Keep a vocabulary notebook to list the words you most often misuse or misspell (for example, *who's*, *whose*) and note details or examples of their proper use.
- ➤ Learn the techniques of brainstorming and outlining plans for a project before beginning your first draft of a writing assignment. Be prepared to edit, get a peer review, and revise what you write through two to six more drafts before printing out the final version.
- ➤ Use stick-on notes or tabs to mark book pages temporarily during research; use them to write brief notes to be consolidated later.
- ➤ When studying a textbook or reference book, read a section of text at least three times.
  1. Get an overview of the topic by reading the headings, skimming the body of text, looking at the graphics and captions, reading any summaries, and noting your questions.
  2. Read the text a second time, concentrating fully and keeping in mind your initial questions and any study guide questions already provided for you.
  3. With the third reading, try to answer all your own questions during homework.
- ➤ Take 5- to 10-minute breaks every 45 minutes or hour to stretch your whole body.
- ➤ Ask your teachers for help when you need it.

Developing Social Skills

Some kids with learning disabilities need specific instruction in socially acceptable behaviour. The adults in their lives can help by describing social behaviours, modelling those behaviours, and role-playing with them to provide practice. Some schools may offer classes, or the guidance counsellors may have information about such classes in the community. There are summer day-camp programs that are designed for kids with learning disabilities and that teach social skills in an engaging setting. Your local Y or Boys and Girls Club of Canada is likely to offer something similar.

Kids who fear failure are reluctant to join group activities. Parents can help by asking the coach or instructor if their teen can attend a couple of sessions or practices as an observer or helper to give him a chance to overcome his reluctance. Encouraging your teen to sign up for a sports team or another group activity gives him the chance to interact casually with peers. Alternatively, your teen might offer her own skills to coach or tutor a younger child.

Computer Literacy

High-school students' access to computers varies by school, by community, by province. Some high schools offer a few computer courses as electives; others integrate computers into every class and maintain a computer lab for courses in computer programming and computer repair. Some provinces and school boards have chosen to fund computer programs in their schools. In others, service groups and corporations donate money to the same purpose. Not all provincial ministries of education can afford to keep updating the hardware and software they've been purchasing since the early 1980s, so few provinces have made computer studies compulsory. But for certain courses at some colleges and universities, computers are a necessity for students. At Acadia University in Wolfville, Nova Scotia, it's mandatory for each student to use a computer, so a laptop is included in the cost of tuition fees.

Buying a Computer

Since most workplaces require employees to have skills in one or more software programs, many parents want their teens to have basic computer knowledge and skills in order to advance their education, to get summer work during college or training, and to get jobs after graduation.

Teens need basic computer skills to advance their education.

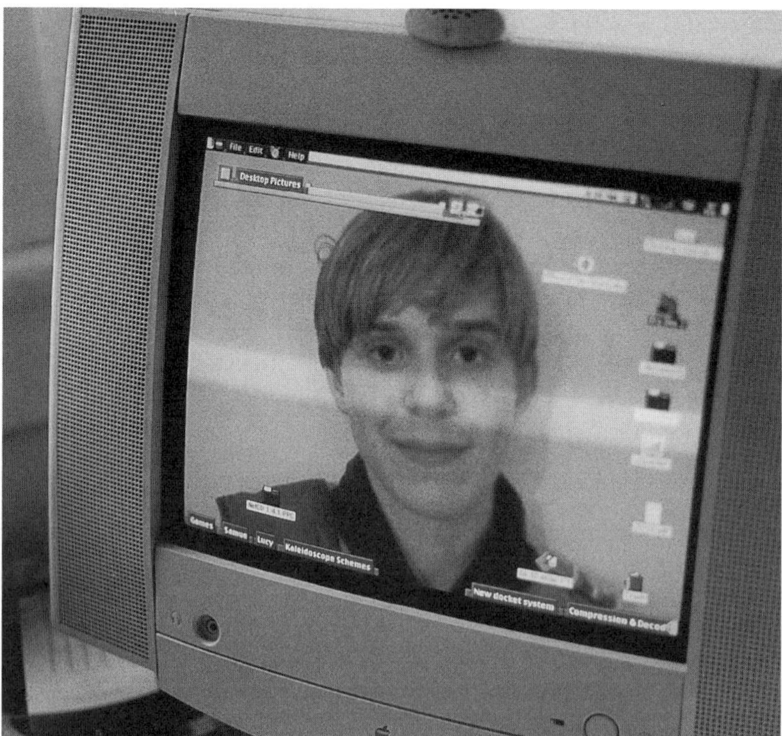

These skills include keyboarding and facility with at least one word-processing program for essays and reports. Other software applications like a browser for E-mail and research on the Internet, financial spread-sheets, database organization, graphic arts, computer-assisted design (CAD), and multimedia presentations are also useful to many students, no matter what their area of specialization.

"Even though we're in a fairly affluent neighbourhood, our school doesn't have much in the way of computers. Parents come up to me and say, 'Oh, there are no computers at school,' and I say, 'Well, do you have a computer at home? Yes? Well, then they're using them.'

When we got on-line at home, my son was the one who came up to me and showed me how to work the Internet. But I'd rather they were out shooting hoops or talking on the phone to their friends than in on-line chat groups.

I keep telling both my kids that if you're a good reader and a good writer and you know how to research, then you don't have to memorize—the important thing is knowing where to go to get the information you need."

SANDRA, MOTHER OF TWO

Many families are wary about buying their first computer. Like any other appliance, it's a major financial outlay, but one that apparently requires upgrading every two or three years. It's true that the value of a computer system decreases substantially as soon as you carry it out of the store. But you're buying the equipment you need to do a job, and you're making an investment in yourself and your family's opportunities for learning and for future work.

Do some solid research. Check out a few computer stores, read the freebie computer newspapers available in libraries and at drugstore exits, talk to teachers or consultants at your teen's school, talk to your neighbours and co-workers about their systems. Talk to the staff at a computer shop. Their first question will be "What do you want to do with the computer?"

Typically, first-time buyers want a machine for word processing, for income tax programs, for E-mail and access to the Internet, for their kids, and for playing some games. Most stores offer a basic package with a standard central-processing unit (CPU), which incorporates a hard drive, a disk drive, a CD-ROM drive, and a modem (to attach to a phone line and link up with the Internet). The package also includes a keyboard and mouse and may include a colour monitor, an audio system, and an inkjet printer.

You can upgrade each of the components of this basic package according to your needs. If you can afford it, you might want to buy greater speed, extra memory, extra storage, and a larger monitor (a 15-inch monitor is easier on the eyesight than a 14-inch one). If you think you'll print more than 50 pages a week and don't require colour printing, a low-end laser printer may be more economical to maintain in the long term, although it costs more than an inkjet printer.

Deal with a reputable manufacturer or computer shop that offers customer support and additional services like training. Again, check with your peers to find out which one has a good reputation. Ask the Better Business Bureau how long a store has been in operation and what its track record with customer complaints is like. Find out what kind of warranty is offered on each element of the computer system and if the store operates an in-house service department. You won't want to ship your computer long distances if you have to send it in for repairs. Be sure to check the documents supplied with each component to find out if they have 1-800 lines or other help lines and how long the service is offered free, if at all.

Most computers now come with a standard operating system (OS)—Windows for the PC or the equivalent for a Macintosh—and the appropriate software to see you through the next few years. Don't worry about every new upgrade that hits the market. The basic computer skills of file management and page formatting that you learn from one software program will apply to later word-processing programs. If the software supplied on the hard drive doesn't include a graphics program and a spreadsheet application, you may want to buy them separately.

For an alternative to computer games, check out programs that enable you to create Web pages, edit videos or music, or produce multimedia presentations or projects. These tend to be more expensive than games, but they are the computer equivalent of a Meccano set—lots of creative play value for teens. Many Web sites have downloadable software for kids and parents to use. In your cost analysis, be sure to factor in the cost of some guidebooks or training sessions for some of the software programs. The computer stores and many bookstores are other good sources for creative programs and for books that help you unlock the secrets of software programs. Once you learn to use E-mail and the Internet, you will find mail lists that also offer tips and peer-to-peer help.

It's possible that you'll only get five years of use from your new computer and two or three upgrades before technology changes significantly enough for you to purchase a new system. By that time, your hard drive might not be performing at an optimum level any longer or the latest upgrade to your most-used software programs may demand more memory than your computer has. But you'll be able to conduct your own needs assessment before deciding to buy a new computer. Is the old one still fulfilling your needs? If not and you decide to buy a new computer, the skills you've acquired in the past year or two will have prepared you to research which bells and whistles you'll need this time around. Your old computer, which may have no resale value but which can still do everything it used to do, will come in handy when one kid is exploring the three-dimensional modelling program and the other one needs to prepare the final copy of her essay.

One interesting aspect of a new computer in the home, especially if Mom and Dad aren't comfortably computer-literate themselves, is that it turns the tables on the family social order. Your teen may well become better versed in its operation, and you may be the one asking for her help. But if none of you knows how to copy a file, ask the computer studies teacher for the name of a student who might be interested in home tutoring. There are always a few in each class who are so knowledgeable they can teach the teacher a few key moves. If you've bought a computer primarily for the benefit of your teens, it's important that you know how to use it, too. Without some guidance and examples from parents, the computer may end up as an expensive games machine. A computer used in this way is as much help to students as an encyclopedia that functions primarily as a paperweight.

Internet Savvy

The World Wide Web offers remarkable resources for everyone, and it offers a lot of fun, too. Kids love to send E-mail to friends and far-off cousins. But then there's the scary side. Youngsters can get drawn into an intense relationship with a person in a chat group purporting to be someone he's not. You or your teen might unwittingly access Web sites filled with hate messages against particular groups or devoted to pornography. But there is too much that's useful to forbid your teens access to the Internet. There are programs that teachers can use to preview sites by downloading and viewing them off-line and programs that protect youngsters from accessing pornography. Some schools have developed Intranet programs, through which students have access only to internal school Web sites.

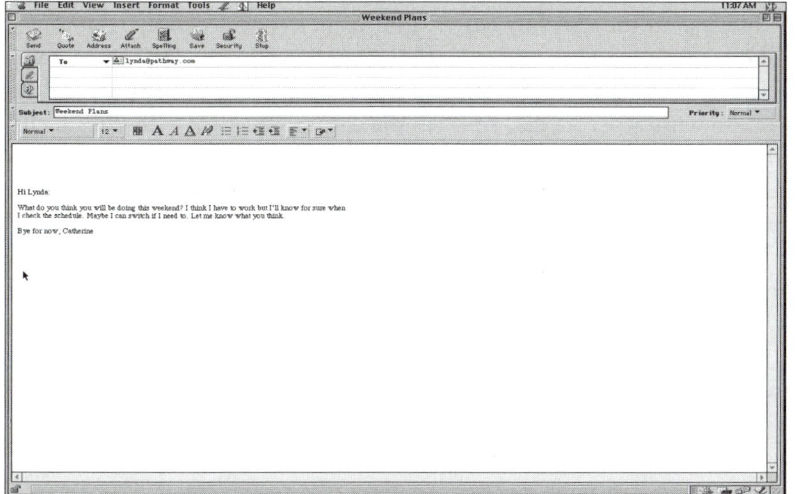

Teens love E-mail about as much as they love the telephone.

Mind

The best method of protecting your kids from the seamier side of the Internet, whether at home or at school, is by being aware of what they're working on. Set up your home computer in a high-traffic area so that you can wander by regularly and check out what your kids are viewing. Tell younger teens that they may log on to the Net only while a parent is at home. Let everyone in the family know that the browser (Netscape, for example) program can track where each user has ventured online. Simply go to Location, type in "about:global" or "about:cache" or look under "History" and you'll see a list of sites most recently used. Let your kids know about your using this feature, but as you do with other media, keep up the communication with your teens, and teach positive techniques. The Media Awareness Network offers several programs to help kids of different maturity levels develop Web literacy. <http://www.media-awareness.ca>

If you have a son and daughter in your home vying for computer time, recent studies at the University of British Columbia and Simon Fraser University may interest you. Since they showed that it's usually the boys who win out, you might set time limits so that each child gets his and her fair share of time. Also, remind your teens that just as it's unacceptable and illegal to copy text from an encyclopedia into a project without giving proper credit, so is it to cut and paste material from a Web site into a project.

Fostering Talents

More personal freedom, better purchasing power, and a stronger ability to focus mean that teens can pursue their hobbies, interests, and extracurricular activities with vigour. Some teens build on interests they developed as children, but many teens jump on new hobbies and activities. Whatever they choose, they gain a deep sense of self-worth and expand their knowledge base with leisure pursuits that they choose for themselves.

Parents may believe that their young teens neither want nor require their support and encouragement as they pursue new hobbies. But, in fact, parental support is still necessary and important. Even when he seems to suffer acute embarrassment just walking down the street with you, you are still the most important adult in your teenager's life. Although your teen may not articulate it, she still wants you as a cheerleader on the sidelines.

"My parents are really supportive of all the stuff I do. I went on a band trip to Toronto and we had to raise $700. Mom helped out by taking stuff in to work to sell. When I went for my last karate belt, we had a six-hour testing in front of a formal board. Both my parents were there for the whole thing. What that means to me is that I don't walk out to the car afterward and say, 'Hey, I got my belt'—they were there; they know what I went through to get it.

I've been collecting comics since I was in grade two. I depend on my parents to drive me to Halifax to my favourite comic book shop. They aren't always as supportive about this hobby. But at last count I had 1,152; I spent one afternoon cataloguing them by name and publisher. I used to like them for the art, but now it's more about the writing. I read every one of them. I think if you just put them in a box without reading them, it takes the fun out of it."

JOSH, AGE 15

Your encouragement may only take the form of driving him to and from band practice without griping, attending his concerts with wild applause, or a private "I'm so proud of the way you've been practising that difficult piece, and it's really paying off—you're sounding great!" Encouragement can also be a resolute affirmation of a child's potential when she develops cold feet at the doorstep of the art studio on the first day of class. But try not to step over the line into coercion. It will create resentment and possibly a lifelong aversion to the activity. You should share your expectations about your investment in and your teen's commitment to particular activities, but activities should enrich a child's life, not become a resented chore. Both parents and teens should feel free to change situations that turn out to be less than expected.

You Have to Do Something!

You might be faced with the worrisome prospect of a youngster devoting fewer hours to once-enjoyed activities and more time just hanging out with friends. While you may view this as little more than a time-waster, refrain from comment. A teen who previously filled several evenings a week with different activities sometimes hits an age when she decides to drop everything. Don't push, but let her know that she can try something new when she's ready.

Teens need to see the good example of their parents choosing to spend time in active physical pursuits as well as quieter leisure interests like gardening or reading. Teens need exposure to a wide range of interests in order to find ones they like. Community associations and family clubs like the Y offer a variety of activities for all age groups. Their fee structure may vary, but teen rates are often about half the adult rate. Fees for youths (age thirteen to nineteen) range from $20 to $28 per month. Most municipal recreation programs are even cheaper. If cost is an issue, such community service groups as the Lions Club, Rotary International, and the Kinsmen might be willing to help fund youth activities under certain circumstances. Contact the secretary of your local club for information about funding procedures.

Let your child know she can try new activities when she's ready.

Activity Overload

Some teens have so many activities on the go that parents fear they will burn out. If they appear to be happy and keep up their grades, should you allow them to continue at full speed? Yes, but pay close attention and try to determine whether or not they're truly happy. Some kids, like some adults, are high-energy types who are happiest when they're constantly in motion. Others might have a jam-packed schedule only because that's what they've been accustomed to since early childhood.

Obviously, a teen who's often tired, frazzled, forgetful, and failing to keep commitments needs to put on the brakes. Sometimes they feel they need our permission to do a little less. If they resist, insist: "Hey, you're just too busy these days. I want you to drop one activity, and you can let me know at the end of the week which one you've chosen. If you can't decide, I'll be happy to decide for you." Your teen might feel relieved.

A teen struggling with a serious problem—anorexia, for instance—sometimes tries masking the trouble with a schedule that is crammed with structured activities. She may use constant busyness to control her weight or help disguise weight loss from her family. A problem such as this needs expert care and guidance, and if you suspect serious underlying trouble, you should consult your family doctor immediately.

"What is fascinating to me is that just when I thought I should be pulling back and not standing on the sidelines screaming and cheering him on, he is asking, 'You're coming, right? You're going to be there?' He still needs us, and he's able to verbalize that. My own parents tended to back off and not pressure us as kids if we balked at following through on something. But I think that kids secretly want their parents to say 'Oh, come on now, you can do it!' I want my kids to be better risk takers than I was, so my husband and I make a point of saying 'Nothing ventured, nothing gained.' Our rule for activities is if you start in September, you can't quit before June."

SANDRA, MOTHER OF TWO

Quiet leisure and time for reflection are also important for most teens. An adolescent who makes no time for introspection during these years may not develop the capacity to do so as an adult. But if your teen appears to be thriving at home and school, maintains a sense of humour, and fits some quiet time into his hectic schedule, then he's very likely to be in control of his active agenda.

Mind

From High School to Higher Learning

You probably began planning for your child's post-secondary education soon after her birth and revisited those plans on many occasions throughout elementary school. But the courses she selects in high school should allow her to keep open for the future as many options as possible that match her interests. In most Canadian provinces and territories, the secondary school system provides avenues for students to move on to apprenticeships, to training schools, to colleges, and to universities. Availability is still somewhat limited, but opportunities for cooperative education during high school give students a chance to experience different workplace environments for a few weeks to a few months each year without having to take on the responsibility of a part-time job.

Emphasize the importance of acquiring skills and achieving their best academically during high school. It's important for everyone to do their best at any job. And most jobs offer possibilities for eventual supervisory work, for training others, for management, for ownership, and for exercising business or entrepreneurial management skills. The more versatility one develops in knowledge and life skills, the more opportunities will open up for earning a living and adapting to the changing economy.

Find opportunities for both you and your teens to acquire information about all kinds of jobs in particular fields of interest. Food and hospitality services? Consumer marketing and customer service? New home construction and decorating? Animal care or training? High-tech software and multimedia games? Park architecture or management? Prepare webs or collages of related work interests, and scan advertisements for descriptions of current requirements and salaries offered. Your teen might speak to career counsellors at employment centres operated by trade unions or provincial and federal governments. Find out about working conditions, about unions, about training programs, about work experience. Some jobs require additional schooling, but the training is primarily practical and hands-on.

> **Help your teen talk out his feelings about how he would fit into various work situations.**

Talk about your own and your friends' jobs and how they've changed and evolved over the years. Focus on the quality-of-life issues: work you enjoy; working environment; building personal financial security; time commitment required for training and upgrading; levels of responsibility and autonomy; lifetime earning potential. Help your teen talk out his thoughts and feelings about how he would fit into various kinds of working situations. A seventeen-year-old who doesn't want to pursue academic studies after high school still needs lots of support from you to find

the right path for him. If he's been feeling societal and peer pressures to pursue a college diploma or university degree, chances are that his self-esteem has been taking a beating. Help him find other options and let him know that choosing not to go to a college or university immediately after high school does not close the door on higher education forever. In time, he may return as a mature student who knows what his interests are.

Many adults return to school to learn new skills or to keep up-to-date in their field after they've worked for several years. Encourage your teen to understand that learning is a lifelong process, that he can learn new skills throughout his life. Point out examples of others who are lifelong learners. Work can also be viewed as a means to an end. If your teen has many interests and hobbies, a weekly paycheque may be all she needs to pursue her passion for music, travel, or anything else her heart desires. Not everyone wants to live for her work; some people work to live.

Choosing a College or University

For a teen who has developed a keen interest for the future and is confident that college or university is for her, help her explore her options early. She might begin by obtaining materials from the guidance department. Many high-school guidance departments have videos and course catalogues for local colleges and universities. If they don't have current calendars outlining the courses that interest your teen, they probably have contact information for telephoning, writing, faxing, or sending E-mail messages for further information.

Pick up the latest edition of a book like *The Complete Guide to Canadian Universities* by Kevin Paul (Self-Counsel Press, 1996) for up-to-the-minute information and to help your teen get a sense of a particular campus. There are also annual publications that rank the services and qualities of Canadian universities from several points of view, including those of students. In fact, talking to older relatives or to friends' older siblings who are university students about their experiences brings a more personal touch to the information. What do they like about their college or university? Would they do anything different if they could plan their education again? Or find one of the many university guides written by students for students. These somewhat irreverent looks at campus life are as entertaining as they are informative.

Your teen needs to gather lots of information in order to choose among programs offered at college or university.

Even though high-school graduation is a year or two away, your teen should attend information sessions and meet university recruiters when they come to his high school. As a family, you might make an effort to visit some campuses on a vacation trip. Most can easily arrange a tour for students and parents. Other good sources of information are the Web sites that each institution maintains.

By the final year of high school, your teen should have an idea of where and what she would like to study. She should nevertheless attend university or college recruitment presentations. Canada has over forty universities and over one hundred colleges, and each one has its own specialties and its own personality. If her plans change or she isn't accepted in her first-choice school, she needs to know what's available elsewhere. But what if they all sound interesting and she can't make a decision? You can help her narrow the choices by asking:

➤ Can I afford to live away from home? What are the tuition costs? the costs for books and other learning materials? costs of living? What scholarships or bursaries are available? What student grants and loans are available?

➤ Do I like big cities or small towns?

➤ Do I want to attend a big university where I'll meet people from all over the country and possibly all over the world?

➤ Would I prefer a smaller school where I'm more likely to receive more personalized attention?

Even though your teen is almost independent, take a more proactive role in the application process if he needs support.

When recruiters come to the high school, your teen might ask:

➤ How big are first-year classes? Are they small enough so that professors can learn students' names?

➤ Is there an orientation program for first-year students? Are there specific services designed to help students make the transition from high school to university?

➤ What academic support services are available (study skills workshops, writing assistance, counselling, tutors)?

➤ Will I need to have my own computer? Are student residences wired for computers?

➤ What sports or physical training facilities are available for general use even if I'm not on a team?

The Nuts and Bolts of Applications

In most high schools, guidance counsellors are available to help students with the application process both by individual counselling when possible, and by arranging group sessions at the school to which all interested students are invited. Some arrange information sessions about university and college applications for parents as well. Attendance at such sessions is voluntary; students need to know about them in advance, register for them, and remember to attend them. Even though your older teen is almost independent, you may want to take a more proactive role in this stage than you have been taking in her life recently.

High-school guidance departments usually have materials only about local or provincial colleges and universities. In all provinces except Ontario, students apply directly to the colleges or universities that interest them. Ontario has centralized and standardized the application system because of the large number of universities and colleges in the province. The following is a summary of what is expected when application time rolls around for the coming school year. Although similar computerized systems do not yet exist in other provinces, many of the stages and processes are the same, and may be considered general guidelines, although costs and timing may vary somewhat.

> **Canada has over forty universities and one hundred colleges, each with its own specialties.**

College Applications

> As early as grade nine, schools begin holding general information sessions for students at which they explain such things as the different requirements for, courses offered in, and diplomas or degrees obtained from, colleges and universities.

> In September, guidance counsellors begin talking to students in their graduating year and recording the names of those who plan to go on to college the next year. They ask them to gather information and be ready to make their final choices by February.

> In December, Ontario high schools receive a batch of Ontario application forms, preprinted with the names of and other information about the students who had expressed their interest in colleges.

> Outside the school, the colleges offer a community information session for both parents and students.

> Before Christmas, the guidance counsellors set a time for a group session at the school to hand out the application forms and help students complete them. Attendance is voluntary, and it might mean skipping a class or lunch to attend. The students can usually take the forms home for parents to review and assist with.

- ➢ In Ontario, the school sends the completed applications to the centralized application centre in Guelph by March 1. In other provinces, students are responsible for sending in their own applications. The fee is $65 for up to five colleges. The school also sends a transcript of grade twelve midterm marks for each student applicant.
- ➢ Students usually receive letters of acceptance or rejection from the colleges by May 15.
- ➢ The deadline for students to inform the college of their choice is June 1.
- ➢ It's still possible for students who missed the above process to apply in May or June, but they are placed at the end of the list of applicants.

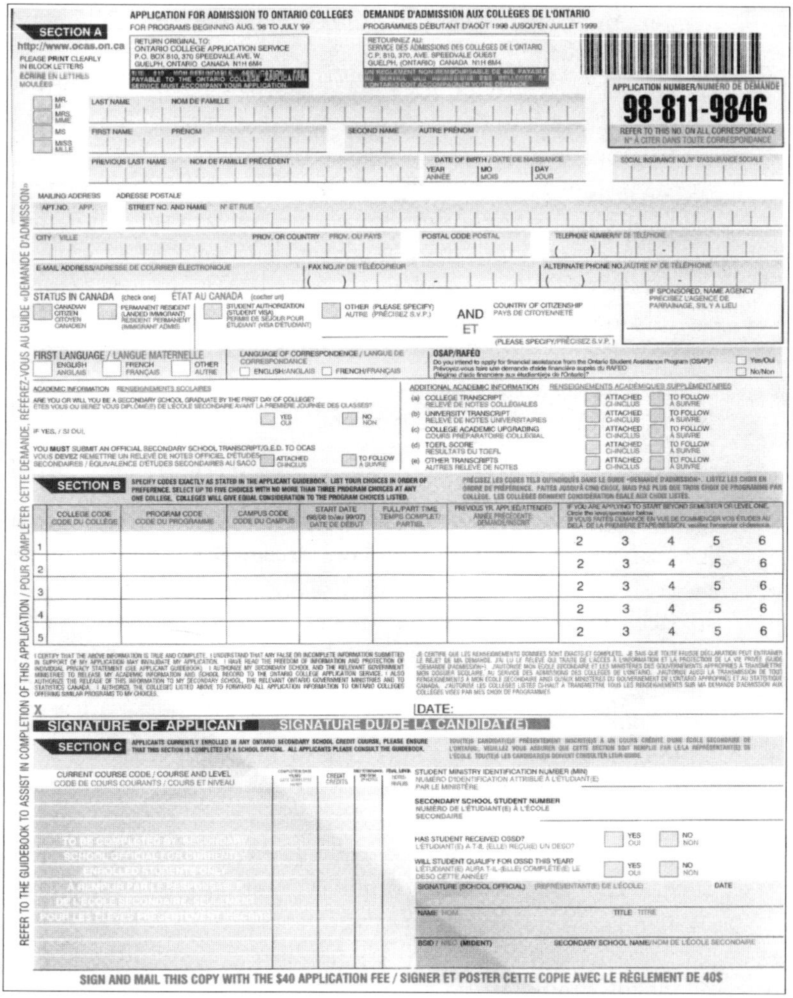

SECTION A
http://www.ocas.on.ca
PLEASE PRINT CLEARLY IN BLOCK LETTERS
ÉCRIRE EN LETTRES MOULÉES

APPLICATION FOR ADMISSION TO ONTARIO COLLEGES
FOR PROGRAMS BEGINNING AUG. '98 TO JULY '99
DEMANDE D'ADMISSION AUX COLLÈGES DE L'ONTARIO
PROGRAMMES DÉBUTANT D'AOÛT 1998 JUSQU'EN JUILLET 1999

RETURN ORIGINAL TO:
ONTARIO COLLEGE APPLICATION SERVICE
P.O. BOX 810, 370 SPEEDVALE AVE. W
GUELPH, ONTARIO CANADA N1H 6M4

RETOURNEZ AU:
SERVICE DES ADMISSIONS DES COLLÈGES DE L'ONTARIO
C.P. 810, 370, AVE. SPEEDVALE OUEST
GUELPH, (ONTARIO) CANADA N1H 6M4

APPLICATION NUMBER/NUMÉRO DE DEMANDE
98-811-9846
REFER TO THIS NO. ON ALL CORRESPONDENCE
N° À CITER DANS TOUTE CORRESPONDANCE

MR. M / MRS. MME / MS / MISS MLLE
LAST NAME NOM DE FAMILLE
FIRST NAME PRÉNOM | SECOND NAME AUTRE PRÉNOM
PREVIOUS LAST NAME NOM DE FAMILLE PRÉCÉDENT | DATE OF BIRTH / DATE DE NAISSANCE: YEAR ANNÉE | MO MOIS | DAY JOUR | SOCIAL INSURANCE NO./N° D'ASSURANCE SOCIALE

MAILING ADDRESS ADRESSE POSTALE
APT.NO. APP. | STREET NO. AND NAME N° ET RUE
CITY VILLE | PROV. OR COUNTRY PROV. OU PAYS | POSTAL CODE POSTAL | TELEPHONE NUMBER/N° DE TÉLÉPHONE ( )
E-MAIL ADDRESS/ADRESSE DE COURRIER ÉLECTRONIQUE | FAX NO./N° DE TÉLÉCOPIEUR ( ) | ALTERNATE PHONE NO./AUTRE N° DE TÉLÉPHONE ( )

STATUS IN CANADA (check one) ETAT AU CANADA (cocher un)
CANADIAN CITIZEN CITOYEN CANADIEN | PERMANENT RESIDENT (LANDED IMMIGRANT) RÉSIDENT PERMANENT (IMMIGRANT ADMIS) | STUDENT AUTHORIZATION (STUDENT VISA) PERMIS DE SÉJOUR POUR ÉTUDIANT (VISA D'ÉTUDIANT) | OTHER (PLEASE SPECIFY) AUTRE (PRÉCISEZ S.V.P.)
AND ET
COUNTRY OF CITIZENSHIP PAYS DE CITOYENNETÉ (PLEASE SPECIFY/PRÉCISEZ S.V.P.)
IF SPONSORED, NAME AGENCY PRÉCISEZ L'AGENCE DE PARRAINAGE, S'IL Y A LIEU

FIRST LANGUAGE / LANGUE MATERNELLE: ENGLISH ANGLAIS | FRENCH FRANÇAIS | OTHER AUTRE
LANGUAGE OF CORRESPONDENCE / LANGUE DE CORRESPONDANCE: ENGLISH/ANGLAIS | FRENCH/FRANÇAIS
OSAP/RAFÉO
Do you intend to apply for financial assistance from the Ontario Student Assistance Program (OSAP)? Yes/Oui No/Non
Prévoyez-vous faire une demande d'aide financière auprès du RAFEO (Régime d'aide financière aux étudiant(e)s de l'Ontario)?

ACADEMIC INFORMATION RENSEIGNEMENTS SCOLAIRES
ARE YOU OR WILL YOU BE A SECONDARY SCHOOL GRADUATE BY THE FIRST DAY OF COLLEGE?
ÊTES-VOUS OU SEREZ-VOUS DIPLÔMÉ(E) DE L'ÉCOLE SECONDAIRE AVANT LA PREMIÈRE JOURNÉE DES CLASSES? YES OUI | NO NON
IF YES, / SI OUI,
YOU MUST SUBMIT AN OFFICIAL SECONDARY SCHOOL TRANSCRIPT/G.E.D. TO OCAS
VOUS DEVEZ REMETTRE UN RELEVÉ DE NOTES OFFICIEL D'ÉTUDES SECONDAIRES / ÉQUIVALENCE D'ÉTUDES SECONDAIRES AU SACO
ATTACHED CI-INCLUS | TO FOLLOW À SUIVRE

ADDITIONAL ACADEMIC INFORMATION RENSEIGNEMENTS ACADÉMIQUES SUPPLÉMENTAIRES
(a) COLLEGE TRANSCRIPT RELEVÉ DE NOTES COLLÉGIALES — ATTACHED CI-INCLUS | TO FOLLOW À SUIVRE
(b) UNIVERSITY TRANSCRIPT RELEVÉ DE NOTES UNIVERSITAIRES — ATTACHED CI-INCLUS | TO FOLLOW À SUIVRE
(c) COLLEGE ACADEMIC UPGRADING COURS PRÉPARATOIRE COLLÉGIAL — ATTACHED CI-INCLUS | TO FOLLOW À SUIVRE
(d) TOEFL SCORE RÉSULTATS DU TOEFL — ATTACHED CI-INCLUS | TO FOLLOW À SUIVRE
(e) OTHER TRANSCRIPTS AUTRES RELEVÉ DE NOTES — ATTACHED CI-INCLUS | TO FOLLOW À SUIVRE

SECTION B
SPECIFY CODES EXACTLY AS STATED IN THE APPLICANT GUIDEBOOK. LIST YOUR CHOICES IN ORDER OF PREFERENCE. SELECT UP TO FIVE CHOICES WITH NO MORE THAN THREE PROGRAM CHOICES AT ANY ONE COLLEGE. COLLEGES WILL GIVE EQUAL CONSIDERATION TO THE PROGRAM CHOICES LISTED.

	COLLEGE CODE CODE DU COLLÈGE	PROGRAM CODE CODE DU PROGRAMME	CAMPUS CODE CODE DU CAMPUS	START DATE (98/08 to/au 99/07) DATE DE DÉBUT	FULL/PART TIME TEMPS COMPLET/PARTIEL	PREVIOUS YR. APPLIED/ATTENDED	IF YOU ARE APPLYING TO START BEYOND SEMESTER OR LEVEL ONE. Circle the level/semester below				
1							2	3	4	5	6
2							2	3	4	5	6
3							2	3	4	5	6
4							2	3	4	5	6
5							2	3	4	5	6

X | DATE:
SIGNATURE OF APPLICANT SIGNATURE DU/DE LA CANDIDAT(E)

SECTION C
APPLICANTS CURRENTLY ENROLLED IN ANY ONTARIO SECONDARY SCHOOL CREDIT COURSE, PLEASE ENSURE THAT THIS SECTION IS COMPLETED BY A SCHOOL OFFICIAL. ALL APPLICANTS PLEASE CONSULT THE GUIDEBOOK.
CURRENT COURSE CODE / COURSE AND LEVEL
CODE DE COURS COURANTS / COURS ET NIVEAU
CREDIT CRÉDITS
STUDENT MINISTRY IDENTIFICATION NUMBER (MIN)
NUMÉRO D'IDENTIFICATION ATTRIBUÉ À L'ÉTUDIANT(E) PAR LE MINISTÈRE
SECONDARY SCHOOL STUDENT NUMBER
NUMÉRO DE L'ÉTUDIANT(E) À L'ÉCOLE SECONDAIRE
HAS STUDENT RECEIVED OSSD? L'ÉTUDIANT(E) A-T-IL (ELLE) REÇU(E) UN DESO? YES OUI | NO NON
WILL STUDENT QUALIFY FOR OSSD THIS YEAR? L'ÉTUDIANT(E) AURA-T-IL (ELLE) COMPLÉTÉ(E) LE DESO CETTE ANNÉE? YES OUI | NO NON
SIGNATURE (SCHOOL OFFICIAL) (REPRÉSENTANT(E) DE L'ÉCOLE) | DATE
NAME NOM | TITLE TITRE
BSID (MIDENT) | SECONDARY SCHOOL NAME/NOM DE L'ÉCOLE SECONDAIRE

REFER TO THE GUIDEBOOK TO ASSIST IN COMPLETION OF THIS APPLICATION / POUR COMPLÉTER CETTE DEMANDE, RÉFÉREZ-VOUS AU GUIDE «DEMANDE D'ADMISSION»

SIGN AND MAIL THIS COPY WITH THE $40 APPLICATION FEE / SIGNER ET POSTER CETTE COPIE AVEC LE RÈGLEMENT DE 40$

In most high schools, guidance counsellors are available to help students with their college or university applications.

University Applications

> As part of the centralized and computerized system, in September, Ontario high-school guidance counsellors begin talking to students and recording the names of those who plan to go to university the following year. They also suggest that the students gather information on the universities that interest them, so they can make final choices by November.

> During the months of September, October, and November, many universities send representatives to the schools to give short informative presentations, typically less than an hour long, and distribute brochures.

> Some schools also offer special information sessions for Parents' Night. Outside the school, many universities offer a community information program (daytime and evening) for parents and students.

> In Ontario, the universities publish a very useful guidebook called *Info*, which outlines the entrance requirements for all the universities' programs. They also provide similar information on CD-ROMs to the high schools and maintain Web sites on the Internet.

SEE PAGE 221

> At the beginning of November, Ontario high schools receive a batch of Ontario application forms, one for each student identified as a potential university applicant that year. These forms are preprinted with the student's name and other known information.

> In early to mid-November, the guidance counsellors set a date and time for a group session at school to hand out the application forms and to help students complete them. Attendance is voluntary, but it might mean skipping a class or a lunch hour to attend. The students can take the forms home as well for parents to review and assist with.

> Ontario high schools send the completed forms to the centralized application centre in Guelph by December 1. The application fee for one to three universities is $80, with an additional $25 for each new university the student adds. The school sends a transcript of the students' final marks in grades eleven and twelve. In other provinces, students are responsible for submitting their own applications.

> In mid-April, the school sends a transcript of any final marks up to the end of the first semester, plus midterm marks for these students.

> Students may sometimes make amendments to their application, such as changing or adding a university selection up until mid-March. Fees are charged after two changes.

> Universities can start accepting applicants as conditional pre-admission candidates on March 10.

If your teen is considering out-of-province schooling, he will need to contact those schools directly.

➤   Students usually receive letters of acceptance or rejection from the universities by May 15.

➤   The deadline for students to inform the university of their choice is June 1.

➤   Students who missed the above process may still apply in May or June, but they are at the end of the applicant list.

Out-of-province applications

If your teen is considering an out-of-province or out-of-country college or university, she will likely have to write or telephone directly to the registrar's office for current information, course calendars, and the application forms for her graduating year. You can usually find contact information from guidance counsellors, from the library, or on the Internet.

SEE PAGE 221

Mind

Give It a Year

What do you want to be when you grow up? Lots of teens graduate from high school without an answer to this question, which makes planning their next step difficult. For some teens, taking a year away from academic studies to explore a variety of possibilities may be the best option. Agree to this, provided your teen plans her time to include work, volunteering, or travelling. Both you and your high-school graduate could look at this as a year of discovery. If she hasn't before undertaken aptitude tests and interest inventories, now's the time to explore what analyses and insights educational psychologists can provide through such tests and forms.

Another option she might want to consider is a work-experience program such as Katimavik. This federal government program under the Canadian Heritage department sends 600 teens each year to work on 54 different nonprofit projects. Katimavik covers the cost of room and board and pays teens $3 a day to cover personal expenses. At the end of the eight-month program, teens receive $1,000. For more information on this program, contact Katimavik toll-free at 1-888-525-1503. To find out about other educational opportunities that provide work experience, your teen might talk again to her high-school guidance counsellors.

Lots of teens graduate from high school not knowing what they should do next.

Read carefully all the information sent by the college or university, including all pages of the application forms and the instructions and deadlines for filling them out and for the documents that must accompany the application or be sent separately. Make sure your teen fills out the application properly—check, double-check, and recheck. Pay special attention to the due dates, and mail materials on time. It's best to apply as early as possible because some programs with limited enrollment fill up early. Call the institutions that your teen applied to just to confirm that the application was received. Follow up with your teen's high school to make sure the transcripts of his marks were sent to each institution.

When an admission offer arrives, it's usually conditional on your teen's final marks being acceptable. The admission offer usually also includes information about campus housing and residences, which should also be handled as soon as possible to avoid disappointment. If your teen's application is rejected, tell her not to take the rejection personally and not to give up hope. Each year, thousands of students are turned away, not because of their marks but because courses and programs have reached full enrollment. A rejection in one year has no bearing on future applications.

> **When an admission offer arrives, it's usually conditional on your teen's final marks being acceptable.**

A Teen's Point of View: My Mind

My abilities to think abstractly and to absorb information are growing quickly. I need you to respect my new intellectual powers.

- I'm critical of you. It's not that I don't love you, but I need to see that my parents have flaws. Finding out that you're not perfect helps me in the process of becoming an individual who is separate from you.

- I watch you like a hawk to see if you still appreciate me.

- I can be critical of my friends, too. I'm struggling to understand what friendship means and who my real friends are.

- I'm aware of my growing intellect. I'll feel insulted if you try to deceive me or hide the complete truth from me. I'm quick to detect the tiniest hint of insincerity.

- I appreciate sarcasm, as long as it's not directed at me. I can be quite cutting.

- I have an imaginary audience that's constantly watching me, criticizing me, and judging me. For instance, I imagine that everyone is looking at the pimple on my nose. It's a result of my new ability to think about other people's thoughts.

- I generalize. I say, "Everybody's going to the concert" or "Nobody else has a curfew."

- I can be hypocritical. I might criticize you for being materialistic, then lust after an expensive pair of designer running shoes.

- I like verbal pursuits, such as using slang terms and playing word games.

- I enjoy computers, not just for the games but for what I can learn.

- Instead of seeing issues in black or white, I'm starting to see shades of grey.

- Although I lack confidence, I sometimes act smug, as if I know all the answers that others aren't bright enough to think of.

- I'm often so lost in thought that I don't notice when you talk to me.

- I'm so involved in myself and my own world that even my handwriting becomes smaller.

Age Fourteen

- I'm still struggling to establish my identity as distinct from yours or anyone else's.

- I'm beginning to develop a way of thinking that's closer to an adult's than a child's. I can form ideas about things that I have no direct knowledge of. I can visualize, hypothesize, and conceptualize. I can picture a historical event, for instance, and understand how and why it happened.

- A whole new world of thought opens up now that I can picture implications, possibilities, and alternatives.

- I enjoy evaluating subjects and teachers.

- I love the ridiculous, the incongruous, the absurd.

- I'm still critical, both to people's faces and behind their backs.

- I make a lot of demands on my family and often fail to show appreciation. It's not that I'm ungrateful; I'm just so focused on myself that I forget to take other people's lives into account.

- While I may be inconsiderate of my family, I'm developing more compassion for society's downtrodden.

- If there's an issue that I feel strongly about, I'll stand up for what I believe in, even if I go against the crowd.

- I'm ready to make a lot of my own decisions about clothes. I can handle a clothing allowance and I can learn from the consequences of my decisions.

- I may be less interested than I used to be in reading and more interested in my social life.

- As my interests change, I might want to rearrange my room to reflect the new me.

- I know right from wrong, and I don't always need somebody to tell me. In most situations, I need to weigh the alternatives to arrive at the right decision by myself.

Age Fifteen

- My intellectual curiosity continues to grow. I might develop an interest in areas of study that I never considered before.

- I like to match wits with people in authority, like teachers. If my teachers see this as a form of rebellion, it could interfere with my learning. But if they respect my intellect and help me to construct my arguments, it may enhance my learning.

- I have an answer to every social problem. The solutions seem straightforward, clear-cut, and workable.

- I'm extremely concerned with fairness and justice. It's important not only that I receive fair treatment but also that others do, too, including younger brothers and sisters. I'll stand up for people who have been wronged, in my opinion.

- As my identity continues to form, I'm often immersed in my own opinions, ideas, and thoughts. Sometimes it's impossible for me not to argue. I might enjoy a debating club or an issues-oriented chat line.

- I don't necessarily want you to agree with my opinions and ideas, but I do need you to listen to them and respect them.

- I believe in my own personal fable—that I'm invulnerable, invincible, even immortal. I think that rules and laws that apply to the adult world don't apply to me. This belief makes me feel special, but it can be dangerous. I'm sure that I can drive before I have a single lesson, that I can drink and stay sober, that I can have sex with no fear of disease or pregnancy. I still need parents to set clear guidelines for me around my physical safety.

- I view every protective parental measure as an indication that I'm being treated like a child. But at the same time, I don't want you to take that protection away. I need it.

Age Sixteen and Up

- I'm less argumentative than I used to be. I can laugh things off now.

- My relationship with my parents may range from friendly to hostile. Over time, I'm becoming less critical and more accepting of you, with all your faults.

- I'm more tolerant when someone criticizes me.

- I love humour, especially when it's spontaneous. I can often see the funny side of a situation.

- I probably think I'm a more capable driver than I really am. I need clear rules around the use of the family car.

- I continue to delve into new ideas in religion, politics, and philosophy. I want to be able to discuss these issues with you.

- I'm still confused by the discrepancies I see between what people say they believe and what they actually do.

- I know that I'm unique, and I firmly believe that. But sometimes I think that I'm far more different and special than everybody else. I think that I'm the only one who has ever felt happiness so deeply, ever suffered loss so keenly, or been affected so profoundly by a book or a movie. If I'm in love, I'm sure that no one in history has ever experienced a love such as this.

- My world view is broadening. I'm more interested in newspapers, magazines, public affairs shows on radio and TV, and international news on-line.

- I'm still egocentric, but I'm starting to show a little more consideration of other people, including my family.

- I'm interested in the truth.

- Even if I don't always obey the house rules, I need to know what they are. It's better for me to break a rule than to have no rules to break.

- I'm planning more seriously for the future. I may change my mind several times about post-secondary education, courses, and careers.

Mind

Heart and Soul

3

Your teen is working hard toward independence. As he explores who he will become as an adult, he may try different personas, different hair colours, different friends. He may also experiment and take risks in ways you won't approve of. But behind the bold exterior, your teen feels insecure and defensive much of the time. Although his friendships are crucial to the development of his adult self, his relationship with his parents is still the most important in his life. He needs and wants your encouragement.

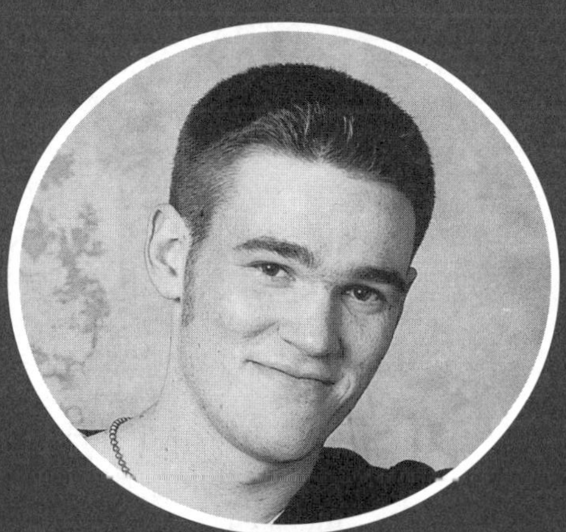

ll your friends and all the media warn you about the difficulties of parenting through the teenage years. While it's true that the whole family rides an emotional roller coaster when a teen is working toward independence, the flip side of the coin is that everyone's life gets more exciting. Your daughter is thrilled by her driving lessons. Your son has just discovered Jimi Hendrix, and "Purple Haze" blasts from the stereo. The phone is always ringing. Your home bursts with energy and activity.

Being a Family with Teens

Parents need to realize, though, that all teens feel insecure and constantly question their self-worth. Am I attractive? Am I fun to be with? Am I smart enough? Am I sexy enough, or am I sex-crazed? Let your teen know that she's not only OK, she's fabulous. Adolescents want their parents to listen to their stories, their concerns, their feelings. They don't like to be questioned—your questions put them on the defensive. If your son's stories spark a lecture from you, he'll be less inclined to share his experiences with you another time. Do as your teen instructs—stay cool. If your child tells you he wants to have his eyebrow pierced or confesses to having had a beer on a school trip, express your concerns, but realize that it's not only normal for teens to experiment, it's part of the adolescent's job description.

Because teens have shaky self-esteem, they need lots of approval from

their parents. It's important to offer kind words about his work on a science project or how well he told an anecdote at dinner. He needs and wants encouragement even more than he wants that new pair of jeans.

At times, it may seem as if your younger teenager doesn't want your love. She seems to be pushing you away all the time. But if you react to your teen's defiant glare by turning away, you may be in for problems—all teens need to feel that they're a valued member of the family. Nevertheless, both parents and their teens need to loosen their embrace. It's not uncommon for parents of older teens to feel that while they love their kids dearly, they won't be sorry to see them leave to live independently. It's as if, when the time comes for your child to try his wings, you are as ready as he is.

Fast friends

Beginning at about age twelve, kids need their peers more intensely than at any other time in their lives. They constantly need to compare themselves with their friends to make sure they're OK. The family has to make room for a teenager's friends. That means setting more places around the dinner table or negotiating the use of the phone so that nobody in the family misses an important phone call.

Families need to support their teens in their quest for friendships. You may miss doing things with your daughter now that she prefers to be with her friends. But it's a normal and healthy progression, so don't make her feel guilty. Instead, look for other ways you can enjoy each other. Maybe it's flipping through a catalogue together, or watching her favourite sitcom with her every week.

The way teens forge friendships tends to be gender-dependent. Boys tend to make friends by participating in an activity together—by playing baseball or being a member of a computer club, boys bond with one another. Girls tend to make friends by talking to one another. As if you haven't noticed, the phone is crucial in these relationships. On the phone and at sleepovers, girls become best friends by gossiping, sharing secrets, and giggling together.

My kids don't like me anymore

The job of a teen is to push off into her own life. By the age of fifteen, your teen may tell you that you don't understand her. After all you've done for her, your daughter has the nerve to unabashedly adore her ballet teacher, who can do no wrong, rather than you. You, she says, are hopelessly old-fashioned. Your son tells you that he can't wait until he's eighteen so that he can get his own apartment.

Throughout their adolescence, your teens gradually expose a part of yourself that you may not like. At age forty, you may find out how immature you are. You become jealous of the ballet teacher, and you can't believe how you let your daughter's comments about your stodginess really get to you. The messy bathroom that your child leaves behind can send you into a tantrum.

Your child used to cuddle beside you on the couch, look up at you with adoring eyes, and tell you all about her day. Now her bedroom door is closed—tight. Every parent of a teenager has stared at that closed door and wished for X-ray vision. What's she doing in there? She's probably listening to music, or exploring her new body, or writing about her feelings in a diary. Or maybe she's off in a fantasy.

By the time your child reaches her late teens, she's again more willing to spend time with you, as her peer friendships lessen in intensity. She finally feels secure enough in her identity and self-worth to return to a more connected family relationship. Once again, she'll sit with you and talk about her day. She may not put you on a pedestal anymore, but that doesn't matter. She likes you just the way you are.

Help wanted

In the second decade of parenting, your job is to be involved without intruding.

Sure, you've taught your son how to brush his teeth, do long division, and make lasagna. Now he needs you to help him learn how to drive, apply for a job, choose an apprenticeship program, and separate the whites from the colours when he does the laundry. He can also use a little help managing money, time, and stress. Of course, he might not ask for your help, but offer it anyway. Don't wait until things go wrong to step forward—not that you should take over his job or fill out his college application for him. And if you insist that he do it the way you did, you can count on his stomping off. In the second decade of parenthood, your cue is to be involved without intruding. You'll know when you've overstepped that elusive line because he'll ask you to butt out of his life.

As your teen masters the final tasks that lead to adulthood, families should mark these milestones. In a society with few rites of passage, you may need to invent your own rituals. Celebrate your daughter's getting a driver's licence by letting her drive the family out for ice cream. Have a corn roast to mark your son's finally getting his braces off. Being accepted into that apprenticeship program is definitely worth a celebratory dinner.

When Your Teen Pulls Away

Developing his adult identity is your teenager's priority. And along with that identity must come autonomy. As your child pushes to become more independent, it's normal and natural for him to put distance between you and him. Your teen wants to leave behind his preteen identity, and he's likely to show less interest in family activities and more need for privacy. If you invade his privacy, he may tell you to stay out of his business. It's quite natural for you to feel hurt, confused, or frustrated by these efforts to pull away. It's unsettling when a gulf begins to develop between you and your child and changes your relationship.

"My husband comes from a loving family, but they were very restrictive about what they were allowed to do. We had more opportunities in my family. I don't fear losing my children to the world."

PATTY, MOTHER OF FOUR

For argument's sake

As part of their search for identity, teens often experiment with different ways of being. They try on different personas, behaviours, and beliefs that may be exactly the opposite of those of their parents. In the process of finding and defining herself, your daughter may adopt political and religious beliefs or hairstyles and clothing that seem outrageous or offensive to you. You might even apply those terms to your teens' friends and their conversations.

Try not to take these actions or beliefs personally or as criticisms of your own lifestyle and beliefs. Although it's normal to feel some resentment when your child makes critical judgments, it's important to see her experiments as a necessary part of her development. A hypercritical, idealistic teen may label as hypocritical the compromises that her parents make in life. The challenge for both of you is to find ways to debate and acknowledge your differences without being dismissive and disrespectful of each other's opinions.

That's not easy when your sixteen-year-old son makes snide, sarcastic comments about your boring job. You may be tempted to snap back about how much time he wastes at the mall. You may disagree about many things—business, politics, the environment, or music—but listen to each other's point of view, acknowledging that you might learn something new. Or at least agree to disagree rather than push each other's buttons until you get into heated arguments.

Your teen's job is to develop her adult identity.

Separate, but not disconnected

Healthy rebellion does not mean that a child wants to completely break the connection with his parents. In fact, as parents, you remain the single most important force in your teen's life. The goal of parent-teen relations is to find new ways of connecting that acknowledge the teen as a different, self-defined person. There is a huge difference between a teenager who separates from his parents to create more space to grow and one who becomes totally disconnected.

"Your kids are the people you want to be with—and they're gone more and more."

TOM, FATHER OF TWO

Adolescents need to push against their parents in order to break free of the container of childhood, but they also need to retain the connection with their parents in a way that's appropriate for adolescence. If you can find ways to make that sometimes elusive connection work, you help your teen develop into an independent person.

Chapter Three

Being connected to your teen means knowing what's going on in his world without being too intrusive. If you take a rigid approach that doesn't give your child the scope to become his own person, you may rupture your relationship. The opposite approach—letting your teen do as he wishes without setting any limits, without providing any direction, and without maintaining your emotional connection—will have the same result, especially if your teen interprets it as a sign that you don't care.

"Teach your children that life is dynamic. They're learning from me. I'm learning from them. It's not a one-way street. We do some of our best talking in the car. You hear a lot of what's going on."

PATTY, MOTHER OF FOUR

It's the parent-teen connection that keeps your teen grounded as she grows and develops, that allows her to try her wings with a family safety net around the nest, and to test herself in her expanding world. This constant moving out to the new and back to the familiar helps her define herself. She'll feel safer when venturing out if she has the security of your known values and limits to refer to and push against. It's this connectedness, the knowledge that you love and care about her, that is an essential ingredient of the resiliency that a teen needs in order to cope when her behaviour goes awry.

It's the parent-teen connection that keeps your teen grounded as she grows and develops.

Heart and Soul

Mood Swings

In early adolescence, your teen's emotional system is still immature, although her ability to feel emotions has deepened. Her emotions may be extreme and variable. Small events might trigger elaborate reactions, whether it's a missed phone call or an innocent question from you about her new friend. Your teen may experience wild swings between elation and depression, shifting from emotional highs to lows in a matter of minutes. She may take a melodramatic approach to solving problems, viewing the possible solutions in terms of either-or—either black or white.

"The mood of the house is set by Emma. Emma's really needy. If she's on our side, there's nothing we can't accomplish as a family."

PATTY, MOTHER OF FOUR

It's important for you to know your kids, to be able to read their moods. Not all adolescents experience wild mood swings, but some teens do mark their attempts to separate from parents with moodiness and irritability. A fifteen-year-old boy may need to create some emotional distance in order to find out who he is. He may quickly plunge into deep despair or even fury at what he perceives as a threat to his autonomy—when all you asked was that he baby-sit his brother for an hour. Your rather tricky job is to strike a balance between setting appropriate limits and increasing his freedom to choose and to act. At age seventeen or eighteen, your teen's emotions may become less volatile, and you may both be more confident about her taking independent action, especially if you established and maintained open communication from childhood through adolescence. If you talked through your conflicts without recrimination, you likely established a firm basis of respect for one another.

Feeling out of control

During the physical changes and surging hormones of puberty and early adolescence, teens feel that their bodies are out of control, which makes them feel even more confused and anxious. But as your teen grows more comfortable with her new body and as the physical changes stabilize, her mood swings become less extreme.

When they do occur, mood swings can be frightening even to your teenager. A fifteen-year-old may wonder why his feelings of sadness or anxiety are so intense—one minute he's excited about being elected student council representative, the next minute he's paralyzed by nervousness about his first speech. Listen to him and help him acknowledge his emotions. He may not be able to express what he feels, so you may have to try to read between the lines. Don't dismiss his feelings or you risk sending the message that you don't care.

To help your teenage daughter deal with her intense emotions in healthy ways, stay cool and calm and offer emotional support when she's upset. It's helpful to her to have someone acknowledge and help her describe what she's feeling. If she's devastated because a friend said something nasty about her behind her back, say, "Tell me about it. How do you feel about what she did?" Get her to tell you what happened and how she feels, and discuss what she might do about it. Let her know that you care and want to help.

> **Don't dismiss your teen's feelings, or you risk sending the message that you don't care.**

Escaping the Pain

Sometimes, a teen's extreme moods or behaviours are really a cry for help. If her bleak mood persists, a teen may get trapped in a downward spiral. Just like adults, some teens become depressed or even suicidal. The following symptoms, if they persist for months, are signs of clinical depression: sadness, apathy, complete lethargy, inertia, carelessness about her appearance and well-being—especially if there is no sign of her bouncing back. Be alert for these signs, especially after a teen suffers a major loss—the breakup of a relationship, a death in the family, or a personal failure in school or sports activities or in her social life, and talk to your doctor. If your daughter hints at suicide or writes a despairing farewell letter, seek immediate help.

Some teens are so overwhelmed by their mixed emotions that they try to escape from their feelings, and these may be destructive escapes. They may take dangerous risks with drugs, drinking, unprotected sex, or violence—these actions may be a sign that your teen wants your attention or may need professional intervention.

The teen years are the time when a genetic predisposition to certain illnesses such as depression, manic depression, schizophrenia, or alcoholism first appear. If your daughter shows uncharacteristic mood swings or disturbing behaviour for a prolonged period, find out what's causing it. If you don't understand what's happening to your son or how to help him, seek the advice of your doctor or other professionals. Objective professionals have experience in recognizing the severity of a teen's moods and turbulent emotions and assessing their implications.

"I have mood swings all the time. One bad thing happens to me and I'm depressed. One good thing happens to me and I'm happy. I'm more moody than my friends are. I have more things to get me happy and get me depressed."

MAX, AGE 15

She may have a variety of responses to her intense emotions. She may need to talk for an hour to her best friend, play sad songs at top volume, work off some steam at the gym, tell gross jokes and laugh hysterically with her brother, or pour it all out in her journal. Gradually, she'll learn to sort out her feelings and make emotional experiences a vital part of her true self and who she really is. Your teen will learn to share her intense, intimate feelings and experiences with friends, siblings, and sometimes her parents. Give teens some freedom to be moody and have their own space. When they seem receptive, take the opportunity to communicate in a low-key, non-intrusive way, but let them do most of the talking. Mastering moods is part of their process of developing emotional maturity. The emotional changes your teen goes through and the changes in your relationship will probably shake you up, too. If you're honest about your feelings and show your own vulnerability, your teens may be more open with you.

A Teen's Fears and Worries

Next to the loss of a parent through divorce or death, nothing worries a teen like losing the acceptance of his friends. Especially in the early and mid-teen years, when a teen struggles to establish his identity, he worries that his friends will reject the person he's working to become.

When a teen begins to develop some independence from his parents and focuses on fitting in with his peers, he nevertheless worries about losing his parents' approval. There's often a big gap between the behaviour, music, clothes, speech, and attitudes that he and his friends express and what you approve of. A teen may be torn between the fear of losing his friends and the fear of his parents' disapproval. Parental resistance to a teen's changing preferences may give rise to tension and conflict. A teen grows as an individual as he develops his own balance between the values of his parents and his peers.

> **A teen may be torn between the fear of losing his friends and the fear of his parents' disapproval.**

Self-conscious fears

Teens' self-consciousness about their rapidly changing bodies often extends to self-consciousness in thoughts and feelings. They usually think that people who look at them are criticizing and judging them. When a thirteen-year-old feels a new sense of privacy, he may become intolerant of his younger brother. A fourteen-year-old girl who's developing at a slower rate than her peers may worry that she's not normal. A seventeen- or eighteen-year-old may feel intense pressure to make choices about his future when he doesn't feel ready.

"I worry about the impression I give my friends. I don't have the balls to do something that they would look down on. I should."

MAX, AGE 15

Take me seriously

Many teens are reluctant to talk about their fears or they prefer to keep them private. If you have created an atmosphere that lets your teen know you take her feelings seriously, she may be more inclined to try to express her anxieties and fears. From an adult perspective, a teen's fears about a situation may seem over-dramatized, but be careful not to dismiss the feelings. If you dismiss, downplay, or tune out the concerns, your teen will shut you out. Listen while your child talks through the current dilemma, and help him gain some perspective.

A teen wants his parents to treat him more like an adult than a child. Although he may sometimes still act like a child, he needs you to respect the person he's becoming. Open the door for discussion, and leave it open. You might say, "I know it's not easy to talk about the things that bother you, but when you're ready to talk, I'll always listen." When the time is right, your teen may come to you.

"If I'm mad, I get angry at anyone in the vicinity."

MAX, AGE 15

Think back to the pressures and confusion you felt when you were a teen. Share some of your worries, too, when the two of you do eventually talk. This is one of the healthiest ways to establish mutual respect. It gives teens a grounded, secure zone if they know they can come to you for help in dealing with their worries and fears.

A teen wants her parents to treat her more like an adult than a child.

Teens have worries that you, as a parent, can help dispel. Your sixteen-year-old daughter might worry that you'll get angry if she calls you at 2:00 a.m. from a party because there's trouble. Assure her that she can call you whenever she's in a jam, that you'll always be there to help. Let your older teen who's worried about the choices that face him know that you'll support his taking time to make decisions. Many decisions made at seventeen are not irrevocable; there's usually the possibility of changing direction or adjusting details.

"Teens worry about humiliation in front of their peers, about not being cool, about the way they look. They worry about looking like a nerd or a geek, or looking out of place. They want to be respected by their friends of both sexes."

TOM, FATHER OF TWO

Stress Management

As a parent, you can't eliminate stress from your teen's life, but you can help him learn to cope effectively. Acknowledge to your teen that the pressures he feels are real. Learn how to monitor his behaviour under stress, and keep the lines of communication open. Show an interest in your teen's world without being judgmental. Most teens already feel they're being judged by peers and teachers and society at large. Helping him feel good about himself provides a strong antidote to stress.

Develop your role as a consultant to let him know that you're an ally, not an enemy. A good consultant listens well, offers considered opinions, but lets the teen make up his own mind. Teach him that it's OK to make mistakes and sometimes fail—that's how he learns and gains experience to solve future problems. If failure occurs despite your advice, don't say "I told you so." Despite all their bravado and rebellion, teens need their parents' support when the chips are down.

"The biggest stress for Shannon is not being accepted by friends. She has a thinner skin than her brother. She's more brittle. The good thing is she'll talk about it. Jealous girls can be cruel. When these things happen, you can give lots of love. We talked every night after school."

LYNETTE, MOTHER OF TWO

Stress management involves knowing what to do to alleviate stress. Energy-demanding sports, music, journal writing, and private time are some outlets that help teens reduce stress. Talking with sympathetic and supportive friends, siblings, teachers, and parents also helps. Parents

"Good friends help alleviate stress. It's tough to talk to parents about some things. My daughter writes in her diary. A journal is a good method of dealing with stress. I use it often. It lets you unload all kinds of things. When your child is really in distress, you have to intervene and offer comfort. Shut up. Get them to start talking. Once they talk, you can deal with it."

TOM, FATHER OF TWO

can help teens manage stress by subtly suggesting certain techniques and modelling good stress management themselves.

One strategy to help kids put their stress in perspective is to ask them to rate their problems on a scale of one to ten. Where does the breakup with a boyfriend or girlfriend rate on the scale? Where does a bad hair day score? By ranking problems, a teen gains some perspective on what triggers her stress reactions and can set priorities for a plan of action.

Help your teens learn that thinking and feeling are two separate processes and that they should consider both when making a decision. Ask "How do you feel about this? What do you think about it?" Show your confidence in their ability to handle a new problem by recalling how they handled a similar problem effectively in the past. Even if they aren't ready to talk, offer a neck massage or a hot cup of herbal tea. Reinforce the idea of positive stress relievers that work for them. Regular exercise and participation in vigorous physical activities can be a powerful tonic and antidote to stress for many teens. Others may prefer the soothing or distracting qualities of their favourite music. Some even get the urge to clean up their room or reorganize their closet just to regain a sense of control.

Teens mature, in part, by challenging and testing their parents' values and guidelines, so sometimes the source of your teen's stress is the parent-teen relationship. If you're feeling pretty stressed yourself about the relationship or other responsibilities, it may be harder for you to help.

"Other people get really stressed out. I don't that much now. I used to back in grade nine. That was a more crazy time. I moved to an all-girls school. You had to get in with the old girls, and it was hard to fit in. When I'm stressed, I get more hyper. I have a lot on my mind, but I'm not in a bad mood."

DEBRA, AGE 18

Even if you can't eliminate the challenges that your teen's struggles create, you can convert them into opportunities to help your teen grow and mature. In between times, shore up your relationship with your shared sense of fun. An open, sometimes heated and combative relationship is healthier than a resentful or indifferent silence in which the lines of communication between parent and teen shut down.

New relationships can be both a source of joy and a source of stress.

Heart and Soul

Siblings

Sibling relationships are complex. Siblings may become close friends or bitter rivals, or they may shift back and forth from one to the other. They may spend a lot of time together, or they may want as little as possible to do with each other. A younger sibling who is in the throes of early adolescence may look up to his more confident, cooler older sister. Or he may resent the older brother who enjoys the privileges of independence and dismisses his younger brother's problems or interests.

"Debra and Max are close when you're not around. They act out more when you're there. They care for each other and support each other. Max worships her. He would never admit it, of course. She's protective of him. There's a tone when they talk, a caring tone."

TOM, FATHER OF TWO

Younger siblings can look up to their cool older brothers.

During their teen years, siblings may talk about all kinds of things—music, dating, sex, drinking, drugs—that they would never, or rarely, discuss with their parents. At a time when many teens want to put a distance between themselves and their parents, siblings often deepen an already close relationship by sharing confidences and advice, worries and feelings.

If siblings are close, the relationship may provide a safer place for a fifteen-year-old girl to be herself. She doesn't feel the same pressure to make an impression, perhaps by putting up a front, as she does with peers. Siblings know one another too well and can't easily reject one another, whereas friendships can come and go, especially in the impressionable teen years. Teens sometimes try on friends like new clothes, wearing them for a month and then discarding them in favour of the next person who interests them. But siblings, in a trusting relationship, may find it easier to acknowledge what they're really thinking and feeling. If they're not sure about resisting peer pressure or about dating someone whom their friends snub, their sibling may give them strength to go their own way.

Sibling rivalry

In some families, the differences in age, style, or popularity between two siblings may create a great emotional distance between them. Their sibling rivalry may go sour and develop into major rifts during which the siblings don't even talk to each other for years. In other families, the cocky sixteen-year-old might simply not want anything to do with his younger brother.

Siblings can't easily reject one another whereas friendships can come and go.

"Emma wants to be cool. She calls her sister Kate a nerd. She says to her, 'You think you're so perfect.' But Emma's friends like Kate."

PATTY, MOTHER OF FOUR

Parents cannot and should not try to force siblings to be friends, but they also shouldn't allow one to be mean to the other. Parents can insist that they act respectfully toward each other. As the older sibling matures, parents can encourage him to be more of a mentor to younger siblings.

With the privileges of driving and more independence come some responsibilities, too. If the seventeen-year-old wants to demonstrate his growing maturity, he can do it by being more supportive toward his nervous, awkward fourteen-year-old brother.

If one child is a star athlete, student, or musician, or has extraordinary good looks, other siblings may feel second-class. That's a sure way to sow the seeds of envy and create a sour relationship. If one teen genuinely feels that another is a favourite, pay attention to those feelings. Don't exacerbate the problem by making comparisons, by praising the one for whom things come easily, or by showing disappointment in the one for whom things are more difficult. Every child is special and has a right to feel special. Make sure each receives an equal share of your attention and time.

"My sister makes me who I am. I look up to her. I know the kind of person I would like to be. I'd like to be the kind of person who doesn't care what other people think about me. My sister's like that. I don't always take my sister's advice, but I often do. Our relationship has always been the same. It just made sense."

MAX, AGE 15

Bonding in Crisis

If one teen struggles with depression, drugs, or other serious problems, his sibling may provide the best way for you to offer support to the child who is in need but seems incapable of talking to you. Ask your other child for suggestions about getting to the source of the problem and restoring communication.

When the family goes through a crisis like divorce or the death of a close family member, siblings can be a great source of support for one another. The crisis may create a scary, stressful time for them, a time when their whole world seems to be changing. Parents can't force their children to be good friends, but they can shape and share experiences that help their children recognize and appreciate one another's strengths and their struggles to overcome personal problems.

Friends for life

If your children get along well with one another and are close, encourage their relationship and accept that they may spend more time with each other than with you. If your teens become close during their teens, you can be sure that they'll have strong, enduring relationships for the rest of their lives. These are formative, intense years that shape their identities and leave a lasting mark. When siblings go through their rites of passage together, their relationship is transformed to a new level and they become friends as young adults. They form an enduring bond that they can count on through the triumphs and crises at each stage of their lives.

"I'll go to my brother when I need an unbiased opinion. He'll give me what he thinks, without worrying about hurting my feelings. I'll ask him, 'Does this look good?' He'll tell me. There's no blackmail, like in other families. We talk about stuff, Mom and Dad, what's happening with us, new friends, boyfriends, girlfriends. We do stuff together, go to a show or an art gallery. He asks me for advice. I'm glad I have a brother. I'm glad I'm not an only child."

DEBRA, AGE 18

Making the Big Steps

Your thirteen-year-old is emerging from childhood still dependent on and controlled by you in many aspects of his life. The main developmental task that lies ahead of him in the next few years is to successfully make the transition to a much more independent adolescent who controls and takes responsibility for many, if not all, aspects of his life.

Driving, managing personal time, and managing money are three major areas in which your teens will face exciting challenges and major risks, but they'll also have many opportunities to grow and become more independent. In each area, the adolescent needs to learn how to handle the increased freedom and responsibility, preferably with your guidance and encouragement.

Driving

Getting a driver's licence is a big step toward adulthood. The first time your daughter slides behind the wheel for a solo drive, she's experiencing a sense of independence and freedom that she may never have felt before. You're probably experiencing major anxiety, and not without cause. Driving is a huge responsibility that poses new risks for your teen. Successfully passing the driving tests gives her the licence to drive—it's still up to you to decide whether she has the appropriate skills and maturity to drive in particular situations.

"Driving worries me—there's greater potential for them to be hurt. But you only get better by doing it. My son has got so much testosterone pumping through his system—I've got to deal with it."

TOM, FATHER OF TWO

Let your son know well before he says he wants to apply for his licence that driving is a privilege that he must earn. Let him know that before you allow him to drive the family car on his own, he will have to prove to you that he can be responsible for a tonne of metal moving at high speed. Let him know that you'll judge his readiness by how he handles responsibilities in other areas of his life that might affect his driving. Does he show good safety sense when he's on his bike, on his blades, on the ski hill? Does he keep you posted on his whereabouts when he's out? Does he meet curfew? Does he come home sober?

If you believe he isn't ready yet, let him know why and negotiate some goals for him to meet bin order to be ready. Set a time in the near future to re-evaluate his readiness. When it's time for your teen to learn to drive, take the advice of the Canada Safety Council and sign him up for formal driving instruction. Look for a school that is approved by a

recognized association—some insurance companies may reduce premiums for young graduates of these schools. Also, choose a school that offers students both hands-on driving instruction and classroom instruction, including defensive driving and emergency procedures. Check that the school offers reports on the student's progress and codriver information for parents to use when driving with their teens. Although you should encourage your teen to enroll in a driver education program, you play a crucial role in helping your teen become a good driver by giving him lots of practice behind the wheel. You may find it nerve-wracking at first to be in the passenger seat, but look upon the time you spend practice driving with your teen as a special time together.

It takes a couple of years for a new driver to gain adequate experience, which is why almost half the provinces have instituted a graduated licensing program with two or three levels of licensing. Usually the applicant has to pass a written test to receive the first licence, a beginner's or learner's permit to practice drive. It stipulates when, where, and with whom a new driver may drive. In some provinces, recognized driver training can shorten the time between the tests for each level leading to a permanent licence. It's best for your teen to have clocked 2,000 km practice driving before he tries the test for his licence. Make sure he learns to drive with an experienced driver in the different kinds of conditions he'll encounter—driving at night, in the rain, and in snowy or icy conditions.

The high cost of driving

Before your teen is old enough for a learner's permit, be sure he is aware of the additional costs for the family and for his own driving. If your teen will use the car regularly, especially for a part-time job, work out an agreement about who pays and how much for gas and oil, car washes and maintenance. You might establish a fair contribution toward the insurance since the family's insurance rates usually increase

Drinking and Driving

It's ostrich-like to avoid the subject of drinking and driving just because your family guideline is that your children can't drink alcohol until they reach the legal age. Consider the following from the Addiction Research Foundation's *Ontario Student Drug Use Survey*. Your child might be one of these students.

Grade	Per cent drinking alcohol
grade seven	31.9 per cent
grade nine	55.3 per cent
grade eleven	80.6 per cent
grade thirteen	78.7 per cent

Drinking and driving is so dangerous that you must discuss it explicitly with your teens and agree upon specific rules. Your teen must never drive when he or she has been drinking. That doesn't mean only when they feel drunk. The rule is simple: If they've had a drink, they must not drive. Nor should they get in a friend's car if that friend has been drinking. This is the standard for their safety.

Discuss with your teen in detail the alternative ways he can get home if he has been drinking. You may want to make this in the form of a contract that you discuss together. Your teen can take public transit, call a cab, or get a ride with someone who hasn't been drinking. Assure him that he can also call you, that you'll take a cab to meet him, then drive him home in the family car, or, if you have a second car, that you'll pick him up that night and retrieve the other car the next day.

If your daughter can't reach you by phone or chooses to take a cab, have a plan for where she can find cash or use a card to pay for the cab. Reassure your teen that her safety is the most important thing in the world to you, that she can call you for a ride at any hour, and you'll come get her.

Set the same example yourself. Don't ever drink and drive. Let your children hear you discussing who will be the designated driver if you're going to an event at which alcohol will be served. Let your licensed teen be your designated driver after you've all been at a family function where the adults have had alcoholic drinks.

when a teenager is added as a driver. Tickets for speeding or other moving violations also increase the cost of insurance, and an accident boosts rates even higher or may disqualify the driver from future coverage.

Once your teen has a licence and is driving regularly, you may find that you're in constant negotiations over the use of the family car. Set the ground rules early about how often he can have the car, when, and for what reasons. If appropriate, let your teen know that you expect him or her to do some family chores, like picking up supplies, chauffeuring younger siblings to and from their activities, and picking up elderly relatives for family events. You may find that there's an advantage to sharing the job of family chauffeur.

"My older sister doesn't drive, and I don't get it. I think driving would be fun and I'd enjoy it. Driving means independence. My parents both have minivans. I want to get a car, not a minivan. That will make everything easier."

MAX, AGE 15

Managing Personal Time

The teen years are usually high-energy years when kids take on many new activities. They make plans with friends, sign up for the school's charity drive, join intramural volleyball, take three baby-sitting jobs in one week—and then feel completely overwhelmed. They need to learn that they can't do everything at the same time, that they have to make choices, and that their choices have consequences. A teenager has to juggle a lot to find time for school, for peers, for boyfriends and girlfriends, for family and household chores, for part-time work and sports, and for relaxation and private time to discover who he or she is. The demands and pressures can be exhilarating and exciting, overwhelming and confusing. There may be too much happening or too little. How do they make their balancing act work?

"I don't have a curfew anymore. I didn't go hog wild before. Little bits of independence have added up to my becoming independent."

DEBRA, AGE 18

As a parent, you still influence how your early teen spends her time. But she'll do everything in her power to resist that influence, just as she resists your influence in other areas of her life. Your time priorities will differ from those of your child. But the passage from parental decision making to parental influence occurs during adolescence, and it may not be a smooth progression for either you or your teen. A fourteen-

year-old may seem remarkably organized and independent one day, then regress to confusion and tantrums the next. Usually, an eighteen-year-old is more mature and knows her strengths and weaknesses, so you may both be comfortable about her relative independence.

"No one's good at managing their time. I always do it all, but I do everything half-assed. I'd like to do some things really well. There are too many things that I want to do. I can't stand missing out on something. My first priority is to be with my friends. I'm having fun. My life is full."

MAX, AGE 15

For every two steps forward, you'll take one step backward as your teen strives to reach independence. The goal is for her to learn how to handle situations in her own way. If you dictate or she demands, you both lose. When you work out a compromise together, that's a win-win for both of you. Negotiate rather than impose.

Chapter Three

As she learns how to balance her time, sometimes she'll make mistakes. Tie your expectations to her performance in school subjects. If she makes decent grades even though she handles ten phone calls every night, then don't suggest she spend less time on the phone. But if her social life takes over her evenings to the point that her school assignments aren't completed, then negotiate a "no-phone zone" every evening, a time for her to concentrate on schoolwork uninterrupted.

As a parent, you can help your teens learn how to manage their time, their swirling emotions, and their increased responsibilities if you stay on a relatively even keel. Sometimes you'll find it hard to watch as your son takes on too much, propelled by furious bursts of hormones and energy. But you can best help by allowing him to try and to learn eventually to recognize for himself how much he can handle. If you become dictatorial about how your teen spends her time, she may never learn her own limits. In fact, she might expend most of her energy finding ways of resisting your suggestions or restrictions. Expect some conflict as she tests the limits, and try to focus on key issues: your teen needs enough sleep; she needs to handle her schoolwork; she needs to contribute to household chores; but she also needs time to hang out with friends.

> **Tie your expectations to her performance in school. If she makes decent grades, loosen the house rules a little.**

> "Shannon considers consequences, so she gets more responsibilities and goes with it."
>
> ALLAN, FATHER OF TWO

On the surface, her time with friends may seem to you like time wasted. Many parents cannot understand how two teens can spend several hours together, then separate to their respective homes only to get on the phone to each other immediately. But your teen's desire to spend time with peers is natural, valid, and crucial for her growth and development. You should respect that social priority and support it, while encouraging her to meet her responsibilities and pursue other aspects of her development, whether academic, athletic, or artistic. You might, for example, negotiate a curfew that allows lots of time with friends on weekends but keeps weekday evenings for schoolwork and other activities.

If parents set no limits, a teen may have trouble learning how to manage his time and his priorities, feeling lost without parental direction and reminders of his goals. A fifteen-year-old isn't ready for complete freedom of choice. As he demonstrates more maturity through your gradual loosening of limits, he earns the freedom to make more decisions for himself.

School and homework

Help your teens learn to set priorities and allocate their time by working out a homework arrangement at the start of the school year. Get their input on how best to do it—what's expected of them on school nights and on weekends. They need time to complete homework assignments but also for after-school activities, for sports, for friends, and for other entertaining pursuits.

Revisit the plan after each term's report card. If you find that his grades aren't meeting reasonable standards, then discuss how he can give enough time to academic studies. Keep the house rules the same; for example, home after school by 4:30 p.m., except on band practice night; a "no-phone zone" on weeknights; an 11:30 p.m. curfew on weekend nights. But if you find that he's doing well in his schoolwork, you might give him more freedom. Perhaps you allow phone calls between 8:00 and 9:00 p.m. or you don't insist on his being home every school night. You let him choose how to use his time, trusting that he'll balance out his various activities appropriately.

By the time your daughter is eighteen or nineteen, she will probably make all the decisions about her time. Your role is to negotiate the free flow of information. As long as you're living under the same roof, you're entitled to know where each other is and when each of you can be expected home. This is most effective if approached as a courtesy and a safety precaution among adults.

Allow your older teen to set his own priorities and allocate his time.

Family time

It's a painful issue for some parents that their teens no longer want to spend time with them or with the extended family. You may feel slighted when you plan a family event and find that your teen has made a commitment to spend the day with friends. You can't force your teen to spend time with the family; making him feel obligated results in an unpleasant time for everybody. Instead, watch for opportunities to do something else together that he enjoys.

TOM, FATHER OF TWO

Younger teens may act uncomfortable just appearing in public with their parents, so going to the movies together may be out. But driving your teen and her friends to the swimming pool and picking them up later may be just fine. It may not feel like quality time to you but, in fact, you are spending time with your daughter and her friends and you have an opportunity to see how they interact.

Try to find topics that keep your son's interest long enough to have a conversation with you. This usually means showing an interest in his activities and listening while he tells you about them, without prying or being judgmental. Sometimes you need to find a new common ground. If your seventeen-year-old daughter is willing to be seen in public with you (and most older teens are), start checking out movies together again. You may have to compromise on the choices, but as long as you pay for them and avoid prime weekend nights, she'll be happy to go.

Plan your family vacation time so that it incorporates your common interests. If your teen wants to try rock climbing and you enjoy hiking, find a location where you can take part in both activities. Family vacations are an excellent time to reconnect with your teen, provided he's been involved in planning where you're going and what you'll be doing. Respect your teen's need to spend a lot of time with his peers, but also invite him to spend some personal time doing fun things with you.

Managing Money

Most parents give their children a regular allowance, and many teens begin to manage their own spending and saving, especially if they obtain a part-time or summer job. How can parents help teens to become responsible and independent in money management? The best way to teach your children how to manage money is by involving them in some discussions of family spending and to give them a lot of freedom in handling their regular allowance. When establishing the amount of the allowance, have your teens make their case for a particular weekly or monthly amount by outlining their regular expenses, their savings for major expenses, and their discretionary spending.

It's important for teens to have some freedom in spending their allowance on entertainment, clothing, snacks, or whatever interests them. They will learn best from their own mistakes. If they run short of cash, don't bail them out. They must learn to budget for what they need as well as what they want. Show them how to look at different ways of allocating their money so that they learn money management. Over time, your teen must learn to take more responsibility for planning and controlling income and expenses for a greater number of personal and eventual household expenses.

"Giving them a regular allowance each week cuts down on the stress in our relationship. They have to decide how to spend it."

PATTY, MOTHER OF FOUR

When she's thirteen, her allowance might cover bus fare, lunch money, and entertainment. When she's sixteen, you might include in her monthly allowance the family budget for her clothing so that she learns to manage her money over a longer period of time. Remind her that you'll always be willing to provide money for situations that involve her health or personal safety. You don't want your daughter to accept a ride with someone who's been drinking because she doesn't have enough money for cab fare and has no other way home.

Bribery or incentive?

Should you tie allowances to household chores, school performance, and behaviour? No, unless you want your children to see money as either bribery or punishment. Family and school responsibilities should not be tied to money. However, experts suggest that it's OK to pay family members for doing chores and family projects that you usually pay a non-family member to do.

Decide together what tasks or projects deserve payment. These extra tasks may also provide an incentive for teens to learn how to handle tools or equipment they might not otherwise learn. By working with you on such tasks as painting and wallpapering inside the house or gardening and fence repairs outside, they also learn how to do the kind of family and household chores that relatives or neighbours would be willing to pay them for, once they see proof of the quality of their work. Most teens who want extra money are willing to mow lawns, to shovel snowy sidewalks, to deliver newspapers or flyers.

Chapter Three

Saving and investing

You may not like your teens' taste in music or clothes, but respect their need to spend their money on what interests them. At the same time, through your example and guidance, help them understand the concepts of saving and investing and giving to others. If you haven't already done so, introduce your teen to standard banking practices, setting up a savings account for money received as gifts, from earnings, or perhaps as an allowance.

A healthy attitude about money includes saving for gifts and to give to charity. If your teen saves some of her allowance for charity, she should be allowed to choose the charity and see the benefits of her contributions. Talk about the volunteer work that you enjoy, and encourage your teens to get involved in causes that they care about.

If your teens need or want more money than their allowance can provide, help them find part-time and summer jobs, but watch to make sure that their salaried work doesn't interfere with their school performance or prevent their having a healthy social and personal life. More than twenty hours a week of part-time work is linked to decreased academic performance by teens. Try not to put your teen in a position where she works too many hours because she needs money just to cover the basics of her daily school and work life.

Encourage your teens who work part-time throughout the year or during the summer to save some of their money for major purchases or travel or for their post-secondary education. If, for example, your seventeen-year-old daughter wants to buy her own car or travel to Europe, you might offer to match whatever money she is able to save toward one of these goals.

Saving for a school trip can be an appropriate short-term goal.

If your teenagers are keen, you might get them interested in the concept of planning for their financial futures. Some teens become interested in ethical investment funds, others are intrigued by the stock market. Some high schools offer courses in commerce that include an introduction to investing and monitoring the performance of investments, whether real or paper.

Most kids are interested in how their parents earn money, and you may have been involved in career days at their schools or in take-your-child-to-work days over the years. Teens also show an increasing interest in different careers and in the potential earnings for different kinds and levels of work.

The financial facts of life should also be part of the education you offer them. What does it cost to run your house and what does your family spend in a year? If your children develop good financial habits and learn from you how to manage money well, they will be much better prepared to handle life on their own away from home, whether they're fully or only partially independent of your financial aid.

Budding entrepreneurs

If your teen shows an entrepreneurial bent, encourage her. She may be interested in structuring a small business around a part-time endeavour that brought her some spending money in the past—whether it's tutoring other students, writing software, troubleshooting for computer users, teaching tennis, or mowing lawns. You can help her assess the demand for her skills, and help her set up a more official business plan and structure. Undertaking this business, with all its successes and failures, will provide terrific experience for her career development and later entry into the full-time working world.

> **In the current job market, your teen may need to create his own job.**

Of course, she will also learn how to develop both financial and personal independence, and in the current competitive job market, your teens may need to create their own jobs. They will benefit from learning how to identify business opportunities, how to network and market their skills, and how to negotiate satisfactory business arrangements. Although self-employment is a growing trend, industries and corporations also expect their permanent employees to be entrepreneurial in spirit as well as educated and skilled.

Learning how to earn and manage money is an important rite of passage. It can also be fun. Encourage your teens to enjoy not only spending, but making, saving, investing, and sharing money. Help them to put money in perspective as a means to an end, not the key to happiness.

Going from Discipline to Self-Discipline

Like most parents, you wouldn't allow your thirteen-year-old daughter to stay out until 3:00 a.m., nor to date someone who's five years older. But a nineteen-year-old who is living away from home makes her own decisions in matters like these. The teen years are years of loosening your restrictions while not loosening your involvement.

In most families, this is a slow and relatively smooth process with perhaps a few anxious moments for parents and teens. You might give them more responsibility or loosen some restrictions and encourage them to show that they can handle the changes. Have a trial period of a month or two. If you agree to a later curfew on weekends, they have to demonstrate that their school performance won't slip. Renegotiate after you both see how well the deal works.

"We tell our kids, 'Think about your behaviour.' We've given them a meat-and-potatoes upbringing. Do unto others...."

ALLAN, FATHER OF TWO

However, in some families, a crisis situation may severely damage SEE PAGE 184 the parent-child relationship and result in an abrupt disconnection that leaves the teen without family support. If your teen suddenly pushes away from you to establish her right to be an individual, she may do so in ways that spark confrontation. Remain calm and choose your battles on the issues that count. A messy room is not as worrisome as her forgetting to call home when she knows she'll be an hour late. Don't be afraid to say No when it's appropriate. You might legitimately insist that your fifteen-year-old not ride the subway alone after dark or go to parties without adult

Negotiate, Don't Dictate

Parents need to set boundaries and restrictions in the early teen years, but it's better to negotiate than to dictate. Negotiation allows both parents and teens to have input into the rules and the responsibilities. It's an important step toward helping the teen create and observe his own rules, which is the essence of self-discipline. Negotiation can be time-consuming, but the time spent discussing your areas of disagreement and working out compromises is time well spent. Teens need to have a say in creating the rules so that they'll be motivated to live up to them and eventually outgrow them.

Gathering in large groups creates a comfortable teen-only atmosphere that lets kids feel free of the watchful adult world.

supervision. But talk to other parents about what guidelines they give their kids so that you have a sense of what others in your teen's group are allowed to do. Say Yes when you can, but say No when you must.

Doing his own thing

One way for a teen to develop self-discipline is his pursuit of passionate personal interests. He has to work hard to improve or to achieve something special. His goal may be to become a better guitar player, a competitive swimmer, or a developer of computer games. If his interest is truly motivating, he'll work to do the best he can, and in doing so, he'll learn a lot about self-discipline. Applaud his efforts and achievements, and encourage him to keep at it. Be available to help, but don't interfere. Let him do his thing, learn from his mistakes, and shoot for the top.

"My husband believes restrictions are what produce a morally responsible child. In my family, we had more opportunity to go out and taste life. You go on your instinct, what you were raised with, lots of family love and time."

PATTY, MOTHER OF FOUR

During their teenage years, your children are in the process of refining their own values. Teens do need some rules and values against which they can define their own values, but they need room to grow, too. Some teens can handle more freedom than others. Match your level of involvement to your teen's level of maturity. Let him make his own mistakes, if the penalty for the mistake won't be too severe. If you think he paid too much for new skates because he didn't shop around, explain how he could get a better deal next time. If you think he's about to make a poor choice, don't say so. Ask if he's considered other options. Suggest that he make a list of the pros and cons of a particular action or purchase, and then decide. Help him learn strategies for problem solving by looking at possibilities and weighing alternatives instead of making snap decisions.

"When they reach their teens, they have power. They're not little kids. They realize they can do things that have a strong impact on your life. They want to be different very suddenly. A lot of things you think are important, they think are crap. They want to shock you. I want them to be more self-reliant, to have respect for their life and for my life. You never lay a hand on your kid. That's not right."

TOM, FATHER OF TWO

Teens are a gregarious lot. Most love a group.

In their early teens, your children may express criticisms and judgments about your values or actions. Some parents might begin to feel excluded from their teen's world. Although you shouldn't take her comments and opinions personally, ask yourself: Am I doing something that bugs her? Or is there something wrong that she's concealing for fear of my reaction? Your daughter has to test her independence and she may need more privacy now, but trust your instincts and your knowledge of her.

There's a fine line between being involved in and intruding on your teen's social life. If you show interest in your teenage daughter's friends, they will probably appreciate your interest, and your daughter won't keep her social life totally secret from you. Respect for your daughter's friends is a sign of respect for her. Make your teen's friends welcome in your home by giving them some privacy, keeping snacks on hand, and being friendly without being overly involved. You can connect with what's going on without spying or feeling that you're intruding. Young teens can be quite inexpressive with adults, so don't expect long discussions or much information from them. But as your teen and her friends get older, you'll find that they're more willing to spend time actually talking to you.

As they move away from their families to establish their separate identities, teens create a new support system for themselves.

Loyalty is an essential element of teen friendship.

Self-discipline also means developing the confidence to be an individual, to not simply accept everything that your peer group does. A parent can help her daughter see what's going on in her group of friends and help her decide how to behave. If some members of the group are mean to another member, help your daughter see the injustice of ganging up on one person, help her find her own voice. Parents can't be nearby for their teens all the time, or even most of the time. But you can make your presence felt through your influence, as they internalize the values and habits that will enable them to do the right thing. Lively discussions and debates, in which you respect each other's views even when you disagree, may have their impact weeks, months, or years later.

"I would like to be more self-reliant. I look up to someone who has self-discipline. No one looks down on someone who does things well.

My parents were pretty relaxed about discipline. They were ahead of their time. I assume they trust me not to do anything that would cause them not to trust me. I can do anything I want because they know I won't do anything stupid. Not enough parents trust their kids."

MAX, AGE 15

Mutual trust provides the best foundation for a teen to move from parental discipline to self-discipline. Do you trust your teen's judgment and do you let her know it? If so, you give her good reason to trust her own judgment and yours.

Heart and Soul

Teen Culture

Most parents are used to adolescents having their own music, their own tastes in movies and TV programs, and their own style of clothing and hair. If their parents don't like it, well, that's really the point. Teen culture as a world clearly distinct from that of adults is a relatively new phenomenon. Sociologists say that what we describe as teen culture began in the 1950s. And the early years of the baby boom produced a record number of kids who moved into their teenage years in the 1960s.

In previous decades, many teens quit school in their middle teens to begin working life. But with the prosperity that North America enjoyed in the 1950s and 1960s, families were able to extend the level of education provided to their teens. The extended stay in high school gave baby boomers more opportunities to share their thoughts and interests with others their age. Advertising agencies and marketers picked up on their interests and fads and reflected them back to the teens in the mass media, particularly in movies and television. Common themes emerged: Teens crave thrills, whether it's the Blob trying to devour a young Steve McQueen or a death-defying ride on a wooden roller coaster; teens find the outlaw fascinating, whether it's James Dean, the urban rebel, or Marlon Brando, the biker in *The Wild One*; teens set themselves apart from their parents' generation by their behaviour, their clothes, and their slang.

Teens have their own world of music, movies, and fashion.

Tastes have changed, but most of the themes are the same. Marketers research what kids like, and they cash in. Teens still love thrills—think of the millions of dollars raked in on the first weekend of the release of the latest techno-thriller. The outlaw still appeals, too, although it may be a real-life convicted rap artist rather than a celluloid biker.

Adolescents are driven to take risks. They have to break out of the relative security and safety of childhood if they're to become independent and enjoy the tantalizing rewards of the adult world. Without taking some risks, they can't grow. Horror movies, defiant song lyrics, and sexually explicit dance styles satisfy some of that need for risk without exposing them to the world's real dangers. They are both an outlet and a form of practice for the real challenges ahead, whether those challenges are working up the courage to go on a date or to deal with the major step of leaving home. As for their clothes, if someone's feeling vulnerable in their changing world, as many teens do, it helps to make themselves look tougher than they may feel. And identifying themselves with outlaws by dressing like a skinhead or a gang member brings some small degree of confidence.

The other reason for teen dress and speech is one that adults recognize—fashion. Once a particular style seeps into the teen consciousness, those who don't follow it just don't belong. If they're going to have a style, it has to be different from the one that parents prefer. How else can they make themselves distinct and complete the separation process, the teen's primary work?

"This guy Mel runs a really cool and funky shop and he's this really cool guy. He has an eighteen-year-old son and I said to him once, 'Your son must think it's great to have such a hip guy for a father,' and he said, 'Not at all. My son considers me a nerd.' I think it's because teens have this need to rebel and reject parents no matter who you are or what you do for a living. In fact, if you're different from other parents, they find you a little bit embarrassing."

CATHERINE, MOTHER OF TWO

Teen culture is not homogeneous today. Subgroups with particular interests, whether it's skateboarding or heavy metal music, develop and spin off. Each group has its own way of dressing and its own favourite style of music. The groups don't interact much, but they also don't seem to confront one another.

Each teen subgroup has its own way of dressing and its own favourite music.

Of course, teen culture isn't always easy to take. Parents who can grit their teeth through a hip-hop music track may react against the misogynist lyrics. They want to reduce or eliminate the violence not only in music for teens but also in TV programs, movies, and computer games. Should they worry? It's an ongoing debate. Some psychologists fear that exposure to violence desensitizes young people so that they more readily accept violence as part of the normal world. Many sociologists counter that there's little solid evidence linking exposure to violence in entertainment to violence among teens themselves.

Your decisions about the type of entertainment you allow your teens to watch will depend on their ages and their temperaments. Many adolescents in their early to mid teens are highly impressionable and very susceptible to the potential negative effects of some materials available in the different media. Even if they aren't likely to copy the acts of a movie character, they may be disturbed by the violence in so-called entertainment. By the mid to late teens, an adolescent is likely no more susceptible to potential negative effects than an adult. Your personal and family values influence your decisions. If you're uncomfortable about a certain kind of entertainment and don't want your teen exposed to it, tell him your decision and why you made it.

Video games

Canadian kids may not be watching as much television as they used to, but they are still spending lots of time in front of a screen. Although no direct link has been made, teens may be watching less TV because they are playing more video games. The video game industry, which is larger than the children's film and television industries combined, certainly competes for their time.

There are fewer investigations into how video games affect the way users think and behave than there are into children's television viewing. But one recent study by Dr. Stephen Kline, a communications professor at Simon Fraser University, concluded that one in every four kids who play video games becomes addicted. Like television, video games reduce the time your teen spends participating in other activities and interacting with other people. Just because video games are interactive and can be played with friends, they are not more "educational" than television. Research shows that most kids play video games by themselves, especially the ultra-violent fantasy games such as Mortal Combat or Doom.

The rating system for video and computer games, similar to movie rating, takes into account the levels of violence, bad language, nudity, and sex. Check a game's rating before you allow your teen to play. Rent the game first to determine whether it's appropriate before making a purchase. You can also set a daily limit and make it clear to your teen that homework and household chores take priority over games.

Teen Friendships

As they move away from their families to establish their own separate identities, teens create new support systems for themselves. Few interests in the life of many teens are as important to them as friends. Teens believe that only someone going through the same thing at the same time can completely understand how they feel. They want close friends with whom they can share their fears, their hopes and dreams, and their secrets. They need friends who won't betray their confidences, who will provide encouragement and reassure them when they fail, and who will stand by them against any personal attacks or vicious gossip. Loyalty is an essential element of teen friendship. As with every other age group, teens are initially drawn together in friendship by shared interests, but the concept of loyalty dominates their interactions in ways that it didn't in childhood and won't in adult life.

While teens value a close circle of friends, they're also a gregarious lot. Large, loosely structured groups of adolescents enjoy hanging out together at school, in shopping malls, or in parks. Sociologists began studying large groups of teens in the 1920s, so it's not a new phenomenon. Although the settings may have changed, the dynamics are the same.

Few interests in life are as important to many teens as their friends.

Gathering in large groups creates a comfortable teen-only atmosphere that lets kids feel free of the watchful adult world, so they can loosen up and be themselves. It's not unusual for these large groups to include members of both sexes. The large group provides a safer environment for boys and girls to test out their charms on each other without having to face the pressure of a one-on-one encounter. The atmosphere is such that any teen can express interest in someone else. Sometimes it's a real expression of real interest. Sometimes it's just a test.

Whether teens are more likely to belong to mixed-gender groups than they were in the past isn't clear. Some professionals who work with teens say that it is more common, perhaps due to changing attitudes. However, teenage boys still spend most of their time with other boys, and teenage girls spend most of their time with other girls, except in dating situations. Changing times don't seem to have altered friendships between members of the same sex. Many girls are more likely to talk about their feelings to other girls. Boys are less likely to talk about how they feel, preferring to show their friendship during activities together.

The negative side of teen friendships hasn't changed much either. Teenage girls tend to be what sociologists call "relationally aggressive."

> **Allow your teen to choose her own friends, even if they aren't people you want to spend time with.**

If they're angry with others, they're more likely to hurt them by spreading rumours, verbally assaulting them, or persuading others to ignore them. Teenage boys are more likely to cut off or withdraw from a relationship or be physically aggressive.

Parents often have worries about the friends their teens admire or acquire. They may worry that a particular companion exerts a bad influence on their teen, especially if the friend is involved in drugs or criminal activities. If you're worried about such a situation, first ask yourself how your concern developed. Are you concerned for your own child's safety? Or is the friend someone you simply don't like? If it is a case of not liking the other teen, try not to interfere. Allow your teen to choose her own friends, even if they aren't people you want to spend time with. However, if you have concerns that the friend may be influencing your child to try illegal or dangerous behaviour, then you must act. Talk to a school counsellor or other parents to get their opinion of the same teen— is she or he a serious problem to others? Does he or she encourage other teens to try harmful behaviour? Have other parents noticed or sensed trouble?

Parental monitoring is the most effective way to keep teens out of trouble.

When you talk with your daughter, avoid attacking the friend directly; she may feel obliged to defend her. She may also express her independence from you by spending even more time with a friend you disapprove of. Instead, say why you're worried about the friendship and where you fear it may lead. If your child has already internalized your family's values, she's unlikely to maintain a friendship with someone who opposes those values. Kids tend to seek out others with similar backgrounds and values as friends. While curiosity may draw her into spending time with antisocial kids, she won't have enough in common with them to sustain the friendship for long.

You can most effectively head off problems with friends by keeping an eye on what your teen is doing and knowing who her friends are. It sounds simple, but parental monitoring is the most effective way to keep teens out of trouble. Make it a house rule that your teen calls you if he's going to be home late or if he's heading off somewhere else with his friends. Make sure his friends feel welcome in your home, so you'll have a chance to know them.

For some teens, the problem with friends is that they have none. When your kids were younger, you may have helped by creating opportunities for them to meet other children. But that tactic doesn't work with teens. They're more likely to resent having their parents involved—it might further damage their image in the eyes of other teens. Everyone needs to build friendships, but some teens enjoy spending time on their own, especially if they want to pursue personal interests and passions. Talk with your teen about her feelings; if she's genuinely happy with her solitude and doesn't think she has a problem, don't worry.

But it's important to know your child. Would she tell you there's no problem and hide her hurt feelings about a lack of friends or about the disloyalty of someone she considered a friend? If you can talk openly, be supportive and reassure her. Tell her that you understand how hurtful it is to be dropped by someone she considered her friend, but that there are other people she can get to know. Suggest activities in which she might meet other teens with similar interests, but let her decide if she wants to join. Don't be discouraged if your teen seems to reject your reassurances; it's more likely that your comments will bubble away in her mind and become a solace to her. Your influence is much stronger than it may appear from your teen's reactions to your suggestions.

Make sure her friends feel welcome in your home, and you'll have a chance to know them.

Dating and Relationships

Can it even be called dating? Your daughter is "going out" with seven or so other kids. But she has confided to you that now she's "going out" with Michael. He's one of the seven. No invitation to something special. No shy boy on your doorstep arriving to pick her up. No chance to ask him what school he goes to and who his parents are. Instead, Alishe comes to pick up your daughter because she wants to use your curling iron. Then, together, they "go out" to meet the rest of the group, including Michael.

"I'm eighteen. I can live on my own right now, and in a year I'll be at university, so I don't really have a curfew. But I tell my mom when I'm going to be home, or she asks. My mom goes to bed at about 11:00 p.m., but until I get home she keeps waking up and looking at the clock. Then when I do get home, I go into her room to tell her I'm home, so she can go to sleep. I feel guilty when I'm out late because I worry about my mom not sleeping. She should just go to sleep. When I'm just around the corner watching a late-night movie at a friend's, what can happen?"

KAREN, AGE 18

In the last decade, the trend has been for teens to go out in groups, especially adolescents age thirteen to fifteen. One benefit is that it's more inclusive. If a teen is quiet or awkward, he might otherwise be excluded from one-on-one dating during adolescence. There's also a safety benefit to going out to movies, doughnut shops, and parks surrounded by a cushion of friends. But how do parents get to know their teen's significant other? And how can you possibly set and maintain limits when you're dealing with a group of seven or so kids?

Don't hesitate to contact other parents of the kids in the group. All it takes is for two parents to agree that 11:30 p.m. is an appropriate curfew to send the whole group home before midnight. Your teen will probably tell you not to dare talk to her friends' parents, but make your intentions clear. "One of my jobs as a parent is to ensure that you're safe," you can explain. Assure her that you're not prying. You just want to know what the parents of other kids consider a reasonable curfew.

Go ahead and ask about your daughter's boyfriend, too, maintaining an attitude of respect and interest. If you play a supportive rather than a controlling role, your teen may keep you informed. Suggest that your daughter invite Michael (and a few other friends if it's more comfortable) for a family barbecue. You'll get to know him and, just as important, Michael will get to know your family and the behaviours you value.

Don't be surprised if your daughter's boyfriend is older than she is. In adolescent couples, the boy tends to be older than the girl, typically by three years. Girls can approach puberty two or three years before boys do and finish puberty long before boys, so they are more advanced in their desire for relationships than their same-age male peers. But if your daughter is in grade nine and she has caught the eye of a boy about to graduate, you may become panicked and want to put a halt to it. Statistics show that young teens are more likely to be sexually active if they are involved with older partners. Try to express your concerns in an uncritical way to increase your child's awareness of potential difficulties rather than to criticize the boyfriend. Start by expressing your concerns: "I feel a little concerned ..." or "It seems to me ..." or "I wonder if ...." Another way of comfortably discussing the relationship with your child is to use the third person, as in "I knew a girl who ...," or the first person, as in "I once had a boyfriend who ...."

Breaking up

When a relationship breaks up, your teen may feel devastated, especially if it's the first time his or her heart has been broken. Don't trivialize your teen's pain—it may be overwhelming. Brace yourself as your child works through all the stages of grief. There may be tears, but you may have to listen to them through a closed door. She may prefer to lock herself in her room than to talk through her tangled web of feelings with her parents.

Your son or daughter may go over and over what happened and feel shaky about starting a new relationship. The former partner may quickly get involved with someone new. Don't make observations on the now-defunct relationship. Your role is to be available and supportive to your child. Make his favourite dinner or make time to spend with him. He needs to know that he's still lovable.

Forced Sexual Activity

In Canada, any forced sexual activity is considered by law to be sexual assault, which is an act of aggression and a serious crime. More than half of all sexual assaults against women are committed against teenage women. In most cases of sexual assault, the offender is someone the victim, female or male, knows and trusts.

When talking to your teens about healthy sexuality, you should say clearly that choosing to be sexually active carries with it the responsibility of respecting the boundaries set by one's partner. Teens need to understand that while they have strong desires, they can and must control their actions. Both your son and your daughter need to know that one partner saying No—in words or conduct, or just by not consenting— is their legal right and should stop the partner from continuing unwanted sexual activity or behaviour. They may then recognize that a partner who uses physical or psychological threats to exert power over them is abusing the concept of consent.

Helping kids learn to protect themselves in a sexual situation is a proactive approach for a family to take. Kids may find it difficult to say No to someone they like and have trusted to this point. They need to know that one person breaks the trust by trying to impose his will on another person, that each person is in charge of her or his own body, that they can say No and expect the other person to accept their decision.

Both children and teens need to learn how to recognize the dangers of certain situations and the warning signs of potential aggression. If you talk with your teens about sexual assaults and the circumstances that surround such occurrences, you not only help them understand ordinary dangers but you also let them know that they can count on your advice and support if they're ever assaulted. Some teens may not tell you if an assault takes place because the offender is someone you know and apparently like, or because your teen was doing something she knew you wouldn't approve of, or because she fears that you will become over-protective. Teens should, nevertheless, know what their community offers as resources and crisis centres to victims of assault.

If the day comes when your teenage daughter tells you that she's been sexually assaulted, try to remain calm, be supportive, and assure her that she did nothing wrong. Sexual assault is one of the few crimes for which we question whether the victim is guilty and place the onus on the victim to prove that the assault took place. Don't blame your teen's halter-top, her friends, or the places she hangs out. No one brings sexual assault on herself.

The event needs to be talked out, because assault is a traumatic experience for everyone. Your daughter may need some time to deal with her emotions; if it was a case of date rape, she may want to take time off school so as not to face the offender every day. Post traumatic stress response—recurrent nightmares, flashbacks to the assault, acting out with unusual behaviour, intense anxiety—is not unusual. Your other children and extended family may want to know why your daughter's mood has changed. Your daughter may want to keep the details private, but if they know that she's been a victim of violence, they can give their support.

Help your teen feel that it's OK to reach out not only to her family but also to counsellors at sexual assault care centres, women's help lines, and distress centres. Counsellors understand what your daughter is going through and are trained to help her through the crisis. Offer to make an appointment for her, then drive her there. Respect her wishes if she prefers that you stay in the waiting room.

Without an opportunity to talk through her feelings about the assault, the experience may fester. Be sensitive to her responses, and don't try to talk about it when she clearly doesn't want to. But people who have been sexually assaulted and who don't receive the support of family, friends, or community agencies in their recovery tend to suffer low self-esteem, to become distrustful of their own judgment and of other people. Girls tend to feel ashamed or guilty, blaming themselves for the crime; boys tend to lash out. Both may guard against future intimacy because they feel that they can't trust their partners.

It's reliably estimated that only 5 to 10 per cent of sexual assaults are reported. If your teen wants to file an incident report with police, take her to a hospital emergency department to obtain evidence such as semen samples, pubic hair, or vaginal bruising within 72 hours of the assault. After investigating the incident, police decide whether or not to lay charges. If your daughter decides not to report it to the police, it's her legal right. Show your support in other ways.

Alternatives to the legal system are possible. The Toronto Rape Crisis Centre, for example, will write a confidential letter to the assailant to let him know that what he has done is wrong, and to suggest that he seek counselling about his behaviour toward women. Some women, through the help of a sexual assault crisis centre, choose to confront their assailant. This non-violent confrontation is not a conversation. It is carefully planned and includes several people who will support your daughter and assure her physical safety. The man must be quiet and listen. It's the victim's turn to speak and be heard.

Dangerous Experimentation

Adolescence is a time to experiment and take risks. It's the time for teens to define who they are as individuals and to discover for themselves whether all the evils their parents warn against are really so dangerous. As a parent, you may not approve of the experimentation, worrying that one may lead to another and on to more serious problems. You don't want to condone or ignore their experimentation, but at the same time you shouldn't overreact. If you've had good communication and a strong family relationship with your children, you have most likely instilled your values over the years. Most teens emerge from their experimentation none the worse for wear, having learned for themselves the behaviours that are appropriate to the life they want to live.

Adolescence is, however, a time when judgment and self-control are still developing, so experimentation in risky situations can turn into real trouble for them. Here's how to tell whether your child is experimenting or heading for real trouble in two of the most common teen pitfalls, and what you might do about them.

Alcohol and Other Drugs

Most teen drug use involves alcohol, cigarettes, or marijuana. The most comprehensive long-term study of drug use in Canada is the *Ontario Student Drug Use Survey* by the Addiction Research Foundation (ARF). SEE PAGE 223 The ARF has surveyed students in grades seven, nine, eleven, and thirteen about their drug and alcohol use every two years since 1977.

Alcohol is the most commonly used drug among teens—about 60 per cent of the students surveyed in 1997 reported that they had used alcohol in the previous year. Cigarettes were next (a little over 27 per cent), followed by cannabis (about 25 per cent). Drugs like hallucinogens (about 10 per cent), amphetamines (less than 4 per cent), and crack cocaine (a little over 2 per cent) were in relatively low use by the students surveyed.

Why do kids use drugs? In many cases, it's part of the teen social pattern—about 80 per cent of the students in grades eleven and thirteen used alcohol. But when teens show signs of dependence on drinking and drug use, it's usually because the drugs make them feel better, or at least help them forget problems such as depression, a troubled home life, or social difficulties. The roots of dependence and addiction are not well understood, but family history (both genetics and environment) may play a role. These teens are more likely to become addicted once they start.

As parents, you can help by talking with your teens about the facts of both prescription and illicit drugs, the problems they can create, and how improper use can impair both mental and physical health. Discuss the problems of the most common drugs—alcohol and cigarettes—the way you would discuss any concern about their health. Find ways to introduce the topic of other drugs into your conversations. News stories like

A Drug Briefing

Alcohol This drug of choice for teens poses the primary risk of their overindulging, which leads to impaired judgment. If they are of driving age, this impaired judgment causes car accidents and all the attendant problems. Alcohol is also a major factor in other kinds of preventable injuries and in sexual assault.

Amphetamines These stimulants are sometimes called pep pills, bennies, or uppers. Users develop a sense of well-being and become hyper-alert, which makes it difficult for them to sleep. When high, they lose their appetite. Chronic users are more prone to sickness. One Canadian study showed that violence was the leading cause of amphetamine-related deaths.

Barbiturates Also known as "downers," these are powerful depressants that slow down the central nervous system, and are sometimes prescribed to relieve anxiety. By themselves, they give an intoxicating effect, but are particularly dangerous when combined with alcohol.

Cannabis This term includes marijuana, hashish, and hashish oil. As with alcohol, it can be dangerous for anyone using cannabis to drive because reaction time is slowed. There is also the possibility of lung damage after long-term use. As well, some people may develop a psychological dependence on cannabis.

Cocaine Made from the leaves of the coca bush, cocaine is a stimulant. Large doses can lead to bizarre or violent behaviour. Long-term use can lead to strong psychological dependence and depression.

LSD (LySergic Acid Diethylamide) The most powerful known hallucinogen, LSD significantly alters one's perceptions in unpredictable ways. It can cause terrifying hallucinations, even among experienced users who've had no previous bad experiences.

Rohypnol Known as a "roofie" or by other street names, rohypnol is a sleeping pill more powerful than any other. Combined with alcohol, it produces disinhibition and amnesia. When slipped into a person's drink, it is difficult to detect because it's tasteless, colourless, and odourless. These factors mean that it has been associated with date rape. Tests of a person's urine sample can detect rohypnol up to three days after the person may have consumed it, so a teen who has a suspicion that she was drugged and assaulted should be tested as soon as possible.

the near disqualification of a Canadian snowboarder for suspected marijuana use at the 1998 Winter Olympics in Nagano no doubt started more than one family discussion about marijuana. Be honest about your own past experiences with cigarettes, alcohol, or other drugs, but don't feel you must discuss them unless you feel comfortable doing so. Being hypocritical about your current use or abuse of drugs would certainly be problematic.

Role-playing about situations in which peers or others apply pressure to participate in drug use can help your teens find the language to divert "friends" who offer drugs at a party. Make it clear that in situations that present a risk to your teens' safety—if they are incapacitated in any way—they should call you or have someone call you, because you will pick them up at any time.

"Dad and I have an open relationship where we talk about a lot of stuff. Mom's a traditional mom. It's harder to get close to Mom. I totally respect my parents. They had an effective way of disciplining us. We were never grounded, never spanked. Dad would say, 'I'm disappointed.' I'd think, 'Dad's mad at me,' and I'd feel bad."

DEBRA, AGE 18

If your child stumbles home late one night, too drunk or stoned to talk properly, try to ensure his physical safety first by finding out what he has taken, if at all possible. If he's extremely drunk or high on drugs, consider taking him to the hospital emergency ward—alcohol poisoning or a reaction to, or overdose of, a drug can be very serious. The next morning when he's sober, a non-accusatory statement such as "You were behaving strangely last night," followed up with an open-ended question such as "Can you tell me what happened?" are ways of opening the discussion. Make sure he knows you're worried about him. Try to find out if there's something in his life or even in your family life that's bothering him and that might be contributing to his use of alcohol or drugs.

> About 80 per cent of senior students drink alcohol.

Many parents say they're surprised when they discover their child has an alcohol or drug problem, but there are usually signs of trouble, like the following, if you look for them:

> **Problems with school** Look for irregular attendance in some school classes and poor performance in several subjects. She may also start to skip the extracurricular activities that she used to enjoy.
> **Health problems** He may have changed his sleep habits, have lost weight, appear run down, or develop more colds or cases of flu.

He could have bloodshot eyes, appear listless, and speak in a flat monotone.

> **Behaviour changes** A formerly outgoing kid might become withdrawn or very moody, spend less time with the family, and possibly even shut down communication. He may have new friends or have become part of a different group. He may ask you for money but avoid discussing what he needs it for, or you might find that money or articles are missing from the house. He may be secretive rather than just want privacy.

> **Legal troubles** Many kids in trouble with the law also have trouble with drugs. Many teens who get drunk or use illegal drugs do so only once or a few times. But continued excessive use of alcohol or drugs is an indication of a serious ongoing problem, and you might consider seeking help from a professional.

Trouble with the Law

Few things can make your heart sink faster than seeing a police officer bring your teen to your door. About 5 per cent of all youths age twelve to seventeen came in contact with the police for violations of the Criminal Code in 1996. More than half of the young offenders were charged with property offences, particularly shoplifting. They stole the same sorts of items most teens pay for—CDs, clothes, makeup, jewellery, and candies.

There are many reasons that teens break the law. Often they act on impulse, sometimes as a form of rebellion or bravado to show off for friends. In some cases, teen lawbreaking may be a sign of other troubles. The teenager may have an unhappy home life, may be dealing with the death of someone close or the breakup of the family through divorce, or with any combination of stresses or problems.

The most effective way to help your kids avoid trouble with the law is to practise the same kinds of parenting skills that are effective in so many areas of their lives.

> Keep open communication with your kids, and be ready to really listen to and discuss their problems.

> Get involved in their school. Teachers are often the first to spot problems in the making.

> Make sure you know your son's friends, and make your home a welcoming place for them to gather so that you'll have a better idea what they're up to.

> Give your kids appropriate supervision. Make it a house rule that they let you know where they're going and call if they're going to be late or if plans change.

> Help your daughter develop skills in her areas of interest, from sports to hobbies. A child who experiences success and feels competent is less likely to get into trouble of any kind.

Some of the signs that your daughter may be on a collision course with the law are not unlike the signs for drug problems: sudden loss of interest in activities she used to enjoy, a withdrawal from family life, faltering grades, and increasing absences from school. She may also suddenly have stereos, clothes, and cash that can't be accounted for.

Underage drinking is one of the ways that teens may break the law.

Younger teens are more likely to be singled out for intimidation.

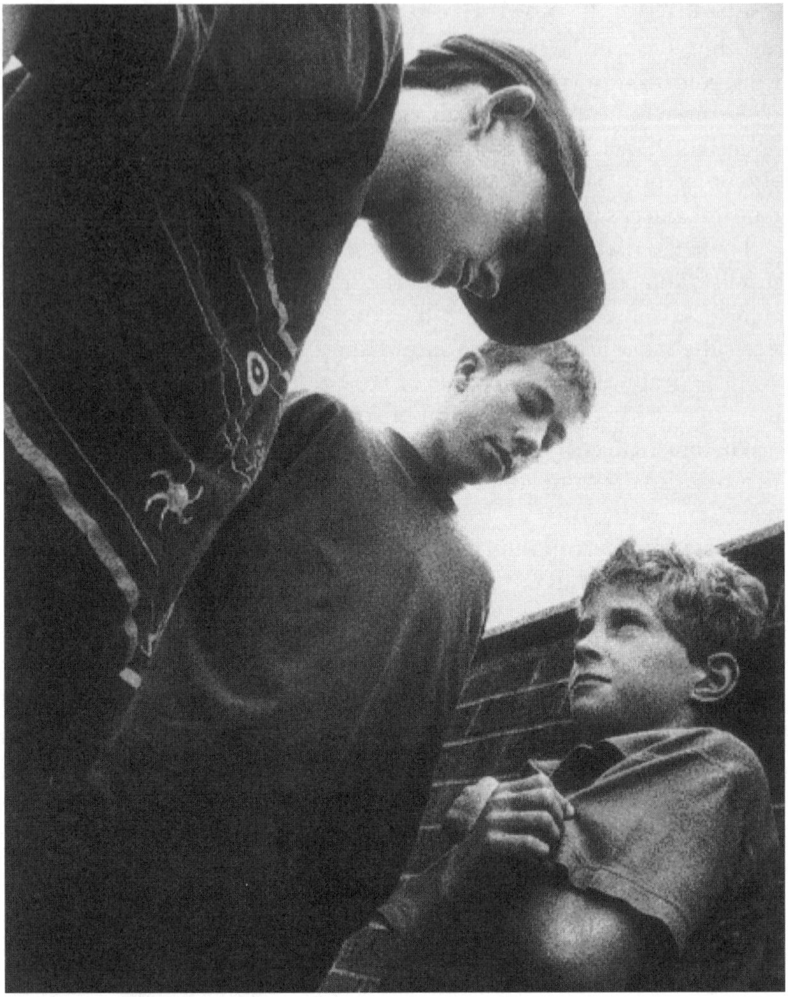

More than 80 per cent of youth crimes are minor, and one brush with the law is enough reason for most teens not to get into trouble again. If your teen does break the law and is charged, be supportive throughout the subsequent legalities. But it's a more significant learning experience if you ensure that your teen deals with the consequences by, for example, fulfilling a community service order as part of a sentence or paying you back for any fine or legal fees connected with the charge. But if you're worried that the crime was a symptom of much larger problems in your teen's life, seek professional help.

Dealing with Violence and Bullies

While youth crime in general has steadily decreased, the number of youth crimes involving violence has increased. In 1986, about 8.5 per cent of all youth crimes were classified as violent. By 1996, it was up to 18.5 per cent. The numbers highlight what a few teens know firsthand— that their world can sometimes be a hostile and dangerous place.

It's during the younger teen years that kids are more likely to be full of uncertainty and be singled out for intimidation. One of the most common forms of violence is extortion. Victims are intimidated into giving up money on a regular basis (sometimes called "taxing") or handing over stereo equipment, clothing, or shoes. There's often a rash of extortion for clothing whenever a new fad comes along. Violence also frequently erupts because of rumours or gossip, particularly about boyfriends or girlfriends.

Be sure your teens know that if they get into an uncomfortable situation of any kind, especially one that has the potential for violence, they can telephone and you'll go get them, no questions asked. Many families find it handy to have a code word their kids can use that tells parents there's trouble. That way, their kids can ask to be rescued even though someone is listening nearby. Good communication within the family means, too, that your kids let you know where they're going and what they're doing. If you're tuned in to your teen's life, you'll be able to react sooner if there's trouble.

"I was harassed for three months at school when I was fourteen. When one guy saw my predicament, he offered to sell me a gun. Three weeks later he told me he had the gun and he wanted $75 for it. I refused, but his threats escalated until he attacked me and I got the police involved. My advice is: Do your darndest to stay away from bullies, but if you do get in trouble, find someone you really trust and tell them. Don't try stalling like I did because it doesn't go away. It's too big to ignore. It just eats away inside you. You aren't a wimp if you go to someone for help."

KEVIN, NOW AGE 19

Some police departments and schools, particularly in larger cities, are taking youth violence and teenage gangs more seriously, but many victims are still reluctant to tell, or to ask for help from, adults. Partly, they fear retaliation from the bullies; partly, they don't believe adults will take the problem seriously. But adult intervention is vital, and it's important for you to recognize some of the signs that your teen may be the victim of intimidation or violence from his or her peers.

In his book *Youth Violence: How to Protect Your Kids* (Communities Against Youth Violence, Toronto, 1997), Toronto police officer Kevin Guest identifies some warning signs.

- Some of your teen's belongings, such as a Walkman or a bicycle, are suddenly missing.
- You notice minor injuries such as a bruise on the arm but are offered no explanation.
- Your child starts skipping school or getting lower marks.
- Your child doesn't eat, isn't talking, and generally withdraws.
- Your child lacks friends or appears to have friends you've never met.

If you spot any of these warning signs, ask your teen if there's a problem. Don't be surprised if you get denials at first. Tell her that saying nothing is the worst approach, because intimidation and violence typically escalate, beginning as verbal threats and building to physical abuse. If a teen doesn't ask for help, the situation will only get worse. Assure your daughter that you won't get angry if she tells you what's happening to her and tell her you're concerned for her safety. Here are some steps in handling the problem.

- Ask your daughter who she would be most comfortable seeking help from at school. It's usually best to start with a teacher she knows; that teacher will probably involve a vice-principal or the principal.
- Make sure the school staff support the victim and keep the discussions confidential.
- Find out from other parents if their kids have been victims. If so, you can go as a group to the school administration. Your son will also feel better knowing that he's not alone.
- Ask the principal what steps he will take and check back later to make sure he has followed through.
- In extreme cases, you may want to work with the school to bring in the police and lay charges.
- Kids are particularly in danger of becoming the targets of bullies if they're unhappy and have low self-esteem. Spending time with your teens and encouraging them to get involved in activities they're good at are ways to boost their self-confidence.

"I think Kevin was afraid we'd be so appalled if we knew what was happening that he wouldn't get any support from us. We were appalled, but if we had known what was happening sooner, we could have done something about it. My advice for other parents who feel upset that their child didn't tell them earlier is to try to understand. They need to know more than anything that they're still loved."

SANDY, KEVIN'S MOTHER

Chapter Three

Spiritual Questing

As your child marches into adolescence, he starts trying on new identities and questioning family beliefs. Even if your family has no religious affiliation, adolescence may be the time when your teen suddenly starts going to a prayer circle or sitting in the back pew of the church on the corner. If your family belongs to a mosque, church, synagogue, or temple, you might expect your adolescent to begin questioning your religious practices. He may drag his feet to worship services or flatly refuse to go.

As part of a teen's questioning of beliefs, she might even consider changing religions. She may wonder whether she really is Roman Catholic, even after a Catholic upbringing and education and confirmation in the Catholic faith. A movie or book may lead her to wonder if under her Catholic school uniform beats the heart of a Buddhist. If your teen studies world religions in high school, she may change religions every few weeks, even if your family are atheists. Consider that this is normal behaviour for a teenager.

As part of your teen's questioning of beliefs, she may even want to change religions.

Of course, you want your children to embrace the religious beliefs and practices that your own family cherishes, and you may feel surprised, hurt, and even threatened by their spiritual questing. But trying to make teens adhere to values and practices they have begun to question usually doesn't work. All religions have a version of the golden rule: "Treat other people exactly as you would like to be treated by them." During his exploration of other beliefs, values, and practices, your teen needs your tolerance and your continued respect and love.

The apparent break with your family's beliefs may not be as significant as your teens lead you to believe. They won't necessarily give up on learned behaviours, showing concern for extended family and neighbours or making efforts to maintain or improve community life and society in general. At some point in their late teens and twenties, young adults begin to consolidate their moral, religious, and ethical beliefs and values. In their adult years, like many people who rejected their family beliefs as teens, they may begin to drift back to and embrace the religion they grew up with, finding that it, too, has changed in some ways to meet the changing needs of its adherents.

Involvement in Cults

In your teenager's quest for identity and beliefs, it's quite possible that he might stumble into a cult. Over the past twenty years, the number of cults in Canada has increased and their influence has strengthened. Some cults are disguised as movements for personal improvement, for maximizing the human potential, for living out an alternative lifestyle, or for expressing the New Age as we approach the millennium. Don't assume that only weak-minded teens can be lured into a cult. Many of the fatalities of the Solar Temple cult, for example, were professional, middle-class, middle-aged people.

Some teens raised in a secure, trusting environment could be more vulnerable to the pitch from the cult's recruiters. Other teens may be street-smart, more sensitized to hustlers of all kinds, and more wary of smiling strangers. The Royal Canadian Mounted Police, in a statement supported by Info-Cult in Montreal, points out that people don't generally seek out a cult—the cult actively recruits them in high schools, colleges, and universities. Their recruiters look for naive teenagers, individuals in need of friendship, or those in transitional situations, perhaps just starting university. Before your teen heads off to college or university, warn him about on-campus recruitment; suggest he be wary of anyone asking him to sign up for a course, join a group, or participate in an event, especially if that person also offers immediate friendship or free meals.

Another time when your teen may be vulnerable to recruitment is when she's travelling alone. Airports and bus and train stations are popular spots for cult recruitment. Cult members may use a technique known as "love bombing." They contrive a sense of family and belonging around your teen through hugging, touching, and flattery. The RCMP notes the following about the people who usually get recruited:

➤ They have been deceived and systematically entrapped.
➤ They don't know the real nature of the organization.
➤ They were lonely and were attracted by the apparent warmth and sincerity of a recruiter.

When your son first gets involved in what he may describe as a Bible study or philosophy group, he may go out and get his long straggly hair cut. He may meditate, something you've always meant to do. In fact, you may be pleased by his behaviour, at first. Then you notice him becoming increasingly distant. Soon it becomes apparent that he has no money and even his great-grandfather's gold watch, inherited as a family me-

> **The key element in freeing a child from a cult is reconnecting him with family members.**

mento, is missing. His conversation seems so bland. Although he used to challenge everything you said, now he seems to lack critical thought.

Ask your teen about his group. If he seems to speak in pat phrases or recite statements that he's learned by heart, you might well worry that his involvement with the group could be harmful. Ask:

➤ Does the group go by any other name?
➤ What is expected of members once they join?
➤ Is the organization considered controversial by anyone? If so, why?

Take responsibility for researching and investigating, but be prepared to find that the group's real beliefs are shrouded in secrecy. If you find that it is a problematic group, talk to your teen about what he does and what he learns and what he values in the group. Listen respectfully and attentively to his answers—an adversarial position gets you nowhere with a teenager. However, the worst thing you can do is nothing if you're concerned there is a problem. As a parent, you are well within your rights to set limits or to intervene so that you don't give your teen tacit permission to stay in the cult. He may subconsciously want a way out, so express your concerns. Set restrictions on his involvement. If he has been meeting with the group three times a week, ask him to restrict his involvement to one meeting every week. Ask him not to take out formal membership. At the same time, it's extremely important to ensure that your teen knows you're there for him. The key element in freeing a child from a cult is reconnecting him with family members.

You may also want to contact Info-Cult in Montreal. One of the SEE PAGE 225 main objectives of this organization is to help families of cult members. Its Resource Centre on Cultic Thinking has the largest library of materials about cults in Canada. It's not open to the public, but it offers a research service for a fee.

A Teen's Point of View: My Heart and Soul

My need for privacy and time with my friends and my hypersensitivity to criticism are all part of my search for my adult self and my growth toward independence.

Age Thirteen

- I often retreat to my room, with the door closed. It's exhausting always being "on," worrying about how I come across to others, and my room is the only place where I can truly relax.

- Privacy is of the utmost importance to me. I might take the phone into the closet, whispering so I won't be overheard. I'll be very upset if I discover that you've read my E-mail, looked through my journal, or listened in on my conversations with friends. I'm usually not hiding anything except my own vulnerable, half-developed personality.

- I'm brooding, sullen, and suspicious. If you ask, "How was soccer practice?" I might reply, "Why do you want to know?"

- I'm extremely sensitive to the slightest criticism. The less you criticize me, the less difficult I'll be to live with.

- I crave isolation so much that I might feel claustrophobic in a crowd.

- I sit at the mirror trying on different looks, expressions, styles, and roles. I affect phony mannerisms, change the spelling of my name, or even try out a new name. I might experiment with dyeing my hair.

- I listen to more music and different music than I used to. I might like to do my homework to music.

- My friends' families seem more appealing than my own. I feel (often wrongly) that my friends judge my parents as harshly as I do.

- It's important to me to hang out with friends. It may look like a waste of time, but this is how I figure out who I am and where I fit in the greater scheme of things.

Age Fourteen

- I may emerge from the protective cocoon of my room, bursting with energy, optimism, and goodwill.

- My days are busy and full with school, friends, and activities.

- I'm feeling less touchy these days. If you've respected my need for privacy over the past year, I'll be ready to start trusting you again.

- My friendships are less intense than they once were. I hang out with friends in various loose, often-shifting groups. I might date, but relationships are rarely long-term.

- My emotions are on a fairly even keel. There might be outbursts of anger or tears, but I get over it quickly.

- I'm less concerned with conformity.

- I don't like it when people brag about themselves. I'm likely to play down my own achievements. When I do boast, I'm usually half joking.

- My areas of interest become more specialized. I'm starting to assess where my talents really lie. When I ask you if you think I'm good at dance or hockey or piano, I'm not looking for reassurance; I want an honest appraisal to help me focus on my strengths.

- I thrive on friendly competition. I don't need to win, but I do want to test my abilities.

- My commitments to my friends take precedence over my commitments to family. Yes, I'll mow the lawn, but only after I spend a couple of hours at my friend's house.

- I might experiment with cigarettes, alcohol, or marijuana. I respond better to parental words of concern than to threats.

- I want you to welcome my friends into our home. Please don't hang out with us, but do say hello and provide snacks.

- I have less need for family interaction and companionship, but I still need to know that I'm a part of the family.

- I explore religious beliefs different from those of my family. I might suddenly decide to stop going to a place of worship or participating in religious ritual, or I might suddenly start. If I've always believed in God, I might now question God's existence. If I've never had a faith, I might seek one now.

Age Fifteen

- I'm reaching a new level of maturity. On the one hand, I'm more settled within myself, but on the other hand, I'm pushing and stretching to be free of parental restraints.

- Friends are more important than ever, but I still need my parents. I want to talk to you, as long as you aren't too anxious to know all the details about where I've been, who I've been with, and what I've been thinking. I want you to be interested in me but not to grill me. Unless you suspect that I'm in trouble, just relax and let me come to you.

- Instead of flying off the handle when we have a disagreement, I can be persuaded to talk things over. However, I still like to practise my debating skills.

- I may still be exploring different styles. I might investigate getting a tattoo or having a body part pierced.

- I have more opportunities for part-time and summer jobs. I might surprise you with how responsible I can be at work. I take on tasks—flipping burgers, bundling up garbage, sweeping floors—with a diligence that I would never show at home.

- I take up causes with fervent zeal, especially when I'm part of a group of people my age. I'll campaign tirelessly to save an endangered species, organize a walkathon, go on a 24-hour fast as part of a fundraiser, or volunteer all weekend in a food bank. I want you to support me in my cause of the moment, even if you don't completely agree with it.

Age Sixteen

- I'm becoming increasingly relaxed with myself and secure about who I am, but this process can take a while. Levels of maturity among my peers vary tremendously.

- I generally have a positive outlook on life. But I can have bouts of moodiness, confusion, and frustration. I have conflicting feelings about my looming independence.

- Even if I've been a good student, my interest in school may drop (along with my marks) while I concentrate on my social life. With your support, I'll gradually get my focus back.

- I no longer feel I have to prove myself at every turn.

- I'm less interested in trying on different roles. If I've been dyeing my hair, I may let it go back to its natural colour.

- I'm better at controlling my temper, although I may still have the occasional outburst.

- I feel very much an adult when I'm at work or school. I'll rebel against being treated like a child at home.

- My world expands considerably as I learn to drive.

- I may be interested in a single romantic relationship, but it's still important for me to spend lots of time with a group of friends.

- I can handle increased responsibilities, especially when it comes to part-time work. I can also help out at home in different ways, like preparing your tax return using a computer program.

Age Seventeen and Up

- As I hurtle toward adulthood—which is the very thing I thought I'd been longing for—I suddenly get cold feet. I might do something risky and dumb, like skipping classes for a week or showing up at my part-time job hung-over. I want you to intervene. It's as though I'm not quite ready to grow up and I need one final bit of proof that I can count on you to protect me. Don't completely bail me out; just show me that you care.

- Once I'm eighteen or nineteen, I'm an adult as far as most laws are concerned. You can expect me to call you if I'll be home late, but don't ask me to account to you for my whereabouts every minute when I'm not at home.

- If I'm back for a visit after moving away from home, I'll probably spend less time with the family and more time catching up with old friends, or sleeping. Don't tease me about using the house as a hotel; a home base is vital to me.

- I may go overboard in impressing you with how grown-up I've become. I might wear clothes that I know you'll disapprove of, criticize your choice of investments, or refuse to eat a formerly favourite dish because it conflicts with my new dietary requirements. The less of an issue you make of it, the less I'll push it.

- I want you to include my boyfriend or girlfriend in our family activities. It's important to me that you take our relationship seriously.

- As I get older, I'm starting to see my family in a different light. You, whom I once saw as hopelessly flawed, are now looking almost decent and may even be endearingly human.

Parenting through Rough Waters

4

When your family faces a problem, your teen may be torn between her family's needs and her growing need for independence. Keep the lines of communication open with your teen as your family deals with a separation, illness, job loss, or substance abuse. Sometimes it's your teen who's at the centre of the family crisis because of substance abuse, an unwanted pregnancy, or criminal behaviour. You may feel that your trust has been broken, but it is possible to find ways to repair your relationship and help your child cope.

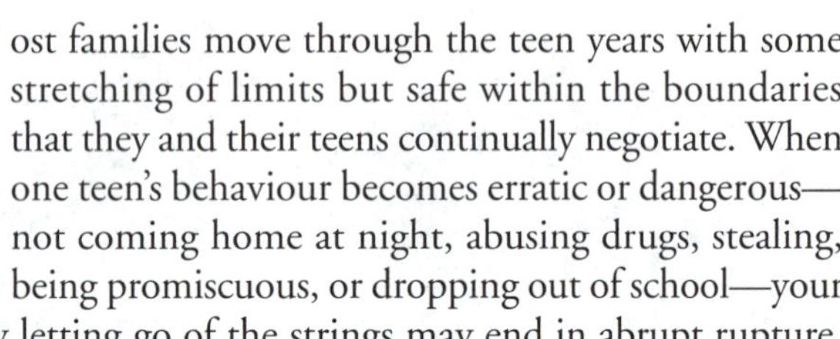

Most families move through the teen years with some stretching of limits but safe within the boundaries that they and their teens continually negotiate. When one teen's behaviour becomes erratic or dangerous— not coming home at night, abusing drugs, stealing, being promiscuous, or dropping out of school—your pattern of gradually letting go of the strings may end in abrupt rupture. And it doesn't matter whether the crisis is about substance abuse or an unwanted pregnancy, there are specific steps you can take as a parent to mend the rupture.

When Your Teen Is in Crisis

Your first job is to assess whether, in fact, you are dealing with a serious crisis. All adolescents go through periods of experimentation and risk taking. But when the dangerous behaviour becomes frequent, your child may be in serious difficulty. Coming home drunk or stoned once or twice isn't a crisis; coming home drunk or stoned almost every night is. Also consider whether your daughter's erratic behaviour in one area of her life is interfering with other aspects of her life. Has her interest in attending all-night raves meant she has broken off contact with former friends and dropped out of activities she used to enjoy? Is your son's behaviour preventing him from moving forward with his life? Is he skipping so many classes that he's in danger of failing a grade and dropping out of school altogether?

The teen crisis quickly becomes the family crisis. As you deal with your teen's problems, the needs of your other children can get shoved aside, and everyday life clouds over with the constant dread that the teen's trouble may turn into tragedy. Big kids can get into big problems. Gone are the days when the consequences of misbehaviour meant no more than a carefully worded note from the teacher or a request to pick up your child early from a birthday party. The problems that a teenager can get into may threaten not only his health and well-being but also his life opportunities from now on. You may even live in fear for his life, worrying whether your child will survive the crisis. If you are dealing with fears like these, you shouldn't hesitate to get immediate professional help; many families attempt to work through major crises on their own when they really need professional support. The first step may be as simple as talking with your family doctor who can help you assess the situation and counsel you directly or refer you to another professional.

Then there's the pressing question that all parents of troubled teens face: How did this happen? Kids are a barometer of family tension. Almost all troubled teens are reacting to some kind of stress at home. Hard as it may be to acknowledge, her life at home may have played a role in her current distress. But the flip side is that her family relationships can also play a role in helping her get back on track.

The task of adolescence is to establish a separate identity, which means establishing a few degrees of separation—even from the people who are most important to him. Although separating from one's parents is a necessary step in a healthy adolescence, it soon becomes complicated if family relationships have gone wrong somewhere along the way. Is there an alcoholic in the family creating a climate of constant uncertainty? Is your troubled teen the child you never really connected with? It could be that difficulties in your child's early life are unresolved. An early trauma, such as the divorce of his parents, that seemed to have been easily dealt with may have been buried only to surface again in adolescence. Sometimes when a teen is acting out, the behaviour masks another problem in the family. But as long as the teen is the one on whom you all focus, the deeper family problem remains untouched and unresolved.

> **The best way to reconnect with a teen who no longer accepts your authority is simply to listen.**

Parenting through a Teen Crisis

The best way to reconnect with a teen who no longer accepts your authority is simply to listen. "What's up?" is a good opener. Fight the urge to interrupt and criticize. It's not unusual for parents to become verbally abusive when a child rejects their authority. If you hear yourself making cruel accusations ("You're so lazy that you'll never get a job") or hurtful criticisms ("No wonder you and Jack aren't friends anymore, the way you're acting these days"), pull back and get a grip on your emotions. You need to set a good example of handling stress. Your role is to act as a solid anchor in the storm. Besides, criticism doesn't motivate any teen to make positive changes. She'll just defend herself and reject you, and she may eventually refuse to talk to you at all.

Listen. Your daughter wants you to know why she loves going to bush parties, not only why she started drinking excessively. From you, your daughter needs to hear—repeatedly—that you value, accept, and appreciate her. She also needs to know where you stand on the crisis. If you think drinking underage is wrong, state your point of view again, but in a calm voice. If you are concerned about her safety and her health, let her know. Explain how worried you are.

Indifference is an even greater rejection than criticism or verbal abuse. It's important not to act as if you just don't care, to imply that you've given up on her. You may have thought you'd be finished parenting by the time your kids reached their teen years, and that you wouldn't have to be at home as much anymore. But teenagers still require your time and attention. In fact, your teen may be rebelling just to get your attention.

"My daughter was only fifteen-and-a-half when she left home to live with her boyfriend. I totally freaked out. At night I didn't sleep. I only had short little naps. I was feeling awful, but feeling awful wasn't getting me anywhere, so I tried to figure out how to make the situation better.

I began hiring my daughter and her boyfriend for all sorts of jobs around the house—like cleaning the garage, weeding the garden, painting the hall. When they came over, I would serve them a good lunch with a salad because I knew they were living on fats. While they cleaned out the garage, I would keep busy doing something in the basement. Since everybody was busy doing things, we could talk in a relaxed way. Having them come over to do these jobs kept us in touch. Everyone was up-to-date on what was happening. But the important part was that I could see my daughter, and see that she was OK."

ANNA, MOTHER OF TWIN TEENS

A teen still needs your help with problem solving, and she needs practice recovering from failure. When she gets caught up in a stressful event, take positive action, don't just react. Your teen will watch you carefully as you respond to the situation. You are still the most powerful role model for your teen, although you may think she emulates her favourite pop star or other teens. While watching you deal with stress, she learns how to solve problems. When she stumbled into this crisis, you may have tightened up on rules and become dictatorial, grounding her for weeks at a time. But try to put the crisis in perspective, and after she has dealt with the consequences of the crisis, move on. We all need a second chance, if not a third, fourth, fifth, or more.

Keeping the family strong

In the midst of any crisis, your family needs the security of its regular routines. Whenever possible, continue with plans for family celebrations, rituals, and vacations. Also, maintain your expectations of your teen's behaviour so that she knows her life and your relationship with one another do not begin and end with the current crisis. Don't define your teen only by her problematic behaviour.

Show your teen that you still value that she's part of the family by asking for her input in family decisions. She may have just been caught shoplifting, but she can still have good ideas about what Grandma would like for her birthday or where to go on a family holiday. It will strengthen your daughter's role in the family to have you act on some of her ideas.

Family meetings may not have worked when the children were young, but they may work now if your family is trying to pull closer together. When kids have a strong sense of family, they're less likely to go from one crisis to the next. Teens still need to find part of their identity in family; with close family ties, they're unlikely to seek part of their identity with a gang.

Sibling alert

The brothers and sisters of the troubled teen may seem to show little inter- est in the problem, but you can be sure that they're upset. Explain to them what their sibling is going through. "Your brother has so much anger, he can't control it" might be explanation enough. If you don't have a solution for the crisis yet, don't pretend that you do. "Right now, we don't know how to help," you might begin, "but we're doing everything we can to find the best way to help your brother."

The teen with serious problems can easily take over and unbalance the family. If this happens, siblings may lose themselves in a dream world or develop attention-getting behaviour. Although the crisis with your teen may demand a lot of your time and energy, continue to share activities with siblings and listen to them, too, in order to prevent future problems with them. If you just don't have the energy, ask for help. A good friend or family member may be willing to make sure that younger siblings pull through the crisis, too.

Some parents with one troubled child react by favouring their other children. If you find yourself saying something like "One of my chil- dren is very well-adjusted, but the other has caused me nothing but trou- ble," you know you're favouring one child and need to reassess your behaviour toward both your troubled child and his siblings.

Some teen problems may be embarrassing, but even if your son has been arrested for joy-riding, don't order your other children not to tell "the family business" to their friends. Kids need to work out what's happening, so don't deny them the opportunity to talk about it with their friends.

Bad timing

For the parents of a troubled teen, all sorts of emotions bubble into consciousness. If you are in your forties or fifties, you may be at a fragile life stage yourself. These decades are a time for introspection. You may be questioning what you've done with your life, or perhaps what you should have done. For some people, this is a time in their lives when they are prone to depression. As a parent, you may feel as if you're suffering from burnout, which some professionals define as situational depression. The crisis may have uncovered a red-hot anger you didn't know you were capable of. You may go from denying the problem to being consumed with guilt to being preoccupied with the troubled teen. On any one day, you may swing from feeling numb to being resentful,

Suicide

A teen who is depressed or has alcohol or drug abuse problems, is violent, has been abused or is experiencing family turmoil is more at risk for committing or attempting to commit suicide. Among teens fifteen to nineteen, the rate of suicide has increased steadily for the past fifty years.

Teens who have suffered a loss of some kind are more at risk for suicide. It could be the loss of a loved one through death or divorce, the end of a relationship, or the loss of friends. When a teen faces several stresses at once, he is more at risk. For example, a teen who leaves friends and girlfriend behind to go to a new school may be more at risk.

For parents, the terror that your child might be suicidal may be so painful that it's almost paralyzing. You don't want to think about it, you don't want to talk to anyone about it, and you don't have any idea how to approach your teen about your fears. But it's only by facing your own fears, by asking for help, and by opening up a discussion that you can help prevent his self-destructive behaviour.

First, you must learn to recognize the signs—the most obvious being that your child actually threatens suicide. Always take such threats seriously. Less obviously, he might refer to his own death by saying something like "Nobody would care if I was dead" or "What's the point of living, anyway?" Other signs that a teen is suicidal are similar to the signs of depression. They are: overwhelming sadness, increased crying, mood swings, loss of appetite, loss of interest in personal hygiene, changes in sleeping habits, isolation or withdrawal from school, friends, family, poor concentration and failing grades, delinquent behaviour, and alcohol or drug abuse.

If your teen threatens suicide or writes a suicide note, treat the situation as an emergency and seek immediate medical help by calling your family doctor or going to your local emergency department. If your son refuses to see the doctor himself, offer other sources of help. Your doctor can guide you to the best course of action.

Parents are often afraid to say the word *suicide* out loud for fear of putting the idea in their child's head. But your child needs to know that you're aware of his pain, that you're there to listen and not to judge. Ask him about his feelings: "You seem really low. What's bothering you?" Ask him if he has considered suicide: "Do you sometimes wish you were dead?" And ask if he has made any plans to carry out suicide: "Have you thought about how you would do it?" Don't trivialize or shrug off anything that your child says. Avoid anger or belittlement. Keep communication open so that your child knows he can come to you any time to talk about his feelings of sadness or his suicidal thoughts.

then ashamed. You may feel so vulnerable that you become distressed over the smallest well-meaning suggestion of a friend. At a time when you've lost your self-confidence, to make matters worse, your teen seems to be turning against you. You're the one on whom he vents his anger, because you're the person with whom he feels safest. He may criticize everything from your hair to how you handled his first day of kindergarten. Worse yet, he may blame you for the crisis: "If only you hadn't been so strict (or permissive, or busy, or too involved), I wouldn't have a problem today." Your teen's crisis may even raise unresolved issues from your own adolescence, and it may also add financial stress.

If your teen's crisis is coinciding with a personal crisis for you, acknowledge to him that you're under a great deal of stress, but don't burden him with your angst. You need someone to talk to, but choose a friend or a professional counsellor, not your teen, who has his own worries right now.

The Parental Relationship

Don't let your son's or daughter's problem absorb all your energy and put too much strain on your relationship with your spouse. More than ever before, you need one another's encouragement and support. Any tension that exists in a marriage can further escalate if you and your partner disagree about the seriousness of the problem facing you and your teen and about how to resolve the situation. In the family life cycle, a marriage may be at its weakest point when the kids are in their teens. Statistics show that divorce is high for partners who have teens.

When dealing with your teen's crisis, take a big step back occasionally. Take time to relax and refuel your marriage; the break will not only benefit you and your spouse but also your teen. This may be the time to do a movie marathon—to rent your old favourites or the latest movies you missed. Or call a halt to discussions about your troubled teen and go out together. It may mean you have dinner in silence, but you still have each other. You may choose to spell each other off the way you did when your children were younger so that each of you gets a break from the tensions at home and spends time with friends or pursuing a hobby. If you're a single parent, make sure to spend time on your own or with friends. If you can be open with your friends and family both about the nature of the problem and how it's affecting you, they may be able to help.

Getting a break

It's possible you don't feel that it's safe to leave your teen at home alone or in charge of his siblings. You may fear that he'll badger them, do drugs, or have irresponsible friends over and trash your home. Your daughter may be so depressed that you even fear that she will commit suicide. But it's essential, whether as a couple or a single parent, for you to take an occasional break from the tensions so that you can continue to cope.

Can Anyone Help?

You don't have to handle your adolescent's crisis alone. Every community offers resources for parents when their love is no longer enough to help their teen. Ask your physician, public health department, school, clergy, or your local chapter of the Canadian Mental Health Association. Don't let embarrassment or shame keep you from seeking help for your teen; go and pick up the phone. Make sure you inquire about cost, although if the service is funded by one level of government, there is usually no charge.

Because a teen's family plays a large part in her life, a professional may suggest family therapy. If your teen refuses to go for help, make an appointment for yourself. You might reach insights about the problem and how your reactions and behaviour affect your teen. The whole family can benefit from one member's therapy.

One or more of the following professionals may be able to help you and your family through a teen crisis.

Family physician or pediatrician Your family doctor can give an overall examination that will determine whether or not a physical disorder is the source of or a contributing factor to the problem. Because she is also concerned with the psychological and social aspects of your family's health, she can refer you to other experts who might help. If your teen refuses to see the doctor, go in yourself to discuss the problem and the options. Your physician can suggest parenting strategies and refer your teen to resources he may be more comfortable with. Doctors with a special interest in adolescent medicine often work in clinics offering a multidisciplinary approach to teens and their families.

School nurse This health professional may be less threatening for your teen. Registered nurses who work full- or part-time in schools usually have expertise in working with teens. Phone the school secretary to find out the times that the school nurse is available and whether she's able to see your teen on a regular basis. As your child builds trust in her, he may agree to her consulting other professionals on his behalf, and then follow through to seek appropriate help.

Psychiatrist These physicians have specialized training in assessing and treating mental health problems; they can prescribe drugs as well as provide various kinds of therapy.

Social worker This professional can help your teen help herself by providing information, support, and practical advice.

Psychologist Trained in assessing people through tests and questionnaires, a psychologist can also offer therapy.

Parent support groups Support groups provide a safe place to share problems and brainstorm solutions. Many groups teach parenting skills and strategies.

It's important for your teen as well. When her life is in chaos, she needs the reassurance that you have your feet firmly on the ground.

Be creative about getting the help you need so you can leave your home for a break. If you're in a parent support group, perhaps you can call on another parent to swap evenings out. You won't have to keep up any pretence with another parent who also has a troubled teen. It's best to drop the pretence with your family and friends, too. If you can trust a few people enough to be honest about the depth and dimensions of the problem, you'll likely find someone—a grandparent, neighbour, or long-time friend—who may be more understanding than you had imagined.

To avoid your teen's rebelling at the idea of being baby-sat, have your friend come over under a pretext—maybe to help younger children with their French homework, or to fix the computer, or to wallpaper the bathroom. Not only will you get the evening off that you desperately need, but your teen will learn that she, too, can turn to people outside the family for help. The knowledge can release her from the feeling that her behaviour is a shameful family secret.

All parents need to know that few adolescents have problems that persist into the future. Adolescence is not a terminal disease; a teen's difficulties usually do subside by voting age. When you're in the middle of a painful situation, it may be hard to view it as an opportunity for growth, but crises are a time for you to take stock and then move on. Traumatic situations are too painful for families not to seek solutions, to try to develop new communication and coping skills, so that members will grow together from the experience.

Handling Violence

If your teen is taller and stronger than you and he becomes physically violent when angry, you must seek help from outside the family. If you or other family members are the target of your teen's physical violence, ask a friend or counsellor for assistance in maintaining order and reinforcing zero tolerance for violence.

If you leave a teen's violent outbursts unchecked, you appear to be condoning the behaviour. Your teen must learn that you won't tolerate violence and that physical violence is punishable under the law. If his comments and actions escalate into physical violence, call the police. Usually in a city, the dispatcher will send officers from the youth bureau of the domestic violence department. If you foresee the possibility that when you head for the phone to summon help your teen might pull the phone right off the wall, take the precaution of talking with a neighbour about your fears and ask if you might come use their phone in such a situation.

Facing a Family Crisis

When your family faces a crisis such as the death of a loved one, your adolescent children may be emotionally torn. They may feel they're too old to rely on parents to guide them through troubled times, but they don't yet have the emotional strength to react like adults. How your teen faces a crisis—whether it's illness or death, divorce or remarriage, discrimination, job loss, or alcoholism in the family—depends on her age, her experiences in life, her temperament, and your parenting style. But no matter how independent she acts, she can feel as battered by the changes a crisis imposes as she did when she was a child.

Teens deserve to know what's going on, though you may not want to tell them everything you would tell an adult friend. If you have established a pattern of communicating openly with your child before he became a teen, you have likely discussed serious issues like sexual mores or unemployment or how people of other races are treated in your community. When you listen to his opinions about these topics, you begin to see the world through his eyes and to understand what he and his friends think. Even if you believe his opinions are wrong, express your views without belittling his. The respect for one another that you demonstrate in family discussions will be invaluable when you have to break bad news to him. He will be able to express his feelings to you or ask basic questions if he knows that you won't put him down or ignore him.

Don't expect your teen to react to a crisis as you would. A thirteen- or fourteen-year-old often has extreme emotions and may react with wild crying or bursts of anger that you never saw in her as an eleven-year-old. Young teens feel intense love and loyalty to their parents and siblings, yet they are beginning the work of establishing an identity separate from their family. When something happens to upset the balance at home, they don't know whether to cling to you or to turn away.

In the middle teen years, your daughter may have her emotions more under control, and she may have a circle of friends to whom she turns in times of trouble, but she will still feel bereft because her peers cannot understand her troubles at home. She still needs you to set limits and to tell her when to come home, especially when the family crisis is driving her away. At eighteen, she may be nearly an adult in the way she speaks and deals with the world, but she may still lack the life experience to put the family crisis in perspective.

Although your teen may have turned from you to his friends for support, your role as a parent is to continue checking in with him regularly. Respect his wish not to talk to you about his emotions, but be alert for signs that he's unable to deal with the crisis. It can be difficult to tell the difference between a moody teenager and an adolescent who is under stress that he can't handle. Don't ignore what's happening with your teenage son because you're preoccupied with the business of finding a new job or nurturing a sick relative. Know your own child and watch for signs of extreme behaviour.

Stress in teens, especially young teens going through puberty, may be expressed as a physical illness—headaches, stomachaches, loss of appetite, insomnia, or the desire to sleep around the clock. Teens may become depressed, appearing to withdraw from life or experiencing periods of irritability, sadness, or flatness. They may act out by becoming defiant or aggressive with others, by taking risks they know they shouldn't, or by coming into conflict with authority. These risks might include taking drugs, experimenting with alcohol, driving recklessly, or sexual experimentation. In extreme cases, teens can develop anorexia, become suicidal, get in trouble with the law, or try prostitution.

> **Stress in teens may be expressed as a physical illness, or they may become depressed, defiant, or aggressive.**

For most teens, a crisis at home won't bring on such extreme reactions. One may have a short period of sadness or irritability when someone dies, without becoming severely depressed. Another may complain of stomachaches and appear to lose her appetite during your divorce, but not develop anorexia. Your son may deal with discrimination by becoming defiant at school, without straying into difficulties with the law. Most teens learn to deal with their emotions and they emerge from adolescence stronger, more experienced, and able to express or act on the values you've instilled in them since childhood.

The teens at risk are those who've experienced several losses almost simultaneously, perhaps a divorce followed by a home move that separates them from friends, and an abrupt change in financial circumstances. Or they may have had to deal with prolonged instability at home because of alcoholism or abuse in the family. If your teen doesn't communicate with you or if you believe the problem is out of control, seek outside help. Have a chat with a school counsellor, a leader in your religious community, or someone who works with teens in your community. Or you may want to seek help through your family doctor or your local mental health clinic. Some employee benefit plans cover sessions with a psychologist or psychotherapist.

When Parents Separate and Divorce

It's unlikely to be a surprise to your teen that her parents are heading for divorce. She will have noticed the tension between Dad and Mom long before you thought of separating. Unlike younger children, your teen needs to know about the impending divorce some weeks before a separation occurs. Although you don't want to put your marriage problems on stage, tell your teen when you seek marriage counselling or when you are seriously discussing a separation. These things will worry her, but at least the news of the divorce won't come as a bombshell. That doesn't make it easier for her to accept. Your marriage is your teen's model of male-female relations at the same time as she's exploring her own feelings about the opposite sex. Your divorce may shake, at least temporarily, her belief in the value of marrying at all.

In his early teen years, your son sees things in black and white and may look for someone to blame. Be careful about how you talk about one another because teens will jump to inappropriate conclusions. At fifteen or sixteen, your daughter may withdraw from you more quickly, spending more time with friends because she's not up to facing the stress at home. At nineteen, your son may have already established his own identity and be genuinely glad for you that you've reached a measure of peace, but your divorce may discourage his own entry into a permanent relationship. Expect some anger, sadness, withdrawal, and denial from all your children, no matter their age.

If you've been an active parent, allowing your daughter more freedom as she demonstrates responsibility, she'll have enough self-esteem to know that your divorce is not her fault. She'll learn to accommodate your separation and divorce as she accommodates all the many changes during her hectic teen years. Her security lies in a close relationship with each parent, not in the place she sleeps each night.

Adolescents in the midst of taking control of their own lives are learning to live with the decisions they make. When it comes time to talk about parental visiting arrangements, involve them in the decisions. Have a family conference in which you all talk about how things might change after the separation. Listen to all suggestions, even if they don't seem workable at first. Make it clear that separate households may have separate rules. Lay out for her the implications of living at Dad's house one week and Mom's the next: "During the week you're at Mom's, you will have to travel by bus for an hour to get to school. That means getting up at 7:00 a.m." Consider your teen's need to be by himself or to hang out with friends when you arrange parental visits. Maybe he can have dinner and watch a movie with Dad during the week so that he can go out with his friends on weekend nights. A schedule that reflects realistic expectations helps everyone in the family.

Don't let your teen avoid curfew by saying he's with the other parent. Teens need more structure, not less, in times of turmoil. Pay special attention that your teens continue regular attendance at school and talk with them about their schoolwork. Studies have shown that teens' interest and academic performance in classes sometimes drop drastically when their parents separate and divorce. Many schools offer counselling groups for the children of divorce.

When parents divorce, they must continue to be civil to one another. If you fight whenever you exchange custody, your teens' loyalties will be torn. They may also think your frustration or anger is their fault or, worse, that you consider them property to fight over. Don't send messages back and forth through your children, and don't complain about your ex when your children are with you. Even if one parent doesn't turn up for a visit, it's better for the teen to direct her anger at the offending parent than for you to complain about your ex's unreliable character. Conflicts that teens have with one parent should not be resolved with the other. Listen to your child's complaints, but don't take sides. Teach them to take their problems with Mom to Mom.

In a separation, don't send messages back and forth through your child.

Telling your teens about a divorce

Tell your teenage children about the divorce in a quiet setting, preferably on a weekend when you're both around and no one has to rush off anywhere. What to say:

- We came to this decision together.
- It was a hard decision for us. We have tried to make our marriage work and we've had many happy times.
- You can't change our minds about separating. It's not your fault or responsibility.
- We both still love you, and we want to spend as much time as possible with you after the separation. Ask what kind of visits might work best.
- You might be embarrassed about the divorce, but it's not shameful.
- Explain details of any new living arrangements, and involve your teen in making plans.

Remarriage and Stepparenting

After the divorce, you and your children have to find a new way to live together or to be together on weekends without the other parent. At the same time as you try to establish a new structure for your family, you must help your teen work through any conflicting emotions about the divorce and consider how she can relate to the opposite sex in a healthy way. If your spouse left you, you may go through a year in which you want nothing to do with the opposite sex, or you may go through a period of heightened sexuality during which you date or become intimate with many partners.

If you do date many partners, keep them all out of your home when the children are there. It sets a poor example for your teen to see a different person eating breakfast in your kitchen on weekend mornings. Teens are intensely interested in male-female dynamics, though they find the notion of their parents' sexuality embarrassing, if not ludicrous. Even as they feign boredom, they watch what you do with great interest. When you believe you've found someone with whom you'd like to have a long-term relationship, then introduce him or her to the kids.

Most of us would like our teens to know they can begin a relationship with a person of the opposite sex by being friends. That friendship may develop into an intimate relationship and later become a serious romance in which both partners think of marriage. To encourage your teen to approach relationships this way, demonstrate that behaviour yourself.

> **It will be easier for your teen to accept your new partner if you make it clear that she doesn't replace Mom.**

If, however, your own relationships are more short-term, it's best to keep your intimacy private. Only after you've become serious about a new partner should you introduce him to your teens as your friend. Begin to include him in family times. Perhaps you can attend an event together or just go out for ice cream. Even if your fifteen-year-old is too cool for outings with you, she still has to eat. Invite your new friend to join your family at dinner.

If you and your adolescent children have lived together without Dad for a few years, you may have begun to rely on them for companionship and be tempted to discuss adult problems with them. But your teenage daughter should not have to take on the responsibility of being your confidante. Call on an adult friend or relative to mull over the question of "whether we're serious or not."

It will be easier for your teen to accept your new partner if you make it clear that she does not replace Mom. Nor should you pump your son for news of a love interest in his mother's life. He's likely to feel his loyalties are being divided. Whatever your plans with your new partner, check in with your teens to find out their own feelings toward her. Your daughter shouldn't dictate to you, her father, that she never wants to see your girlfriend again, but she should have the right to feel angry or confused about her presence. Your teen's reaction will show you how far she has come along in accepting the divorce and in accepting the new choices her parents make. Accept even very negative reactions without criticism, but make it clear to her that your choice of partners is yours alone. Keep checking back with her as your own relationship deepens.

"After Rick and I got married, we discussed our house rules with Mara's mother, Rick's ex-wife. We wrote down our expectations—Mara's chores, how many hours of TV, how late she could stay up—so they would be consistent in both households. Mara knew she couldn't play one parent against the other."

MARY, STEPMOTHER OF A TEEN

A thirteen- to fourteen-year-old has a very black-and-white view of the world and may think that he can't accept a stepdad without betraying his biological father. By the time he's fifteen, he may be striking out for independence and may resent any new authority figure in his life. At eighteen, he may see his mom as a human being who needs support and be happy that someone new loves her. If you find the right person, you won't want to wait for your son to mature before you remarry. But you must discuss with him the role your new partner will play in parenting before you begin a permanent live-in relationship.

You cannot hand over authority for discipline of the children to a new partner without creating resentment. One of the most effective parenting styles for a stepparent to adopt is called "adjunctive parenting." In this style, the stepparent supports the parenting initiatives already established and does not create new rules. This style of parenting allows you and your partner to develop skills in consistent parenting without the children becoming resentful because someone who is "not really Dad" is setting out new rules. If, for example, your new wife has strong ideas about how your daughter should dress, you might raise these at a family meeting. But negotiate with your teen what the rules are going to be, rather than dictate to her. Family meetings to discuss conflicts and work out consequences are essential in a second marriage. Everyone has his or her own emotional baggage, and it will take years before you all accept one another. This is particularly true of blended families, in which two sets of children move among two sets of parents. Teens will respect that you've taken the time to listen to them and work something out that everyone can live with.

When a Parent Loses a Job

When a parent loses a job, there is considerable turmoil for the person involved. But it also affects the rest of the family when the routine of the house changes and everyone adjusts to a tighter budget and the need to accommodate a job search. Teens may become very worried about their family's financial health and future, or they may shrug off the new situation and suggest a raise in their spending money.

When Dad first loses a job, he and Mom should talk privately about how to tell the family and what reason to give for the loss of a job. If possible, get everyone to sit down together to hear the news. Outline for your teens what the financial consequences of the job loss will be. Perhaps the family has to give up a planned vacation. Encourage suggestions from your children about ways to economize. Most teens will be cooperative, particularly if you involve them in the changes.

Mom's job loss and job search will inevitably get teens thinking about the world of work and how it functions. A thirteen-year-old with an exaggerated sense of justice may rail at the unfairness of your being laid off. A sixteen-year-old, in the process of establishing an identity for herself, may develop strong opinions about the moral bankruptcy of corporate life. Don't dismiss their opinions. Treat their ideas with respect, but temper them by discussing your own feelings. Remember that your teen is angry at what has happened to you, but has little life experience to put it in perspective.

A seventeen-year-old may suddenly show less interest in his future education and more interest in taking a part-time job. He may demonstrate an adult sense of responsibility by offering to bring in more money. Let him know that you appreciate his efforts, but that his primary focus must be on his own future. Talk about his options and how, as a family, you will ensure that he reaches his educational goals. Use the opportunity to reiterate the value of a good education and of working

What Teens Can Do to Help

- Scan the classified ads for job leads.
- Do background research on the Internet about the companies placing the ads.
- Help a parent work on her résumé. Try writing one at the same time.
- Stay off the phone until after 7:00 p.m.
- Always answer the phone in a businesslike way.
- Work out a sharing arrangement for the computer.
- Remember that the family doesn't have as much money as before.

Your teen may be very supportive as you go through a difficult transition.

productively. When Mom sticks to her job search or tries some innovative way of getting work, such as starting a home business, she demonstrates to her kids how to approach life's unexpected curve balls.

If Dad is home all day for the first time in years, he may notice many things about his teenage children's behaviour that he hasn't before. This is not the time to reimpose strict discipline, but it might be a good opportunity to work out some house rules that will make life easier. Maybe loud music can be confined to one room of the house or the teens can be given the responsibility of clearing away the dishes so that Dad can make dinner in a clean kitchen.

During a long period of unemployment, you and your partner will have to make money decisions that will affect your teen's day-to-day life. Perhaps your daughter will have to give up an expensive hobby or lessons. You may have to eliminate luxuries like cable, pizza on delivery, or new CDs. If you reach more difficult circumstances and have to sell the house or move to another city to get work, give your teens lots of warning so that they can adjust to the change. Be alert to the teen who is overly worried about your tighter finances. One fifteen-year-old was always absent at dinner time, fearing that it cost her parents too much to feed her. Her marks plunged and her health suffered before her distracted parents noticed there was a problem.

If there seems to be a lot of conflict with your teens during this period or if the person who lost a job is having trouble coping, you might seek counselling. Some outplacement firms offer family counselling. If you can't get outplacement help, you may find that church and temple groups or school counsellors can help you work with your teen to deal with the stress.

When a Parent Is an Alcoholic

Alcoholism in the family will always have an effect on the behaviour of teens, and not only on their attitudes toward alcohol and drug abuse. Families of alcoholics tend to be secretive, hiding their problem from the world and their emotions from each other. Teens are embarrassed to bring friends home because a parent may be drinking.

Children of alcoholics find a role that lets them cope with the problem. A teen may become super-responsible, shouldering more than her share of household tasks to support the parent who doesn't drink. She nurtures everyone at home, including the drinker, and presents an air of calm competence. But that calm masks a fear that she herself is the cause of the drinking and that she has to fix it on her own. She avoids carefree activities with her peers and later in life may become a workaholic or be drawn to a partner who needs taking care of, perhaps an alcoholic.

Sometimes one child of an alcoholic becomes the scapegoat for the family's problems, and attention is focused on him and away from the drinking parent. In his teen years, he may become increasingly reckless, challenge authority at school, refuse to live by home rules, and seek out friends he knows you won't approve of. As he approaches adulthood, he may stray into alcohol or substance abuse himself or be drawn to other high-risk behaviours.

Another teenager may cope with the drinking by withdrawing, by keeping out of the way of the alcoholic, and by trying to avoid the family problem. As a teen, she may have few friends and seldom have fun. As she struggles through her lonely world, she is at risk of developing severe depression or other psychological problems.

Alcoholism: What Teens Should Know

- ➤ It's not a taboo subject. Find someone to talk to about it.
- ➤ It's not your fault that your parent drinks.
- ➤ You can't cure him or her. An alcoholic needs outside help.
- ➤ You can't protect alcoholics from themselves. Don't steal the car keys to prevent them from driving, but also don't get into a car with someone who has been drinking.
- ➤ It's OK to be angry or sad about an alcoholic parent.
- ➤ It's stressful to live with this parent, but you aren't the only teen who has this problem.
- ➤ You will survive. You can learn from the experience and grow stronger.

Although about half of the teens treated for drug and alcohol abuse have witnessed alcoholism and drug use in their own families, having an alcoholic parent does not sentence a teenager to a future life as an alcoholic. The depression and emotional turmoil of having an alcoholic parent means that some teens try to numb their emotions by drinking, the one activity they learned at home. Yet other teens develop an aversion to alcohol and vow never to touch it, while some are able to drink in moderation. Young teens need to learn, at home or at school, about the effects of alcohol on the body; older teens need to learn about the dangers of drinking and driving. But all teens need to hear these messages, not just those who have seen alcoholism firsthand.

It's important to acknowledge that the problem in your family is alcoholism and to allow your teen to express his feelings about it. Attempting to explain alcoholism brings its own difficulties. Describing alcoholism as a disease—"Mom is ill, and we can't make her better without help"—can be beneficial to early adolescents who have a very black-and-white view of the world. They also need to hear that they aren't to blame. Older teens can understand a more detailed explanation of addiction and the effects on the body of dependency on alcohol or other drugs.

When you discuss the place of alcohol in our society and the effects of one person's alcoholism on other family members, you have an opportunity to learn what your own teen and her friends think about alcohol. Open communication between the healthy parent and the teen helps build trust. If she can come to you and say, "I just don't know what to do when I come home from school and Dad has been drinking and yells at me," then you can help ease the burden on her, just by talking. If together you can devise a strategy for this difficult situation, then you free her to look after herself instead of feeling responsible for Dad. Perhaps she can go to a friend down the street or do her homework at the library until you come home and can handle the situation.

Perhaps she'll turn from you to her peers to discuss her problems. It can be difficult to find friends who understand her difficulties, but joining a support group like Alateen may help. You might also encourage her to confide in a school counsellor or a favourite aunt. Your teen needs as many healthy role models and mentors as possible to help her find her way, and to instill hope and a belief in her own healthy resilience.

It can be difficult to be the partner of an alcoholic, and you may be tempted to turn to your newly mature teen for companionship and sympathy, even for sharing the burden of managing the family when your partner is drinking. A drinking parent lets down his side in the parenting

About half of teens treated for alcohol abuse have witnessed alcoholism in their own families.

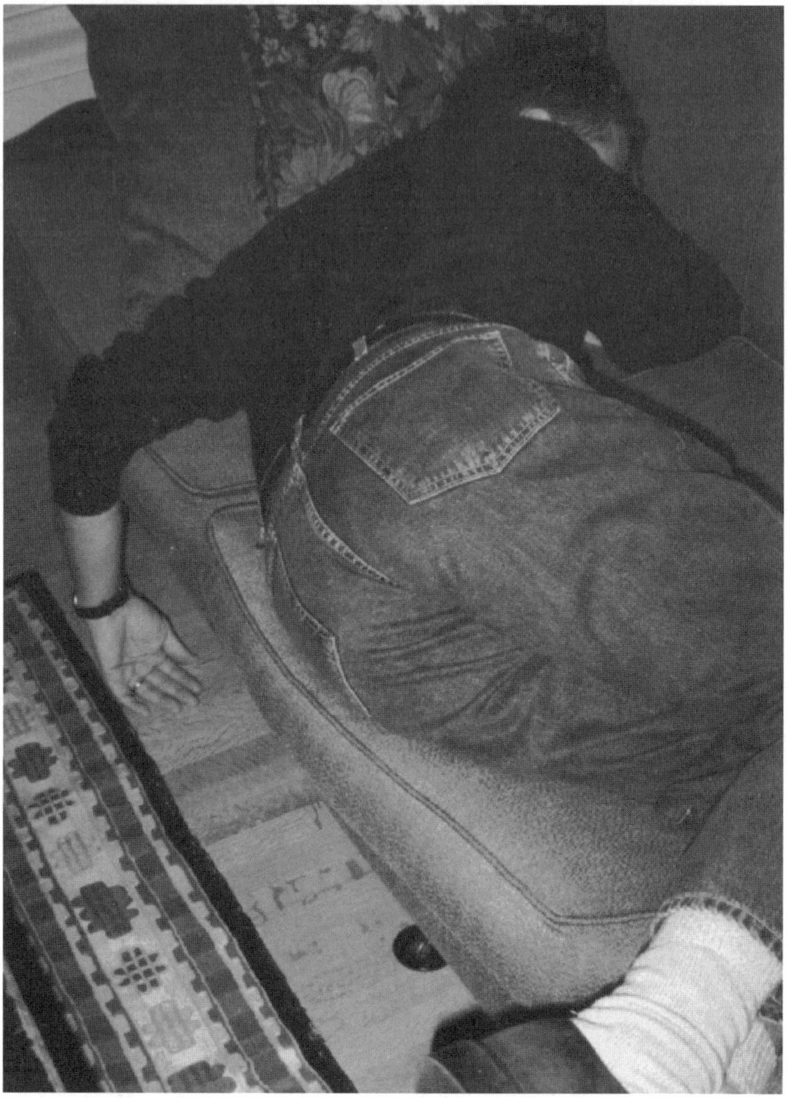

team, and the children will have learned not to trust him. But children of alcoholics desperately need parents who are adults, who take responsibility from them and free them to be kids. Your teen will benefit from regular routines and celebrations and consistent rules consistently applied. Even if it's always up to you, the non-alcoholic parent, to negotiate the perils of teen discipline, don't give up because you have no support from your spouse. You must learn to lean on friends and other family members, or seek support from your doctor, a family counsellor, or your religious leader. You may also find help in a support group such as Al-Anon.

SEE PAGE 218

When a Family Member Is Ill or Dies

When a close family member is ill, it can upset a teen's fragile sense of control over his life. Illness, especially terminal illness, is neither foreseeable nor avoidable, and it changes the balance at home when parents channel their energies into taking care of the sick person. This may be the first time your teen has had to think about the difficulties imposed by a family member's long illness or about the imminent death of someone he loves. He may express his concerns by becoming depressed or angry; he may become angry with the sick person or with you, or frustrated that a situation over which he has no control is interfering with his life. Try to accept your teen's negative emotions without criticism. If you respect his feelings, he'll learn to respect your hurt and grief. Your teen may also find ways to be helpful and want to be part of the family coming together during a crisis.

Early teens are very needy and require much reassurance from you. Middle teens are more likely to confide in their friends or just seek their support by hanging around with the gang. Older teens may know intellectually that the family needs their help and support, but they may be unable to take on a more adult role. Be careful not to load them with responsibilities that prevent them from being with friends or having time alone just to be adolescents. But perhaps they can prepare dinner some nights or take care of younger children in an arrangement that you work out together. You may have to let the housework go or hire some help during this period. When friends and family offer casseroles or to mow the lawn, take up those offers.

LINDA, MOTHER OF TWO

Teens really need to know what's going on when a family member is ill. It's important that you be honest with them, even if the truth is painful. If you don't tell them the illness is terminal, they may feel betrayed when Grandpa dies, as if you didn't trust them with important information that could have helped them prepare themselves. Keep communicating throughout a long illness. As you watch your brother go through the rigours of chemotherapy, you can tell your teen of his progress each day: "Uncle Hal has lost his hair, but he's able to eat now." Some teens are fascinated by illness and begin surfing the Internet for whatever details they can find. This is not a morbid interest; they are genuinely trying to help. Talk about the loved one with them, explaining how difficult it is for you and for everyone touched by the illness: "I find it hard to watch him get sicker every day. He's lost all colour in his face."

When your teen plans to visit the sick person, prepare him. Warn him that Grandma may not know him, and suggest to him what he might talk about and how to behave: "You might tell her about the hockey game you were in last week and hold her hand if you like. You only have to stay half an hour, then you can wait for me in the hospital cafeteria." If a parent or sibling is dying, you may find that your teen avoids visiting. Gently encourage her without pushing. If she cannot face it, suggest she make a card or write a letter to keep connected with the sick relative. When the end is near, let her know clearly: "You should see Joanna now, because the doctors think she might not live through the night."

Breaking Bad News to Teens

Your teen may look as if he's an adult, but he can be quite vulnerable emotionally. When you deliver bad news about a death or serious illness affecting someone close to him, you should choose words carefully. He deserves to know everything, because he will feel you do not trust him if he's kept in the dark. But he needs your support to deal with the shock. Sit beside him, and turn off the music or TV so that you can concentrate on one another.

- First, give a little warning of what you are about to say: "I have some bad news to tell you."
- Then, say what has happened: "Grandpa had a heart attack. He's in a coma in the hospital."
- Third, tell him what it means: "The doctors think he could die today." It's better to use direct words, such as *death* and *die*, whose meanings are clear.
- Guide him by telling him what he could do to help: "I'm going to the hospital. I would like it if you'd come with me."
- Let him absorb all the information any way he wants, whether by crying, by going to his room, or by turning back to the computer.
- Don't censure him if he won't go to the hospital, but prepare him for what he'll see if he does decide to go: "Grandpa's breathing is very uneven, and it's hard to watch." Let him know he can ask questions, either of you or of another relative if you feel overwhelmed by the situation.

An older teen can participate in a family conference to decide whether Mom will come home to die. Work out a role for him that he can sustain throughout her illness, perhaps reading to her every day. Create some important rituals and memories. Perhaps you want to celebrate Hanukkah early because your father won't live until the holiday. If your teen is particularly close to the person who's dying and is having a difficult time, you may want to seek outside support for him. His peers may not know a lot about the stresses of caring for a loved one with a terminal illness. A school or religious counsellor may be able to say the right thing to him. If you know he'll hate missing class for a counselling session, suggest that they meet at lunch or before school so that he doesn't have to miss class.

Facing the Death of a Loved One

It's often during the teen years that your child first experiences the loss of someone he loves. Sometimes it's a grandparent or a friend who has been close to your family. By the age of thirteen, most teens have an intellectual understanding of death, but young teens have quite volatile emotions. As they first experience mortality, even if it's someone they don't know well, teens may feel their grief deeply. They may exhibit their sadness, fear, or anger as physical symptoms, especially if they're going through puberty. An older teen who has put a great deal of effort into rebelling and separating from parents may feel guilty when someone dies. He may recall that he hadn't seen or even spoken on the phone with Grandma for months; he'll need reassurance that his struggle for some independence from the family is normal and that Grandma still spoke of him affectionately before she died. A teenage boy may struggle against other people's expectations of how he should behave. Don't let anyone tell him to "be a man about it." He has the right to cry.

Your teenager may not turn to you for support, but it's important that you talk to your teen about the death, sharing your own feelings about and memories of the person. She will appreciate this, but she may be unable to handle the emotions it raises and flee to her room. She may talk about her loss to a close friend or group of friends and they may want to come to the funeral to support her. If she seems reluctant to talk with family members, accept that reluctance, but raise the subject again as the months pass so that she can explore her feelings with the rest of the family when she's ready.

Give your teens a role in the funeral service, if they can handle it. Ask them whether they're willing, but don't push if they seem reluctant. A sensitive thirteen-year-old may feel too self-conscious to read her poetry, but she may be able to read a passage of Scripture. At

fifteen, your son may fear the job of pallbearer, because he's afraid he'll be too shaky to carry the casket. But he may be able to walk along as an attendant or an escort. A self-confident eighteen-year-old may be able to relate her memories of Grandpa during the service. Whatever age your teens are, prepare them for what will happen at the funeral and guide them in appropriate behaviour.

If your spouse or child has died, you may be emotionally absent to your teen as you struggle with your own grief, and you may be unable to support your teen as he copes with the death of his parent or sibling. Although the support of his friends will help him at the time, they are unlikely to understand if he's still upset one year later. It may help your teen to talk with other teens who've had a similar loss at a grief support group for adolescents. Bereaved Families of Ontario, Compassionate Friends, hospices, and schools throughout the country run such programs.

If your teen was just beginning to establish a separate identity and had frequent conflicts with the parent who died, she may have difficulty separating from someone who's no longer there. If she was the second oldest and is now the oldest living child, her sense of her own place in the family will begin to shift. Parents who have lost one child may develop an extreme fear of losing another and may restrict the freedom of their other teens, even if they had previously led an active social life. Try to negotiate guidelines that are manageable while still putting your mind at rest.

Unfortunately, teens too often experience the death of a classmate or friend through traffic accidents or suicide. Many school boards have plans in place, such as a counselling team for tragic events, to help students deal with tragedies. In the microcosm of a high school, the sudden death of a student or teacher can reverberate, triggering strong emotions and possibly copycat suicide among other teens, even those who didn't know the victim well. Young teens may personalize a death, thinking "It could have been me," or, if a classmate loses a parent, "It could

> **If your teen wants to attend a classmate's funeral, offer to accompany her and a group of friends.**

"I'm a different person than I would have been if my dad hadn't died. It was a wake-up call for me. I don't exist in a bubble in which only good things happen. At my school, there are a lot of airheads who think the world will come to an end if their top doesn't match their pants. They get everything they want, and they don't have any real problems. I wonder if I'd be like that if Dad hadn't died."

MIRIAM, AGE 14

have been my mother." They need to work through their own fear of death, and they may be unable to shake a feeling of foreboding after the event. Some are unable to sleep; others react with anger at the unfairness of a death.

Counselling by slightly older peers and by teachers may help them cope, but parents also play a role. If your teen wants to attend a classmate's funeral, agree to accompany her and a group of her friends. Unaccompanied teens who don't know how to behave at a funeral may make things difficult for the bereaved family, although they may help one another. Tell your daughter what's appropriate in attire and behaviour and what she might say to the bereaved parents. Help your teen gain some perspective on the tragedy by talking it over with her. Resist the impulse to lecture about drinking and driving, but acknowledge that bad things do happen to good people and that the death has been a shocking experience for everyone.

When a Teen Faces Discrimination

The politics of race, religion, and difference become more complex as teens get older. Most Canadian cities have very diverse populations, and teens are accustomed to learning and socializing alongside people of many different backgrounds. Even teens in small homogeneous communities are connected to the wider world by TV and the Internet and are exposed more frequently to religious and ethnic differences. But there is still plenty of insulting name-calling in the halls of high schools, and it can be very hurtful to the young teen who belongs to a visible minority and is so conscious of her appearance. When she is developing a wider circle of friends in her middle teen years, she may struggle with whether to move toward teens who have a similar background or to develop a different circle based on her interests. In her late teens, she may enter the working world and wonder whether prospective employers will judge her on her outward appearance rather than her education and skills.

"My boys know where they come from and their family history. We talk about slavery and segregation and the different ways our people came to Canada. Did you know the first black man in Canada was an explorer who interpreted in Micmac for Champlain? Then people came as United Empire Loyalists and escaped slaves and skilled tradesmen and professionals. I wanted them to know they have the right to be here. When people say, 'You should go back where you came from,' my boys know they are just wrong."

JANIS, MOTHER OF TWO

As your teens become more sophisticated and aware of the world around them, they start to put into context all that they've learned as children about their family history. Do your best to enlarge their understanding by exposing them to books, movies, art, and videos that tell about the history of slavery, the Holocaust, or the turmoils of Southeast Asia. Talk with your teen about how Native Canadians are treated in your town, whether sports stars are realistic role models for people of colour, and whether disabled people have equal access to services in your shopping mall. Be a critic of the media and the positive and negative ways in which they portray people of other races, but refrain from lecturing. Make discrimination the topic of a family discussion in which your son tells what he has seen happen at school or what he has heard his friends say. If you treat his contribution with respect, it will encourage him to continue listening to you and will give you an opportunity to see how he thinks about these issues. Keep bolstering his pride in his own background.

You should continue to monitor what your daughter is learning in classes, though you will probably do it at a greater distance than you did when she was younger. Ask to see her textbooks and homework, get involved with parent groups, and take every opportunity to talk with teachers and administrators at the school. You want to know how inclusive her education is and what attitudes are reflected in the hallways. Teens who don't feel at home in their school, because of discrimination or inadequate curriculum and resources, are at risk of poor academic performance and of dropping out. You can contribute to the diversity of your teen's high school by offering to speak on career days or by chatting with teachers about the curriculum and resources in each discipline. Perhaps you think the course in twentieth-century history should acknowledge the role of the Asian Allies during the Second World War. Sometimes a few words from parents are enough to encourage a teacher to broaden his focus; sometimes it takes hours of work on school curriculum committees or a proposal from a group of parents to the school staff.

Even in communities where children of diverse backgrounds have played at each other's houses since elementary school, the tables in the local high school's cafeteria may readily divide along racial lines. Unless there is intense bullying or racial conflict within your teen's school, you shouldn't worry too much about this division. In their search for identity, teens may hang out only with others of the same background. In general, people overreact about a group of teens who appear to be of one race or ethnic background and who hang out together in one place. Shopping mall managers have expelled groups of visible minority teens, thinking they pose a gang problem. Police, too, may move them out of a park or off the street corner. If your teen had somewhere else to go, he'd be unlikely to get involved in this kind of problem. As a parent, you might offer him opportunities to meet different

Teens need to understand their family history and their roots as they explore the wider world.

DAREEN, AGE 18

groups of kids in safe environments, perhaps in sports at the community centre or in your religion's youth group. You might also be the valiant parent who allows your teen to invite his friends into the rec room for an evening of videos or playing cards, as long as you can provide the appropriate supervision.

"My mother told me to ignore the stereotypes of black people and just be myself. She has supported me in everything I've done and said, 'Go for it.' In the community I live in, blacks have a very bad label. The media blow up every incident of drugs and alcohol. Anything positive they just don't want to hear. I feel I have to do whatever I can to make the black community here stronger and better."

SHAUN, AGE 15

When your teen is the target of derogatory name-calling or exclusion by other kids at school, she may become withdrawn or resist going to school, but still be reluctant to confide in her parents. If she does want to talk with you about such problems, reassure her that the behaviour of the other kids is abnormal and that she won't experience that kind of negative attention all her life. Together, you can work out how she might deal with these comments and still feel good about herself. Perhaps she should just ignore them? After all, "they're the ones who have the problem." Sometimes a little humour dropped into the situation might make everyone laugh and break up the tension. If she is a wit, she might carry that off successfully. Another solution might be for your teen to find allies and form a group of like-minded friends who shrug off negative comments from others. Warn her to avoid confrontation with troublesome groups of kids—too many teens get hurt by others because they fail to ask for adult help against belligerent groups of teens.

SEE PAGE 173

If racism is a serious, ongoing problem, talk with a teacher, a counsellor, or the principal at the school. All provincial ministries of education have anti-racism policies and guidelines for the development of inclusive curriculum and learning resources. Many school boards also have services such as an anti-racism or equity coordinator to promote racial tolerance. Your teen might like to become involved, particularly if he is socially conscious or a good speaker. Above all, don't hesitate to visit the school or work with other parents, if necessary, to ensure your teen's physical and emotional safety.

Family Resources

5

Finding the right information at the right moment is important, and in this chapter parents can find both essential information and contact information on national and specialized resources that will help them develop as parenting experts.

- Selected Canadian Books for Young Teens

  Books about Books and Reading

  Specialized Sources and Web Sites

- Selected Canadian Associations and Organizations

- Selected Canadian Resources for Parents

- Health Canada: Recommended

  Immunization Schedules

- What Teens Can Do When

  without Parental Consent

Selected Canadian Books for Young Teens

Selected and annotated by Janet Abernethy from the recommendations of the librarians of Toronto Public Library, West Region, Spring 1998. The books are listed with title first, but are alphabetized by author as readers would find them in a bookstore or library.

Redwork, Michael Bédard. 1990. Lester & Orpen Dennys, Toronto.
Is the mysterious landlord hiding an evil secret? A perplexing fantasy.

Forbidden City, William Bell. 1990. Doubleday Canada, Toronto.
The fictional diary of a Canadian boy who witnesses the Tiananmen Square tragedy.

No Signature, William Bell. 1992. Doubleday Canada, Toronto.
Bent on finding the father who left him years ago, Wick is shocked by what he discovers.

Another Shore, Nancy Bond. 1988. McElderry Books, CHK Hearst Book Group, Toronto.
Time travel to 1744, when Nova Scotia was French and at war with England.

There Will Be Wolves, Karleen Bradford. 1995. HarperCollins, Toronto.
Condemned at home as a witch, a young girl is forced to join the Crusades.

The Dark Garden, Margaret Buffie. 1995. Kids Can Press, Toronto.
Traumatic amnesia, ghosts, murder, and passion in a highly satisfying story.

The Guardian Circle, Margaret Buffie. 1989. Kids Can Press, Toronto. Reprinted in 1994 as The Warnings, a mass market paperback.
Rachel had always hated her "second sight" until she found out who she really was and what she had to do.

My Mother's Ghost, Margaret Buffie. 1992. Kids Can Press, Toronto.
Who are the ghosts from the past and why is their tragedy happening again? Can the past help heal the present?

Who Is Frances Rain? Margaret Buffie. 1987. Kids Can Press, Toronto.
When Lizzie puts on the old pair of glasses, she witnesses a drama from her family's past and finally puts things right. A most realistic ghost story.

The Dream Carvers, Joan Clark. 1992. Penguin Books, Toronto.
A young Greenlander is abducted from his settlement in what is now Newfoundland and forced to become a member of the Osweet tribe.

Covered Bridge, Brian Doyle. 1990. Groundwood Books, Toronto.
Hubbo needs the help of a ghost to save the old covered bridge from needless demolition.

Spud in Winter, Brian Doyle. 1995. Groundwood Books, Toronto.
Spud's hijinks and nose for mystery lead him on a frozen trail through Ottawa.

Spud Sweetgrass, Brian Doyle. 1992. Groundwood Books, Toronto.
An unlikely lovable hero and some larger-than-life villains tangle in this popular farcical mystery.

Uncle Ronald, Brian Doyle. 1996. Groundwood Books, Toronto.
After fleeing his abusive father, Mickey and his mother find refuge with relatives in a close-knit Quebec town. Deft, impressive, and surprisingly funny.

Up to Low, Brian Doyle. 1996. Groundwood Books, Toronto.
A tender love story in Doyle's inimitable tall-tale, fast-paced, witty style.

The Baby Project, Sarah Ellis. 1994.
Groundwood Books, Toronto.
*Jessica struggles for understanding and
acceptance after the death of her baby sister.*

Back of Beyond, Sarah Ellis. 1996.
Groundwood Books, Toronto.
*Intriguing short stories that take a very different
view of the supernatural.*

Out of the Blue, Sarah Ellis. 1994.
Groundwood Books, Toronto.
*Megan's adjustment to discovering she has an
older half-sister, the baby her mother gave up
for adoption years ago.*

Pick-Up Sticks, Sarah Ellis. 1991.
Groundwood Books, Toronto.
*Polly is frustrated by her artistic,
unconventional mother and opts to live with
more established relatives. Insightful.*

One Thing That's True, Cheryl Foggo. 1997.
Kids Can Press, Toronto.
*At thirteen, Roxanne is doing all right until
everything falls apart when her brother learns
he's adopted.*

Don't Call Me Sugarbaby! Dorothy Joan Harris.
1991. Scholastic, Toronto.
*Alison goes through shock, anger, and despair as
she adjusts to having diabetes.*

Home Child, Barbara Haworth-Attard. 1996.
Roussan, Montréal, Que.
*The heart-wrenching story of one of over
100,000 destitute children sent from Britain to
Canada in the early 1900s. For many of these
children, "a better life" in Canada turned out to
be almost slave labour.*

The Faces of Fear, Monica Hughes. 1997.
HarperCollins, Toronto.
*Virtual reality can have the power of the real
thing in this psychological sci-fi thriller.*

The Golden Aquarians, Monica Hughes. 1994.
HarperCollins, Toronto.
*Beautifully realized science fiction in which a
boy defies his father to save a planet from
destruction.*

Hunter in the Dark, Monica Hughes. 1982.
Reissued 1998. Irwin Publishing, Toronto.
*Diagnosed with leukemia, a young boy goes
hunting, alone, to test his mettle.*

Invitation to the Game, Monica Hughes. 1990.
HarperCollins, Toronto.
*At first it was just diversion in the bleak world
of the far future, but it soon became the only
thing that mattered. Masterful science fiction.*

Adam and Eve and Pinch-me, Julie Johnston.
1994. Reissued 1996. Stoddart, Toronto.
*Sarah, a hardened foster child, can't resist the
pull of love from a farming family.*

Hero of Lesser Causes, Julie Johnston. 1992.
Stoddart, Toronto.
*Keeley heroically tries to revive her brother's
will to live after he is paralyzed by polio.*

Naomi's Road, Joy Kagawa. 1988.
Reissued 1995. Stoddart, Toronto.
*Separated from their parents, Naomi and her
brother are sent to a Japanese internment
camp in British Columbia during the
Second World War.*

Out of the Dark, Welwyn Wilton Katz. 1995.
Groundwood Books, Toronto.
*Torn apart by grief over his mother's murder,
Ben retreats into a fantasy world of
Viking mythology.*

The Third Magic, Welwyn Wilton Katz. 1990.
Groundwood Books, Toronto.
*While on vacation, Morgan is pulled through
time to an alien world where competing magics
do battle in this intriguing take on the King
Arthur legend.*

Witchery Hill, Welwyn Wilton Katz. 1995.
Groundwood Books, Toronto.
*A mesmerizing, terrifying tale in which Mike
pits his courage and wits against an evil coven
bent on human sacrifice.*

The Hollow Tree, Janet Lunn. 1997.
Alfred A. Knopf Canada, Toronto.
The lives of some Loyalist families depend on
Phoebe's getting a secret message to the British
army after her beloved cousin is hanged as a spy.

Shadow in Hawthorn Bay, Janet Lunn. 1987.
Lester & Orpen Dennys, Toronto.
With her "second sight," Mary hears her cousin
calling from Upper Canada, and she sets out
alone from Scotland to find him. A mysterious
romance.

Eating Between the Lines, Kevin Major. 1991.
Doubleday Canada, Toronto.
Jackson escapes his unhappy family life through
his uncanny ability to actually enter the worlds
of his books.

Hold Fast, Kevin Major. 1991. Stoddart,
Toronto.
Michael, recently orphaned, runs away from his
intolerable uncle.

Daniel's Story, Carol Matas. 1993. Scholastic,
Toronto.
Daniel, 14, tells his powerful and horrific family
story, from a normal life in Frankfurt to the
death camps in Nazi Germany during the Second
World War.

Jesper, Carol Matas. 1994. Scholastic, Toronto.
At the height of the Second World War, Jesper
and his friends defy the Germans by publishing
an underground newspaper and embarking on
dangerous acts of sabotage.

Lisa, Carol Matas. 1987. Lester & Orpen
Dennys, Toronto.
Lisa follows her older brother, Stephan, to join
the dangerous world of the Danish resistance as
they work to thwart the Germans during the
Second World War.

Laughs, Claire McKay. 1997. Tundra Press,
Toronto.
A collection of very funny stories, poems, and
riddles.

One Proud Summer, Claire McKay and
Marsha Hewitt. 1981. Women's Press, Toronto.
After the death of her father, Lucie goes to work
in a factory where the union is fighting for the
rights of the workers.

The Druid's Tune, O.R. Melling. 1983.
Reissued 1994. HarperCollins, Toronto.
Two teens visit Ireland and suddenly find
themselves in the ancient past, companions of
the hero Cuchulainn and battling to save Ulster
from invasion by warrior Queen Maeve.

The Hunter's Moon, O.R. Melling. 1993.
HarperCollins, Toronto.
Gwen needs all the magical help she can get to
rescue her cousin from the fairy king before it's
too late. A spellbinding fantasy.

Who Has Seen the Wind, W.O. Mitchell. 1947.
Reissued 1991. McClelland & Stewart, Toronto.
A thoughtful look at life on the Canadian
Prairies just after the turn of the century.
A modern classic that has celebrated its
50th anniversary.

Emily of New Moon, Emily Climbs, Emily's
Quest, Lucy Maud Montgomery. Originally
published beginning 1923. Reissued 1989.
McClelland & Stewart, Toronto.
Orphaned and living with strange relatives,
Emily struggles to overcome her grief with the
help of family and friends. She is passionate,
stubborn, gifted, and determined to become a
writer. Emily has won the hearts of innumerable
readers and inspired many of Canada's writers.
A beloved series not to be missed.

The Black Joke, Farley Mowat. 1963.
Reissued 1987. McClelland & Stewart, Toronto.
A heroic tale of pirates and bootlegging on the
Newfoundland coast during the Great Depression.

Lost in the Barrens, Farley Mowat. 1956.
Reissued 1987. McClelland & Stewart, Toronto.
The heartwarming, gripping classic of two boys
fighting to survive in the Arctic wilderness.

Dead Water Zone, Kenneth Oppel. 1992.
Kids Can Press, Toronto.
*Only Paul's brother has discovered what's been
done to the water, but he has mysteriously
disappeared. A futuristic environmental fantasy.*

The Lights Go On Again, Kit Pearson. 1993.
Penguin Books, Toronto.
In this sequel to Looking at the Moon, *Norah
and Gavin must choose between staying with
their foster family in Toronto or returning to
England with their grandfather.*

Looking at the Moon, Kit Pearson. 1991.
Penguin Books, Toronto.
*In the second book in a series, Norah, now 13,
and her brother, refugees from England, spend a
summer in Muskoka. Insightful and sensitive.*

The Sky Is Falling, Kit Pearson. 1991.
Penguin Books, Toronto.
*Norah and her little brother are sent from
England to the safety of strangers in Toronto
during the Second World War. The first of a
popular trilogy.*

The Boy with an R in His Hand, James Reaney.
1980. The Porcupine's Quill, Erin, Ont.
*The story of William Lyon Mackenzie's
young apprentice and the political upheavals
of 1836–37.*

The West Windsor Nine, Joseph Romain. 1997.
Vanwell Publishing, St. Catharines, Ont.
*An unlikely group of teens form a baseball team
to win the trip to Montreal, all in search of the
unknown father of one of them.*

Beautiful Joe, Marshall Saunders. 1894.
Reissued 1994. Applewood Books, Bedford, MA.
*Loved for generations, a classic animal story
guaranteed to bring tears.*

A Fly Named Alfred, Don Trembath. 1997.
Orca Book Publishers, Victoria.
In this sequel to The Tuesday Café, *Harper is
still writing, but anonymously. One of his
scathing columns brings a bounty on his
anonymous head.*

The Tuesday Café, Don Trembath. 1996.
Orca Book Publishers, Victoria.
*Harper surprises himself when he really "gets
into" writing, although it was intended as a
punishment for a misdemeanour. Quick, funny,
and clever.*

Jasmin, Jan Truss. 1982. Groundwood Books,
Toronto.
*Jasmin is failing because she can't concentrate
or get any peace in her large, boisterous family.
She runs away and survives in the wilderness
until, finally, she finds friends who care.*

Stars, Eric Walters. 1996. Stoddart, Toronto.
*An enforced wilderness experience has no appeal
for a group of young offenders, but it's better
than jail.*

Ran Van, the Defender, Diane Wieler. 1993.
Groundwood Books, Toronto.
*Hooked on video games, Ran sees himself as a
noble knight with a mission to rescue a troubled
girl from a troubled life.*

The Leaving, Budge Wilson. 1990. House of
Anansi Press, Toronto.
*Nine remarkable stories about nine remarkable
girls. Outstanding and memorable.*

The Maestro, Tim Wynne-Jones. 1995.
Groundwood Books, Toronto.
*Running away from an abusive home, Burl finds
refuge and respite at the cottage of an eccentric
musician, but not for long.*

Some of the Kinder Planets, Tim Wynne-Jones.
1993. Groundwood Books, Toronto.
*Unusually clever and funny short stories about
ordinary kids in extraordinary situations.*

Stephen Fair, Tim Wynne-Jones. 1998.
Tundra Books, Toronto.
*Could Stephen's nightmares have anything
to do with the terrible secret that has torn his
family apart?*

Books about Books and Reading

Bibliographies in the following books, whether Canadian, American, or international, identify reading or interest levels and categories—young teens up to age 16 are encompassed in the term "children's literature."

Everybody's favourites: Canadians talk about books that changed their lives, Arlene Perly Rae. 1997. Penguin Books, Toronto.

Great books for boys: More than 600 books for boys 2 to 14. 1998.
Great books for girls: More than 600 books to inspire today's girls and tomorrow's women. 1997. Both books by Kathleen Odean. Ballantine Books, New York.

Kindling spirit: L.M. Montgomery's Anne of Green Gables, Elizabeth Waterston. 1993. Canadian Fiction Studies series. ECW Press, Toronto.

The New republic of childhood: A critical guide to Canadian children's literature in English, 3rd ed., Sheila Egoff and Judith Saltman. 1990. Oxford University Press, Toronto.
Bibliography up to 1990 on pages 315–348.

Only connect: Readings on children's literature, 3rd ed., Sheila Egoff, Gordon Stubbs, Ralph Ashley, and Wendy Sutton. 1995. Oxford University Press, Toronto.

Out of this world: Canadian science fiction and fantasy literature, compiled by Andrea Paradis for National Library of Canada. 1995. Quarry Press, Kingston, Ont.

Specialized Sources and Web Sites

Young teens up to and including age 16 are encompassed in most references to "children's literature."

Canadian Children's Book Centre   CCBC
35 Spadina Rd.
Toronto, ON M5R 2S9
(416) 975-0010
Fax: (416) 975-1839
E-mail: ccbc@sympatico.ca
<http://www3.sympatico.ca/ccbc/>
A national nonprofit organization founded in 1976; promotes and encourages the reading, writing, and illustrating of Canadian children's books; offers the services of a comprehensive reference library of contemporary Canadian children's books as well as background on authors, illustrators, book production and publishing—by phone, fax or mail. A regular newsletter, Children's Book News, *announces annual activities like Children's Book Festival, Freedom to Read Week, and Book Day. Check out the Web site.*

Canadian Children's Literature   CCL
CCL is a bilingual journal of criticism and review covering Canadian books and other media for children and young adults. Provides essential information for everyone who cares about children's reading.
University of Guelph
Guelph, ON N1G 2W1
(519) 824-4120 x3189
Fax: (519) 837-1315
E-mail:ccl@uoguelph.ca
<http://www.uoguelph.ca/englit/ccl/index.html>

Canadian Children's Literature Service
National Library of Canada
395 Wellington St.
Ottawa, ON K1A 0N4
(613) 996-2300 or 996-7774
Fax: (613) 995-1969
E-mail: clsslj@nlc-bnc.ca
<http://www.nlc-bnc.ca/services/eclsc.htm>
The service maintains a collection of books
(in English and French and other languages
published in Canada) for children and young
people age sixteen and under. Services are
offered to the general public as well as to
students and those with a professional interest.
Also promotes its book collections with major
exhibits and publications like "Read Up On It:
Books to Share."

Canadian Society of Children's Authors,
Illustrators and Performers   CANSCAIP
35 Spadina Rd.
Toronto, ON M5R 2S9
(416) 515-1559
Fax: (416) 515-7022
<http://www.interlog.com/~canscaip/>
The largest organization in Canada supporting
creative work for children and young adults,
CANSCAIP works with the CCBC on a variety
of activities, exhibits, and workshops; offers a
newsletter and annual meetings to members.

The Children's Book Store   CBS
2532 Yonge St.
Toronto, ON M4P 2H7
(416) 480-0233
Fax: (416) 480-9345
E-mail: cbs@inforamp.net
<http://www.toronto.com/cbs>
Established in 1974 by former librarian Judy
Sarick, the CBS was the first bookstore in
Canada devoted exclusively to children's books.
Known throughout North America, the CBS
offers many services beyond selling books
and media.

Children's Literature Web Guide
David K. Brown
Doucette Library of Teaching Resources
University of Calgary
Calgary, AB T2N 1N4
(403) 220-6295
<http://www.acs.ucalgary.ca/~dkbrown/>

The LM Montgomery Institute
<http://www.upei.ca/~lmmi/cover.html>

National Library of Canada
Forthcoming Books
<http://www.nlc-bnc.ca/forthbks/efbintro.htm>

New Canadian Library
A continuing series of over 100 reprints of
classics by Canadian authors of fiction and
poetry, under the general editorship of David
Staines. McClelland & Stewart, Toronto.

The 1999 Canadian Encyclopedia CD-ROM
Three editions available, each of which includes
the 1997 Gage Canadian Dictionary. *James*
Marsh, Editor-in-Chief. McClelland & Stewart,
Toronto.

@Sympatico NetLife
Canada's Home Internet Magazine
Links Editor: Adrienne Webb
E-mail: a_webb@bc.sympatico.ca
Six issues a year; a good source of interesting
Web sites for children and young adults. The
magazine comes with a subscription to the
Internet service Sympatico.

Selected Canadian Associations and Organizations

Many of these resources offer information, fact sheets, and publications.

Ability OnLine Support Network
<http://www.ablelink.org/public/default.htm>
Provides links to other disability/health-care Web sites.

AboutFace
123 Edward St., Suite 1003
Toronto, ON   M5G 1E2
1-800-665-3223
E-mail: abtface@interlog.com
<http://www.interlog.com/~abtface>
Provides information and emotional support for individuals and families who are touched by facial differences.

Adult Children of Alcoholics
20 Bloor St. E., Box 75061
Toronto, ON   M4W 3T3
(416) 593-5147
E-mail: ccrumb@passport.ca
<http://www.adultchildren.org>

Al-Anon/Alateen
World Service Office
Virginia Beach, VA
1-800-443-4525
<http://www.al-anon.org>
Provides a calendar for all local groups worldwide.

Al-Anon Information Services
1771 Avenue Rd., Box 54533
North York, ON   M5M 4N5
(416) 410-3809
<http://web.idirect.com/~alanon>
An answering service provided by volunteers.

Alberta Alcohol and Drug Abuse Commission
10909 Jasper Ave., 2nd Floor
Edmonton, AB   T5J 3M9
1-800-280-9616
Youth Services: (403) 422-7383

Alcoholics Anonymous   AA
234 Eglinton Ave. E., Suite 202
Toronto, ON   M4P 1K5
(416) 487-5591
(416) 487-5591
Fax: (416) 487-5855
<http://www.alcoholics-anonymous.org>
Check for local groups in the Business Section of your telephone book.

Allergy/Asthma Information Association   AAIA
30 Eglinton Ave. W., Suite 750
Mississauga, ON   L5R 3E7
(905) 712-2242
1-800-611-7011
Fax: (905) 712-2245

The Alliance for Children and Television   ACT
60 St. Clair Ave. E., Suite 1002
Toronto, ON   M4T 1N5
(416) 515-0466
Fax: (416) 515-0467
E-mail: acttv@interlog.com
<http://www.act-canada.com>

Association for Bright Children   ABC
Ontario ABC
2 Bloor St. W., Suite 100-156
Toronto, ON   M4W 2G7
(416) 925-6136
E-mail: abc_ontario@on.aibn.ca
<http://www.inode.org/abc/>

Association of Canadian Publishers
110 Eglinton Ave. W., Suite 401
Toronto, ON   M4R 1A3
(416) 487-6116
Fax: (416) 487-8815
E-mail: info@canbook.org
<http://www2.publishers.ca/acp/default.html>
Provides contact info on member publishers and their catalogues of books and learning materials.

Asthma Society of Canada
130 Bridgeland Ave., Suite 425
Toronto, ON M6A 1Z4
(416) 787-4050
1-800-787-3880
E-mail: asthma@myna.com
<http://www.asthmasociety.com>

Attention Deficit Disorder Ontario Foundation
<http://www.addofoundation.org/>
Attention Deficit Hyperactivity Disorder
<http://www.mhnet.org/guide/adhd.htm>

Autism Society Canada
2281 Yonge St., Suite 206
Toronto, ON M4P 2C7
(416) 483-3566
Fax: (416) 922-1032

Bereaved Families of Ontario
562 Eglinton Ave. E., Suite 401
Toronto, ON M4P 1P1
(416) 440-0290
Fax: (416) 440-0304
E-mail: BFO@inforamp.net
<http://www.InfoRamp.Net/~bfo/>

Big Brothers & Sisters of Canada
3228 South Service Rd., Suite 113E
Burlington, ON L7N 3H8
(905) 639-0461
1-800-263-9133
E-mail: bbsc@bbsc.ca
<http://www.bbsc.ca/>
For children 6 to 16 years of age.

Boys and Girls Clubs of Canada
7100 Woodbine Ave., Suite 405
Markham, ON L3R 5J2
(905) 477-7272
Fax: (905) 477-2056
<http://www.bgccan.com/>

**British Columbia Confederation of
Parent Advisory Councils**
1185 West Georgia St., Suite 1540
Vancouver, BC V6E 4E6
(604) 687-4433
Fax: (604) 687-4488
E-mail: bccpac@direct.ca
<http://www.bccpac.bc.ca>

Cable in the Classroom Association
350 Sparks St., Suite 909
Ottawa, ON K1R 7S8
(613) 233-3033
Fax: (613) 233-7650
E-mail: information@cableducation.ca
<http://www.cableducation.ca>
*A Web site resource made possible by ROGERS
Communications.*

Call Mom
1-800-993-9984
E-mail: callmom@mts.net
<http://www.mts.net/callmom>
*National help line on parenting dilemmas and
household conundrums.*

Canada Safety Council
1020 Thomas Spratt Place
Ottawa, ON K1G 5L5
(613) 739-1535
E-mail: csc@safety-council.org
<http://www.safety-council.org/>
*Check Traffic Safety Section and Driver
Training.*

Canada's SchoolNet
<http://www.schoolnet.ca>
*SchoolNet's mandate is to facilitate the
connection to the Internet of all 16,500 schools
and 3,400 libraries in Canada by 1999.*

Canadian AIDS Society   CAS
130 Albert St., Suite 900
Ottawa, ON K1P 5G4
(613) 230-3580
Fax: (613) 563-4998
E-mail: casinfo@cdn.ca
<http://www.cdnaids.ca>

The Canadian Association of the Deaf
251 Bank St., Suite 203
Ottawa, ON K2P 1X3
Voice/TTY: (613) 565-2882
Fax: (613) 565-1207
<http://www.cad.ca>

Canadian Association of Family Resource Programs
30 Rosemount Ave., Suite 101
Ottawa, ON K1Y 1P4
(613) 728-3307
Fax: (613) 729-5421
E-mail: info@frp.ca
<http://www.cfc-efc.ca>
A national association of resource centres that offer parenting courses, peer support, and other programs.

Canadian Association for Health, Physical Education, Recreation, and Dance CAHPERD
1600 James Naismith Dr.
Gloucester, ON K1B 5N4
(613) 748-5622
Fax: (613) 748-5737
E-mail: cahperd@itm.activeliving.ca
<http://www.activeliving.ca/cahperd>

Canadian Association of Speech-Language Pathologists and Audiologists CASLPA
130 Albert St., Suite 2006
Ottawa, ON K1P 5G4
(613) 567-9968
1-800-259-8519
Fax: (613) 567-2859
E-mail: caslpa@caslpa.ca
<http://www.caslpa.ca>

Canadian Automobile Association CAA
Check for local groups in the Business Section of your telephone book.
1-800-268-3750
School Safety Patrol Program
<http://www.caa.ca>

Canadian Cancer Society
10 Alcorn Ave., Suite 200
Toronto, ON M4V 3B1
(416) 961-7223
Fax: (416) 961-4189
also **National Cancer Institute of Canada**
Cancer Information Service: 1-888-939-3333
<http://www.cancer.ca>

Canadian Centre for Ethics in Sport CCES
1600 James Naismith Dr., Suite 205
Gloucester, ON K1B 5N4
(613) 748-5755/1-800-672-7775
Fax: (613) 748-5746
<http://www.cces.ca>

Canadian Centre on Substance Abuse CCSA
75 Albert St., Suite 300
Ottawa, ON K1P 5E7
(613) 235-4048
Fax: (613) 235-8101
E-mail: webmaster@ccsa.ca
<http://www.ccsa.ca>
Provides information on the prevention and treatment of substance abuse and other programs.

Canadian Cystic Fibrosis Foundation CCFF
2221 Yonge St., Suite 601
Toronto, ON M4S 2B4
National Office: (416) 485-9149
1-800-378-2233
E-mail: info@ccff.ca
<http://www.ccff.ca/~cfwww/index.html>

Canadian Dental Association CDA
1815 Alta Vista Dr.
Ottawa, ON K1G 3Y6
(613) 523-1770
Fax: (613) 523-7736
E-mail: reception@cda-adc.ca
<http://www.cda-adc.ca>

The Canadian Dermatology Association CDA
774 Echo Dr., Suite 521
Ottawa, ON K1S 5N8
(613) 730-6262/1-800-267-3376
Fax: (613) 730-1116
E-mail: cda.albagli@rspsc.edu
<http://www.derm.ubc.ca/jcms/
CDA-ACD.html#Top>

Canadian Diabetes Association CDA
15 Toronto St., Suite 800
Toronto, ON M5C 2E3
(416) 363-3373
National toll-free: 1-800-BANTING
Ontario only: 1-800-361-1306
Fax: (416) 214-1899
E-mail: info@cda-nat.org
<http://www.diabetes.ca>

Canadian Down Syndrome Society
811-14th St. N.W.
Calgary, AB T2N 2A4
(403) 270-8500
E-mail: cdss@ican.net
<http://home.ican.net/~cdss/index.html
Down Syndrome Association of Metro Toronto
<http://www.dsamt.toronto.on.ca>

Canadian Education Association   CEA
252 Bloor St. W., Suite 8-200
Toronto, ON M5S 1V5
(416) 924-7721
Fax: (416) 924-3188
E-mail: acea@hookup.net
<http://www.acea.ca>
*The CEA produces an annual handbook with
names and addresses of all education entities
across Canada.*

Canadian Education on the Web
<http://www.oise.utoronto.ca/~mpress/
eduweb.html>

**Canadian Fitness and Lifestyle Research
Institute**   CFLRI
185 Somerset St. W., Suite 201
Ottawa, ON K2P 0J2
(613) 233-5528
Fax: (613) 233-5536
E-mail: info@cflri.ca
<http://activeliving.ca/cflri/cflri.html>

Canadian Guidance and Counselling Association
220 Laurier Ave. W., Suite 600
Ottawa, ON K1P 5Z9
(613) 230-4236
Fax: (613) 230-5884

Canadian Liver Foundation   CLF
National Office
#200, 365 Bloor St. E.
Toronto, ON M4W 3L4
(416) 964-1953
1-800-563-5483
Fax: (416) 964-0024
E-mail: clf@liver.ca
<http://www.liver.ca>

Canadian Living: Your Family Magazine
25 Sheppard Ave. W., Suite 100
Toronto ON M2N 6S7
(416) 733-7600
1-800-265-5371
Fax: (416) 733-3398
E-mail: letters@canadianliving.com
<http://www.canadianliving.com>
Christine Langlois is Canadian Living*'s Health
and Family editor and moderator of its Health
and Family forum online.*

Canadian Living Foundation CLF
Breakfast for Learning
25 Sheppard Ave. W., Suite 100
Toronto ON M2N 6S7
(416) 218-3540
1-800-627-7922
Fax: (416) 218-3631
E-mail: clf@sympatico.ca
<http://www.canadianliving.com/bfl>
*Founded in 1992, CLF is the only national
organization promoting and helping to fund
school nutrition programs.*

Canadian Lung Association
#508, 1900 City Park Dr.
Gloucester, ON K1J 1A3
(613) 747-6776
Fax: (613) 747-7430
E-mail: info@lung.ca
<http://www.lung.ca>

Canadian MedicAlert Foundation
250 Ferrand Dr., Suite 301
Toronto, ON M3C 3G8
(416) 696-0267 or (416) 696-0142
National English: 1-800-668-1507
Toll-free Fax: 1-800-392-8422
E-mail: medinfo@medicalert.ca
<http://www.medicalert.ca>

Canadian Mental Health Association   CMHA
2160 Yonge St., 3rd Floor
Toronto, ON M4S 2Z3
(416) 484-7750
Fax: (416) 484-4617
E-mail: cmhanet@interlog.com
<http://www.icomm.ca/cmhacan>

Canadian National Institute for the Blind   CNIB
1929 Bayview Ave.
North York, ON   M4G 3E8
(416) 486-2500
E-mail: irc@lib.cnib.ca
<http://www.cnib.ca>

Canadian Naturopathic Association
4174 Dundas St. W., Suite 303
Toronto, ON   M8X 1X3
(416) 233-1043
Fax: (416) 233-2924
E-mail: cdnnds@interlog.com
The professional association of registered naturopaths in B.C., Man., Ont., and Sask.

Canadian Network for New Media Learning
Suite 1002, 10611–98 Ave.
Edmonton, AB   T5K 2P7
(403) 424-4433
Fax: (403) 424-4888
E-mail: clc@mrg.ab.ca
<http://www.mrg.ab.ca/clc>
Offers services and courses for distance education learners.

Canadian Paediatric Society   CPS
2204 Walkley Rd., Suite 100
Ottawa, ON   K1G 4G8
(613) 526-9397
Fax: (613) 526-3332
E-mail: info@cps.ca
<http://www.cps.ca>

Canadian Parents Online
<http://www.canadianparents.com>
Offers chat forums, product information, and Canadian experts to answer questions.

Canadian Parks and Recreation Association   CP/RA
1600 James Naismith Dr., Suite 306
Gloucester, ON   K1B 5N4
(613) 748-5651
Fax: (613) 748-5854
E-mail: cpra@activeliving.ca
<http://activeliving.ca/activeliving/cpra.html>

Canadian Publishers' Council   CPC
250 Merton St., Suite 203
Toronto, ON   M4S 1B1
(416) 322-7011
Fax: (416) 322-6999
<http://www.pubcouncil.ca/>
Provides contact info on member publishers and their catalogues of books and learning materials.

Canadian Red Cross
National Office, 1800 Alta Vista Dr.
Ottawa, ON   K1G 4J5
Western Zone: (403) 541-4400
Ontario: (905) 890-1000
Quebec: (514) 362-2929
Atlantic: (506) 648-5000
<http://www.redcross.ca>

Canadian Resource Centre on Children and Youth   CRCCY
180 Argyle Ave., Suite 316
Ottawa, ON   K2P 1B7
(613) 788-5102
Fax: (613) 788-5075
E-mail: crccy@newforce.ca
<http://magi.com/~crccy/>
The CRCCY amalgamates the resource collections of the former Canadian Council on Children and Youth and the former Canadian Child Welfare Association.

Canadian Sleep Society   CSS
380 Yonge St., Suite 5055
Toronto, ON   M3N 3N1
(416) 483-6260
<http://bisleep.medsch.ucla.edu/WFSRS/CSS/css.html>
A professional association of clinicians, scientists, and technologists.

Canadian Teachers' Federation   CTF
110 Argyle Ave.
Ottawa, ON   K2P 1B4
(613) 232-1505
Fax: (613) 232-1886
E-mail: info@ctf-fce.ca
<http://ctf-fce.ca>

Canadian Toy Testing Council
22 Hamilton Ave. N.
Ottawa, ON K1Y 1B6
(613) 729-7101
Fax: (613) 729-7185
<http://www.toy-testing.org/>
The 1998 Toy Report lists 1,700 toys, including educational software.

CanConnect
<http://canconnect.globalx.net/>
Part of Industry Canada's SchoolNet, CanConnect offers such programs as Computers for Schools and the SchoolNet Youth Employment Strategy.

Centre for Addiction and Mental Health
In 1998 incorporated the
Addiction Research Foundation   ARF
33 Russell St.
Toronto, ON M5S 2S1
INFO-ARF: (416) 595-6111
Ontario only: 1-800-463-6273
<http://www.arf.org/>
One of North America's pre-eminent facilities for research into addictions. Offers an Information Package on Youth and Alcohol.

Centre for Health Promotion
University of Toronto
The Banting Institute
100 College St., Room 207
Toronto, ON M5G 1L5
(416) 978-1809
Fax: (416) 971-1365
E-mail: centre.healthpromotion@utoronto.ca
<http://www.utoronto.ca/chp/>

Child & Family Canada   CFC
<http://www.cfc-efc.ca>
An umbrella organization committed to the well-being of Canada's children and their families.

Child Find Canada
PO Box 6611, RR4
Cornwall, PE C0A 1H0
(902) 626-3152
In Canada and U.S.: 1-800-387-7962
Fax: (902) 626-3153
E-mail: childcan@aol.com
<http://www.childfind.ca>

Childhood Cancer Foundation
Candlelighters Canada
55 Eglinton Ave. E., Suite 401
Toronto, ON M4P 1G8
(416) 489-6440
1-800-363-1062
E-mail: staff@candlelighters.ca
<http://www.candlelighters.ca>
Offers a TeenNetwork.

Child Welfare League of Canada   CWLC
180 Argyle Ave., Suite 312
Ottawa, ON K2P 1B7
(613) 235-4412
Fax: (613) 788-5075
E-mail: cwlc@newforce.ca
<http://www.cwlc.ca>
The CWLC's 71 member agencies offer services and programs on issues relating to the well-being of children and youth.

The Children's Wish Foundation of Canada
95 Bayly St. W., Suite 404
Ajax, ON L1S 7K8
(905) 426-5656
1-800-267-WISH
Fax: (905) 426-4111
E-mail: wishes.national@sympatico.ca
<http://www.childrenswish.ca>
Dedicated to fulfilling a favourite wish for children ages 3 to 17, afflicted with a high-risk, life-threatening illness.

The Clarke Institute of Psychiatry
250 College St.
Toronto, ON M5T 1R8
(416) 979-2221
E-mail: webmaster@cs.clarke-inst.on.ca
<http://www.clarke-inst.on.ca/>
A division of the Centre for Addiction and Mental Health.
Child and Family Studies Centre
(416) 979-2221 x 2255
One of Canada's largest child centres for research, education and treatment of attention deficit disorder, the epidemiology of language disorders, learning disabilities and anxiety, gender identity disturbance, oppositional defiant disorders, and children at risk for mood disorders.

The College of
Family Physicians of Canada   CFPC
2630 Skymark Ave.
Mississauga, ON L4W 5A4
(905) 629-0900
Fax: (905) 629-0893
E-mail: info@cfpc.ca
<http://www.cfpc.ca>

Communities against Youth Violence
621 Milverton Blvd.
Toronto, ON M4C 1X8
(416) 422-4806
1-800-498-CAYV
Fax: (416) 422-1579
E-mail: cayv@interlog.com
<http://www.interlog.com/~cayv>

Concerns Canada
Alcohol and Drug Concerns, Inc.
4500 Sheppard Ave. E., Suite 112
Toronto, ON M1S 3R6
(416) 293-3400
Fax: (416) 293-1142
E-mail: concerns@sympatico.ca
*Offers services, publications, and educational
programs for drug education in grades 4–6
and 7–8.*

Council of Ministers of Education, Canada
252 Bloor St. W., Suite 5-200
Toronto, ON M5S 1V5
(416) 964-2551
Fax: (416) 964-2296
E-mail: cmec@cmec.ca
<http://www.cmec.ca>
*Provides links to provincial ministries and
departments of education.*

Crohn's and Colitis Foundation of Canada
#301, 21 St. Clair Ave. E.
Toronto, ON M4T 1L9
(416) 920-5035
1-800-387-1479
E-mail: ccfc@netcom.ca
<http://www.ccfc.ca>

Dads Can
St. Mary's Annex, Room 411
35 Grosvenor St.
London, ON N6A 1Y6
(519) 646-6095/1-888-DADS CAN
E-mail: ncampbell@julian.uwo.ca
<http://www.dadscan.org>
Promotes responsible and involved fathering.

Dietitians of Canada
480 University Ave., Suite 604
Toronto, ON M5G 1V2
(416) 596-0857
Fax: (416) 596-0603
E-mail: centralinfo@dietitians.ca
<http://www.dietitians.ca>

Easter Seals Society Canada
511-90 Eglinton Ave. E.
Toronto, ON M4P 2Y3
(416) 544-1715
Fax: (416) 932-9844
E-mail: national.council@esmodnc.org

Educational Computing Organization
of Ontario   ECOO
<http://www.oise.on.ca/ecoo>

Epilepsy Canada
#745, 1470 rue Peel
Montréal, QC H3A 1T1
(514) 845-7855/1-800-860-5499
Fax: (514) 845-7866
E-mail: epilepsy@epilepsy.ca
<http://www.epilepsy.ca>

Families in Transition
2 Carlton St., Suite 917
Toronto, ON M5B 1J3
(416) 585-9151
For families going through divorce.

Family Service Canada
383 Parkdale Ave., Suite 404
Ottawa, ON K1Y 4R4
(613) 722-9006/1-800-668-7808
Fax: (613) 722-8610
E-mail: fsc@igs.net
<http://www.cfc-efc.ca/fsc/>
A network of over 100 family-serving member
agencies in communities across Canada.

Hamilton Health Sciences Corporation
Family Resource Centre
Children's Hospital at Chedoke McMaster
Box 2000, Hamilton, ON L8N 3Z5
(905) 521-2632
<http://www.cmh.on.ca/~frc/frc.htm/>
Offers services and publications for parents.

The Hanen Centre
252 Bloor St. W., Suite 3-390
Toronto, ON M5S 1V5
(416) 921-1073
Outside GTA: 1-800-380-3355
Fax: (416) 921-1225
E-mail: info@hanen.org
<http://www.hanen.org>
Offers program materials, workshops and pre-
sentations, and training for speech-language
pathologists as well as for parents and early
childhood teachers of children with developmen-
tal delays and specific language impairment.

Health Canada
<http://www.hc-sc.gc.ca>
Health Protection Branch   HPB
Product Safety Directorate
Vancouver (604) 666-5003
Toronto (416) 973-4705
Montreal (514) 646-1353
Health Promotion & Programs Branch   HPPB
<http://www.hc-sc.gc.ca/hppb/>
Canadian Hospital Injury Reporting and
Prevention Program   CHIRPP
National Clearinghouse on Family Violence
1-800-267-1291
Not a crisis line; offers referrals and
information on family violence.

Publications Branch
Health Canada
Ottawa, ON K1A 0K9
(613) 954-5995
Also check the Blue Pages for regional offices of
Health Canada.

Heart and Stroke Foundation
National Office
222 Queen St., Suite 1402
Ottawa, ON K1P 5V9
(613) 569-4361
<http://www.hsf.ca>

HeartSmart Kids
<http://www.hsf.ca/funpack/index.html>
Check the 1998 Heart and Stroke Report Card
on the Health of Canada's Kids.

The C.M. Hincks Treatment Centre for
Children's Mental Health
440 Jarvis St.
Toronto, ON   M4Y 2H4
(416) 924-1164
Fax: (416) 924-8208
E-mail: centre.hincks@utoronto.ca
<http://www.interlog.com/~hincks/homex.htm>
Hincks-Dellcrest Centre
Specializes in the treatment of adolescents who
suffer from mental illness and offers support to
their families.

The Hospital for Sick Children
555 University Ave.
Toronto, ON M5G 1X8
(416) 813-1500
<http://www.sickkids.on.ca/>
Adolescent Substance Abuse Outreach Program
(416) 813-5265
Centre for Health Information & Promotion
(416) 813-5819
Poison Information Centre
1-800-268-9017

Info-Cult
5655 Park Ave., Suite 208
Montréal, QC H2V 4H2
(514) 274-2333
Provides information on cultic thinking and
support for ex-cult members and their families.

Katimavik
édifice du port de Montréal
L'aile 2, Office 3020, Cité du Havre
Montréal, QC H3C 3R5
1-888-525-1503
E-mail: katimavik@camitael.com
<http://www.katimavik.org/>
*A community service and alternative training
program for youth ages 17 to 21.*

The Kidney Foundation of Canada
5165 Sherbrooke St. W., Suite 300
Montréal, QC H4A 1T6
(514) 369-4806
1-800-361-7494
Fax: (514) 369-2472
E-mail: comm-mktg@kidney.ca
<http://www.kidney.ca>

Kids Help Foundation
439 University Ave., Suite 300
Toronto, ON M5G 1Y8
How to help, to volunteer, to contribute:
(416) 586-5437
Fax: (416) 586-0651
E-mail: info@kidshelp.sympatico.ca
<http://kidshelp.sympatico.ca>

Kids Help Phone/Jeunesse J'écoute
1-800-668-6868
*A national Toronto-based, bilingual telephone
service available 24 hours a day free of charge
to any child or teenager in distress.*

**Learning Disabilities Association
of Canada** LDAC
323 Chapel St., Suite 200
Ottawa, ON K1N 7Z2
(613) 238-5721
Fax: (613) 235-5391
E-mail: ldactaac@fox.nstn.ca
<http://educ.queensu.ca/~lda>
LDAC publishes helpful materials for parents.

Media Awareness Network
1500 Merivale Rd., 3rd Floor
Nepean, ON K2E 6Z5
(613) 224-7721
1-800-896-3342
Fax: (613) 224-1958
E-mail: info@media.awareness.ca

<http://www.media-awareness.ca>
*A Canadian nonprofit organization offering on
its Web site resources to help teachers, students,
parents, and others better understand media
information, electronic entertainment, and the
new technologies.*

Multiple Sclerosis Society of Canada
#1000, 250 Bloor St. E.
Toronto, ON M4W 3P9
(416) 922-6065
1-800-268-7582
E-mail: info@mssoc.ca
<http://www.mssoc.ca>

Muscular Dystrophy Association of Canada
#900, 2345 Yonge St.
Toronto, ON M4P 2E5
(416) 488-0030
1-800-567-CURE
Fax: (416) 488-7523
<http://www.mdac.ca>
*Offers information on neuro-muscular disorders
and on regional offices and chapters.*

National Eating Disorder Information Centre
200 Elizabeth St., College Wing 1-211
Toronto, ON M5G 2C4
(416) 340-4156
Fax: (416) 340-4736
<http://www.infonautica.com/nedic>

National Institute of Nutrition   NIN
265 Carling Ave., Suite 302
Ottawa, ON K1S 2E1
(613) 235-3355
Fax: (613) 235-7032
E-mail: nin@nin.ca
<http://www.nin.ca>
*Offers a wide range of information on food and
nutrition to Canadian consumers.*

The Neurological Centre
2805 Kingsway
Vancouver, BC V5R 5H9
(604) 451-5511
E-mail: tnc@iSTAR.ca
<http://home.iSTAR.ca/~tnc>
*Looks after children with physical challenges or
developmental delays.*

New Directions
542 Mount Pleasant Rd., Suite 203
Toronto, ON M4S 2M7
(416) 487-5317
Fax: (416) 487-5170
An organization focused on divorce and remarriage.

One Parent Families Association of Canada
National Office
6979 Yonge St., Suite 203
Willowdale, ON M2M 3X9
(416) 226-0062
E-mail: oneparent@titan.tcn.net
<http://www.tcn.net/~oneparent>

Osteoporosis Society of Canada
33 Laird Dr.
Toronto, ON M4G 3S9
(416) 696 2663/1-800-463-6842

Parentbooks
201 Harbord St.
Toronto, ON M5S 1H6
(416) 537-8334/1-800-209-9182
Fax: (416) 537-9499

Parenting Today
2762 Wall St.
Vancouver, BC V5K 1A9
(604) 258-9074
Fax: (604) 258-9075
E-mail: k_lynn@home.com
<http://members.home.net/kathylynn>
Offers parent education services.

Parents against Drugs
7 Hawksdale Rd.
Toronto, ON M3K 1W3
(416) 395-4970
E-mail: pad@sympatico.ca
<http://www3.sympatico.ca/pad/>
Provides education on drug abuse, and supports adolescent drug users and their families.

Parents, Families and Friends of Lesbians and Gays   P-FLAG
Check for local groups in the Business Section of your telephone book.
<http://www.pflag.ca/index.htm>

Parents of Multiple Births Association   POMBA
240 Graff Ave.
Stratford, ON N5A 7V6
(519) 272-2203
E-mail: office@pomba.org
<http://www.pomba.org>

Parents without Partners
Check for local groups in the Business Section of your telephone book.

Planned Parenthood Federation of Canada
1 Nicholas St., Suite 430
Ottawa, ON K1N 7B7
(613) 241-4474
Fax: (613) 241-7550
E-mail: admin@ppfc.ca
<http://www.ppfc.ca>

The Renascent Centres
1240 Bay St., Suite 404
Toronto, ON M5R 2A7
(416) 964-1207
<http://www.cleanandsober.com>
An Ontario resource that offers counselling and a 21-day live-in program at no charge for alcohol and addiction treatment for men and women.

Ronald McDonald Children's Charities of Canada
McDonald's Place
Toronto, ON M3C 3L4
(416) 443-1000/1-800-387-8808
Fax: (416) 446-3650
Provides information on R.M. Houses across Canada.

**Royal Canadian Mounted Police   RCMP
Drug Awareness Program**
(613) 993-2501
Missing Children's Registry
PO Box 8885
Ottawa, ON K1G 3M8
(613) 993-1525
Fax: (613) 993-5430
E-mail: mcr.nps@sympatico.ca
Child CyberSEARCH™ Canada
1-888-326-5352
<http://www.childcybersearch.org/>

Safe Communities Foundation   SCF
64 Charles St. E., Suite 201
Toronto, ON M4Y 1T1
(416) 964-0008
Fax: (416) 964-0089
E-mail: info @safecommunities.ca
<http://www.safecommunities.ca>
Launched in 1996, SCF focuses on community-
wide, long-term health and safety programs.

St. John Ambulance Canada   SJA
National Headquarters
312 Laurier Avenue E.
Ottawa, ON K1N 6P6
(613) 236-7461
Fax: (613) 236-2425
E-mail: nhq@nhq.sja.ca
<http://www.sja.ca>
Check for local branches in the Business Section
of your telephone book. SJA offers First Aid
products, training, and services.

**The Sex Information and Education Council of
Canada**   SIECCAN
850 Coxwell Ave.
Toronto, ON M4C 5R1
(416) 466-5304
Fax: (416) 978-8532
E-mail: sieccan@web.net
A publicly funded council of sexuality
researchers and counsellors.

Sleep/Wake Disorders Canada   SWDC
National Office
3080 Yonge St., Suite 5055
Toronto, ON M4N 3N1
(416) 483-9654/1-800-387-9253
Fax: (416) 483-7081
E-mail: swdc@globalserve.net
<http://www.geocities.com/~sleepwake/>
A national charitable organization providing
information, encouraging research, and
establishing self-help groups.

SmartRisk Foundation
658 Danforth Ave., Suite 301
Toronto, ON M4J 5B9
(416) 463-9878/1-888-537-7777
E-mail: choose@smartrisk.ca
<http://www.smartrisk.ca>
A national injury-prevention organization.

Sport Medicine and Science Council of Canada
1600 James Naismith Dr., Suite 314
Gloucester, ON K1B 5N4
(613) 748-5671
Fax: (613) 748-5729
E-mail: smscc@smscc.ca
<http://www.smscc.ca>

Transport Canada
<http://www.tc.gc.ca>
Canadian Motor Vehicle Safety Standards
<http://www.tc.gc.ca/actsregs/mvsa/tocmvs.htm>
Keep Them Safe
<http://www.engr.usask.ca/tc/crs/keep.html>
Road Safety Information Centre
<http://www.engr.usask.ca/tc/tcanada/rsic.html>
Road Safety Directorate
330 Sparks St., Tower C
Ottawa, ON K1A 0N5
(613) 998-1978
1-800-833-0371
E-mail: RoadSafetyWebMail@tc.gc.ca
<http://www.engr.usask.ca/tc/tcanada/rsd.html>

The Vanier Institute of the Family
94 Centrepointe Dr.
Nepean, ON K2G 6B1
(613) 228-8500
Fax: (613) 228-8007
E-mail: vif@compuserve.com
<http://www.cfc-efc.ca/vif>

World Health Organization
<http://www.who.ch/>

World of Dreams Foundation Canada
999 De Maisonneuve W., Suite 675
Montréal, QC H3A 3L4
(514) 985-3003
1-800-567-7254
Fulfills dreams for critically and chronically ill
children across Canada.

YM/YWCA
Check for local branches in the Business Section
of your telephone book.

Selected Canadian Resources for Parents

alphabetized by title

All shapes and sizes: Promoting fitness and self-esteem in your overweight child, Teresa Pitman and Miriam Kaufman, MD. 1994. HarperCollins, Toronto.

Anaphylaxis: A handbook for school boards. (Booklet, 58 pages). Canadian School Boards Association, Ottawa. (613) 235-3724.

Anne Lindsay's new light cooking, Anne Lindsay in cooperation with Denise Beatty, RD, and the Canadian Medical Association. 1998. Ballantine Books, Toronto.

Battling the school yard bully: How to raise an assertive child in an aggressive world, Kim Zarzour. 1994. HarperCollins, Toronto.

Becoming vegetarian: The complete guide to adopting a healthy vegetarian diet, Vesanto Melina, RD, Brenda Davis, RD, and Victoria Harrison, RD. 1994. Macmillan Canada, Toronto.

Beyond the mirage: A documentary video on the cult phenomenon, by Info-Cult and Vidéographe, directed by Jorge Martinez. Vidéographe-Distribution. (514) 521-2116.

The Body image trap: Understanding and rejecting body image myths, Marion Crook. 1991. Self-Counsel Press, North Vancouver, B.C.

Bone vivant! Jan Main with the Osteoporosis Society of Canada. 1997. Macmillan Canada, Toronto.

- Canada's food guide to healthy eating. 1992
- Using the food guide.
- Using food labels to choose foods for healthy eating
- Food guide facts: Background for educators and communicators

- Vitalité: Healthy eating and self-esteem: The body-image connection

Publications, Health Canada
Ottawa, ON K1A 0K9
(613) 954-5995

The Canadian allergy and asthma handbook, rev. and updated by Canadian allergists Dr. Barry Zimmerman, Dr. Milton Gold, Dr. Sasson Lavi, Dr. Stephen Feanny, ed. by Eleanor Brownridge, RD, FCDA. 1996. Random House Canada, Toronto.

The Canadian babysitter's handbook: The essential guide for everyone entrusted with the care of babies & young children, Caroline Greene, St. John Ambulance. 1995. Random House Canada, Toronto.

Canadian child welfare law: Children, families, and the state, ed. Nicholas Bala, Joseph P. Hornick, and Robin Vogl. 1991. Thompson Educational Publishing, Toronto.

Canadian Living's Best: Kids in the kitchen, 30 Minutes and light, Vegetarian dishes (and others in the series), Elizabeth Baird and the food writers and test kitchen of *Canadian Living* magazine. 1998. Ballantine Books, Toronto.

Career intelligence: Mastering the new work and personal realities, Barbara Moses. 1997. Stoddart, Toronto.

Changes in you and me: A book about puberty, mostly for boys. 1997.
Changes in you and me: A book about puberty, mostly for girls. 1997.
Both by Paulette Bourgeois and Martin Wolfish, MD. Consultant: Kim Martyn. Illus. by Louise Philips and Kam Yu. A Somerville House Book, Andrews and Mcmeel, A Universal Press Syndicate Company, Kansas City, KA.

Child care: A practical guide, 3rd ed. 1991. St. John Ambulance.

Children as peacemakers, Esther Sokolov Fine (York University), Ann Laccy, and Joan Baer. 1995. Teacher to Teacher Series, Heinemann, Portsmouth, NH.

Children with school problems: A physician's manual, ed. A. Mervyn Fox, MD, BS, FRCPC, MRCPCH, DCH, and William J. Mahoney, MD, FRCPC. 1998. Canadian Paediatric Society, Ottawa. (Professional)

A Child's grief, videocassette, 54 min. English or French. 1994. Bereaved Families of Ontario. Magic Lantern Communications Ltd., Oakville, Ont. 1-800-263-1818.

Child well being: A guide for parents and children. An animated interactive CD-ROM. 1996. Canadian Paediatric Society, Ottawa.

Cinderella revisited: How to survive your step-family without a fairy godmother, Peter Graham Marshall. 1993. Whitecap Books Ltd., North Vancouver, B.C.

Clueless in the kitchen: A cookbook for teens, Evelyn Raab. 1998. Key Porter Books, Toronto.

The Complete breast book, June Engel and the University of Toronto Faculty of Medicine. 1996. Key Porter Books, Toronto. (Reference)

The Complete Canadian health guide, June Engel and The University of Toronto Faculty of Medicine. 1993. Key Porter Books, Toronto. (Reference)

Cooking vegetarian, Vesanto Melina, RD, and Joseph Forest. 1996. Macmillan Canada, Toronto.

Could do better: Why children underachieve and what to do about it, Harvey Mandel. 1995. HarperCollins, Toronto.

Crohn's disease & ulcerative colitis, Fredric Saibil, MD. 1996. Key Porter Books, Toronto.

Cybersense and nonsense. 1998. A computer-animated game to develop players' critical capacities. Downloadable from Media Awareness Network: <http:www.media-awareness.ca>

Dads Can Video Series:
The Masculine mystique   (Images of men in society). 24 min. 1997.

Taking our measure as dads   (Fathers with older children). 24 min. 1997. Magic Lantern Communications Ltd., Oakville, Ont. 1-800-263-1818

Dear diary, I'm pregnant, Anrenée Englander. 1997. Annick Press, Toronto.

Easy for you to say: Q & A's for teens living with chronic illness or disability, Miriam Kaufman, MD. 1995. Key Porter Books, Toronto.

Eating for performance, videocassette, 24 min. Sport Nutrition Advisory Committee, Sport Medicine Council of Canada, Ottawa.

Ghosts from the nursery: Tracing the roots of violence, Robin Karr-Morse and Meredith Wiley. 1998. Publisher's Group West Inc., Toronto.

God in the classroom: The controversial issue of religion in Canada's schools, Lois Sweet. 1997. McClelland & Stewart, Toronto.

The Green teen: Help for parents in preparing meals for a vegetarian teenager, Valerie McRae. 1995. Children's & Women's Health Centre of British Columbia, Vancouver, B.C.

Growing up in Canada: National longitudinal survey of children and youth, D. Ross, K. Scott, M. Kelly. 1996. Human Resources Development Canada and Statistics Canada, Ottawa.

Harassment: Take positive action, Scarborough Board of Education brochure. Student and Community Services, (416) 396-7516, Toronto.

The HeartSmart shopper: Nutrition on the run, Ramona Josephson. 1997. Douglas & McIntyre, Vancouver, B.C.

HIV/AIDS and child care: Fact book and facilitator's guide, A project of the Canadian Child Care Federation; funded by Health Canada through the National AIDS strategy. 1995. (Professional)

How to break bad news: A guide for health care professionals, Robert Buckman, MD, and Yvonne Kason. 1992. Johns Hopkins University Press, (University of Toronto Press, Toronto).

I can't stop crying: It's so hard when someone you love dies, Rev. John D. Martin and Frank D. Ferris, MD. Foreword by Robert Buckman, MD, PhD. 1992. Key Porter Books, Toronto.

I don't know what to say: How to help and support someone who is dying, Dr. Robert Buckman. 1988; 16th printing, 1998. Key Porter Books, Toronto.

I'll be the parent. You be the kid, Paul Kropp. 1998. Random House of Canada, Toronto.

Interior passages: Obesity and transformation, Francine Saillant, translated by Myriam Jarsky. 1994, 1996. Second Story Press, Toronto.

An Introduction to food and weight problems, National Eating Disorder Information Centre.

Keys to parenting your anxious child, Katharina Manassis, MD, FRCP, The Hospital for Sick Children. 1996. Barron's Educational Series, Inc., Hauppage, N.Y.

Kid culture: Children & adults & popular culture, Kathleen McDonnell. 1994. Second Story Press, Toronto.

The Lactose-free family cookbook, Jan Main. 1996. Macmillan Canada, Toronto.

Learning Disabilities Association publications
A guide to understanding learning and behavior problems in children
Making the most of the law: Education and the child with disabilities

Minding the set: Making your television work for you and your family. 1994. The Alliance for Children and Television with Rogers Cablesystems.

The Mother zone: Love, sex, and laundry in the modern family, Marni Jackson. 1992. Macfarlane Walter & Ross, Toronto.

Mothering teens: Understanding the adolescent years, ed. by Miriam Kaufman, MD. 1997. gynergy books, Charlottetown.

New guide to prescription and over-the-counter drugs, Canadian Medical Association. 1996. Reader's Digest, Montreal, Que.

Now I know why tigers eat their young, Peter Marshall. 1992. Whitecap Books, North Vancouver, B.C.

Nurturing independent learners: Helping students take charge of their learning, Donald Meichenbaum (University of Waterloo) and Andrew Biemiller (University of Toronto). 1998. Brookline Books, Cambridge, Mass.

Ontario student drug use survey, 1997, Addiction Research Foundation, Toronto.

Our strength for tomorrow: Valuing our children, Report on Child Health. May 1997. Based on the Task Force on Child Health, The College of Family Physicians of Canada.

Out of the garden: Toys and children's culture in the age of TV marketing, Stephen Kline. 1993. Garamond Press, Toronto.

Privacy playground: The first adventure of three little cyberpigs. 1998. A computer-animated game to develop players' critical capacities. Downloadable from Media Awareness Network: <http:www.media-awareness.ca>

Racism in Canadian schools, M. Ibrahim Alladin. 1996. Harcourt Brace, Toronto.

The Real guide to Canadian universities, ed. Sara Borins. 1994. Key Porter Books, Toronto.

Really cookin', Carol Ferguson. 1994. Maxwell Macmillan Canada, Toronto.

Religion, Myrtle Langley. 1996. Eyewitness Books, Stoddart, Toronto.

Sleep problems in children: A parent's guide, The Canadian Sleep Society.

Sleep thieves: An eye-opening exploration
into the science and mysteries of sleep,
Stanley Coren. 1996. Free Press, New York
(Prentice-Hall Canada, Toronto).

Social skills and learning disabilities, Jean B.
Schumaker and Donald D. Deshler. 1995.
Learning Disabilities Association of America
Newsbriefs.

Speaking of SEX: Are you ready to answer the
questions your kids will ask? Meg Hickling, RN.
1996; 3rd printing 1998. Northstone Publishing
Inc., Kelowna, B.C.

Surviving your partner's job loss, Jill Jukes
and Ruthan Rosenberg. 1992. Murray Axmith,
Toronto.

Teenage troubles: Youth and deviance in Canada,
Julian Tanner. 1997. ITP Nelson, Toronto.

Teen trends: A nation in motion, Reginald Bibby
and Donald Posterski. 1992. Stoddart, Toronto.

The Vegetarian edge, 1995. British Columbia
Ministry of Health and Ministry Responsible for
Seniors, Victoria.

What every babysitter should know: Babysitting
course, 2nd ed. 1993. St. John Ambulance.

When girls feel fat: Helping girls through
adolescence, Sandra Susan Friedman. 1997.
HarperCollins, Toronto.

When in doubt, eat broccoli, Liz Pearson. 1998.
Penguin Books, Toronto.

Worldviews: The challenge of choice,
Ken Badley. 1996. Irwin Publishing, Toronto.
*A resource for exploring contemporary ethical
issues with teenagers in the context of world
faiths.*

Your child's best shot: A parent's guide to
vaccination. 1997. Canadian Paediatric Society,
Ottawa.

Youth violence: How to protect your kids,
Kevin Guest, Donald Cowper and Andrew
Haynes. 1997. Communities against Youth
Violence, Toronto.

Recommended Immunization Schedule for Infants and Children (including teens)

NATIONAL ADVISORY COMMITTEE ON IMMUNIZATION (NACI),
HEALTH PROTECTION BRANCH, HEALTH CANADA

Routine Immunization Schedule for Infants and Children

Age at vaccination	DTaP[1]	Inactivated polio vaccine	Hib[2]	MMR	Td[3]	Hep B[4] (3 doses)
Birth						
2 months	x	x	x			
4 months	x	x	x			
6 months	x	(x)[5]	x			Infancy
12 months				x		or
18 months	x	x	x	(x)[6] or		preadolescence
4–6 years	x	x		(x)[6]		(9–13 years)
14–16 years					x	

DTaP	Diphtheria, tetanus, pertussis (acellular) vaccine
Hib	*Haemophilus influenzae* type b conjugate vaccine
MMR	Measles, mumps and rubella vaccine
Td	Tetanus and diphtheria toxoid, "adult type"
Hep B	Hepatitis B vaccine

Routine Immunization Schedule for Children under 7 Years of Age Not Immunized in Early Infancy

Timing	DTaP[1]	Inactivated polio vaccine	Hib	MMR	Td[3]	Hep B[4] (3 doses)
First visit	x	x	x	x [7]		
2 months later	x	x	(x)[8]	(x)[6]		
2 months later	x	(x)[5]				
6–12 months later	x	x	(x)[8]			Preadolescence
4–6 years[9]	x	x				(9–13 years)
14–16 years					x	

Routine Immunization Schedule for Children 7 Years of Age or Older Not Immunized in Early Infancy

Timing	Td[3]	Inactivated polio vaccine	MMR	Hep B[4] (3 doses)
First visit	x	x	x	
2 months later	x	x	(x)[6]	
6–12 months later	x	x		Preadolescence
10 years later	x			(9–13 years)

DTaP	Diphtheria, tetanus, pertussis (acellular) vaccine
Hib	*Haemophilus influenzae* type b conjugate vaccine
MMR	Measles, mumps and rubella vaccine
Td	Tetanus and diphtheria toxoid, "adult type"
Hep B	Hepatitis B vaccine

NOTES:

1. DTaP (diphtheria, tetanus, acellular or component pertussis) vaccine is the preferred vaccine for all doses in the vaccination series, including completion of the series in children who have received one or more doses of DPT (whole cell) vaccine.

2. Hib schedule shown is for PRP-T or HbOC vaccine. If PRP-OMP, give at two, four and twelve months of age.

3. Td (tetanus and diphtheria toxoid), a combined adsorbed "adult type" preparation for use in persons seven years of age or older, contains less diphtheria toxoid than preparations given to younger children and is less likely to cause reactions in older persons.

4. Hepatitis B vaccine can be routinely given to infants or preadolescents, depending on the provincial/territorial policy; three doses at zero, one and six month intervals are preferred. The second dose should be administered at least one month after the first dose, and the third dose should be administered at least four months after the first dose, and at least two months after the second dose.

5. This dose is not needed routinely, but can be included for convenience.

6. A second dose of MMR is recommended, at least one month after the first dose given. For convenience, options include giving it with the next scheduled vaccination at eighteen months of age or with school entry (4–6 years) vaccinations (depending on the provincial/territorial policy), or at any intervening age that is practicable.

7. Delay until subsequent visit if child is under twelve months of age.

8. Recommended schedule and number of doses depend on the product used and the age of the child when vaccination is begun. Not required past age five.

9. Omit these doses if the previous doses of DTaP and polio were given after the fourth birthday.

Summary of Selected Immunization for Adults

Teenagers and young adults require special attention. Some may not have received recommended vaccines while others may have received vaccines of lower potency than those currently available. Given the infrequency with which this group seeks medical care, practitioners and health officials should use every opportunity to review and update their protection.

Vaccine	Indication	Further doses if risk continues
BCG	High-risk exposure	None
Hepatitis B	Occupational, lifestyle or environmental exposure	None
Japanese encephalitis	Travel to endemic area or other exposure risk	
Meningococcal	High-risk exposure	
Pertussis	Not indicated	
Poliomyelitis	Travel to endemic area or other exposure risk	
Rabies pre-exposure	Occupational or other risk	Every 2 years
Typhoid	High-risk exposure	Every 3–4 years
Yellow fever	Travel to endemic area or if required for foreign travel	Every 10 years

What Teens Can Do When without Parental Consent

Province	Buy tobacco	Buy alcohol	Drive (car & motorcycle)	Buy life insurance	Work	Leave school	Get married	Vote	Apply for SIN	Apply for passport
Alberta	18	18	16*	18	varies	16	16	18	birth	birth
British Columbia	19	19	16–19* g	18	15	16	19	18	birth	birth
Manitoba	18	18	16*	18	16	16	18	18	birth	birth
New Brunswick	19	19	16* g	18	16	18	18	18	birth	birth
Newfoundland	19	19	17	18	16	16	19	18	birth	birth
Northwest Territories	19	19	16	18	varies	16	19	19	birth	birth
Nova Scotia	19	19	16 g	18	16	16	19	18	birth	birth
Ontario	19	19	16 g	18	14	16	18	18	birth	birth
Prince Edward Island	18	19	16	18	16	16	18	18	birth	birth
Quebec	18	18	16*	18	varies	16	18	18	birth	birth
Saskatchewan	18	19	16 g	18	16	16	18	18	birth	birth
Yukon	19	19	16*	18	varies	16	19	19	birth	birth

g = Graduated licensing program

* = Parental consent

About the Editor

Christine Langlois is *Canadian Living*'s Health and Family Editor. She developed and edited three comprehensive books in the *Canadian Living Family Book* series, designed to guide parents through their child's development from pre-birth to leaving the nest. Christine makes regular media appearances on parenting and family health issues. She lives in Toronto with her husband and two teenagers.

About the Writers

Lynne Ainsworth, a writer specializing in education issues, lives in Hamilton, Ontario, with her husband and their two school-age boys.

Cindy Barrett, a writer and frequent contributor to *Canadian Living,* lives in Kemptville, Ontario, with her husband and two children.

Marcia Kaye, an award-winning senior writer with *Canadian Living*, specializes in parenting issues. She lives with her husband and their two children in Aurora, Ontario.

John Keating, a Toronto journalist and father of two, is a frequent contributor to *Canadian Living* on parenting and family issues.

Susan Noakes is a Toronto mother of two, a journalist, and chair of her local school council.

Susan Pedwell is an award-winning Toronto freelance writer, and the mother of two. She is a frequent contributor to *Canadian Living.*

Laura Pratt is a Toronto freelance writer and the mother of two. She is a frequent contributor to *Canadian Living.*

Mark Witten, an award-winning journalist from Toronto, is a frequent contributor to *Canadian Living* on family issues.

Acknowledgments

The writers and editors gratefully acknowledge the assistance of the following people:
Janet Abernethy, head of the Children's Department, Richview Library, Toronto Public Libraries; Reverend Doctor **Leslee Alfano**; **Greg Anderson**, school principal; **Ethel Archard**, manager of marketing and promotions, Canada Safety Council; Dr. **Harvey Armstrong**, child psychiatrist and founder, Parents for Youth Ltd.; **Marion Balla**, director, Adlerian Centre; Dr. **Leslie Balmer**, psychologist, private practitioner, and chair of the professional advisory committee of Bereaved Families of Ontario; **Frances Balodis**, director, Music for Young Children; **Lynn Barnhardt**, speech-language pathologist, Nipissing-Parry Sound Catholic School District; Dr. **Riva Bartell**, psychologist, Department of Educational Administration, Foundations and Psychology, University of Manitoba; **Dianne Bascombe**, executive director, Child and Family Canada; **Angèle Beaulieu**, communications officer, Canadian Fitness and Lifestyle Research Institute; **David Blankenhorn**, president, Institute for American Values; **Gordon Bullivant**, executive director, Foothills Academy; Dr. **Neil Campbell**, psychotherapist, founder and director, DADS CAN; **David Carmichael**, director of research and development, Ontario Physical and Health Education Association; Dr. **Mary Ann Carter**, psychologist, private practitioner; **Nancy Chapple**, coordinator, Thames Valley School Board; Dr. **Ester Cole**, supervising psychologist, Toronto District School Board, and chair of the Psychology Foundation of Canada; **Robert Conn**, president and C.E.O., SMARTRISK Foundation; Dr. **Betty Davies**, professor, School of Nursing, University of British Columbia; **Jeff Deane**, president, The Canadian Principals' Association; **Sharon Dembo**, child psychotherapist, private practitioner; **Sara Dimerman**, individual marital and family therapist and director, The Parent Education and Resource Centre; **Julie Dotsch**, coordinator, Early Child Diversity Network Canada; Dr. **Jim Duffy**, associate professor, Department of Psychology, Memorial University of Newfoundland; **Frank B. Edwards**, author, and publisher of Bungalo Books; **Resa Eisen**, family therapist and mediator, private practitioner;

Theresa Ferrari, youth development specialist, University of Florida; Dr. Graham Fishburne, professor, Department of Elementary Education, University of Alberta; Dr. Raymond Foui, sessional instructor, Department of Sociology, University of Manitoba; Pat Garrod, guidance counsellor, LaSalle Secondary School, Kingston; Dr. Mark Genuis, executive director, National Foundation for Family Research and Education; Dr. Robert Glossop, executive director of programs and research, the Vanier Institute of the Family; Mary Gordon, parenting expert, administrator of parenting programs, Toronto District School Board; Dr. Joan Grusec, professor, Department of Psychology, University of Toronto; Claudette Gudbranson, information officer, Learning Disabilities Association of Canada; Cheryl Hannebauer, former board member, BC Confederation of Parent Advisory Councils; Merylie Wade Houston, coordinator, Early Childhood Education Program, Seneca College; Helen Jones, spokesperson and co-founder, Association of Parent Support Groups of Ontario Inc.; Jill Jukes, consultant, Murray Axmith and Associates Inc.; Dr. Miriam Kaufman, pediatrician, The Hospital for Sick Children, associate professor, Department of Paediatrics at University of Toronto; Dr. Brenda Kenyon, director, Centre for Psychological Studies, University of Guelph; Patti Kirk, owner, Parentbooks; Dr. Stephen Kline, professor, School of Communication, Simon Fraser University; Dr. Leon Kuczynski, professor, Department of Family Relations and Applied Nutrition, University of Guelph; Joanne Lee, president, Association for Bright Children of Ontario; Dr. Donna Lero, professor, Department of Family Relations and Applied Nutrition, University of Guelph; Dr. Marc Lewis, associate professor, Department of Human Development and Applied Psychology, Ontario Institute for Studies in Education, University of Toronto; May Love, family counsellor, Renascent Centres; Brian Luhoway, counsellor, Alberta Alcohol and Drug Commission; Kathy Lynn, parenting educator; Dr. Katherina Manassis, staff psychiatrist, The Hospital for Sick Children, assistant professor, Department of Psychiatry, University of Toronto; Pauline Mantha, executive director, Learning Disabilities Association of Canada; Dr. Freda Martin, director, Hincks-Dellcrest Institute; Kathleen McDonnell, author of *Kid Culture*; Sue McGarvie, clinical sex therapist; Dr. Harold Minden, professor emeritus,

Counselling and Development Centre, York University; Faye Mishna, social worker, clinical director, Integra Foundation; Dr. Barbara Morrongiello, professor, Department of Psychology, University of Guelph; Dr. Deborah Norris, assistant professor of Family Studies, Department of Human Ecology, Mount Saint Vincent University; Dr. Caroline Piotrowski, developmental psychologist and assistant professor, Department of Family Studies, University of Manitoba; Ellie Presner, author of *Kidtips* and *Familytips*; Lee-Ann Boyd Pringle, doctoral student, Child Clinical Psychology, York University; Dyanne Rivers, former teacher; Dr. Stephen Rivers, psychologist, Adolescent Substance Abuse Outreach Program, The Hospital for Sick Children; Morina Reece, children and youth issue expert, Health Canada; Heather-jane Robertson, director of Professional Development Services, Canadian Teachers' Federation; Dr. Sandy Romanow, kinesiologist, private practitioner; Dr. Norman Rosenblood, psychoanalyst and associate professor, Faculties of Humanities, McMaster University; Dr. Art Salmon, National Technical Director, Participaction; Lori Santyr, special education resource teacher, Upper Canada District School Board; Judy Sarick, owner, Children's Book Store; Laura Sliwin, head of public relations, Canadian Association of Psychoanalytic Child Therapists, and private practitioner; Jerry Smith, president, Playtoy Industries, and former spokesperson for the Canadian Juvenile Products Association; Sheila Urban Smith, program leader, 4H Programs, Michigan State University; Dr. Rosemarie Tannock, Department of Psychiatry, The Hospital for Sick Children; Charlotte Teeple, executive director, Canadian Children's Book Centre; Helen Thomas, associate professor, School of Nursing, McMaster University; Nico Trocmé, associate professor, Faculty of Social Work, and director of the Bell Canada Child Welfare Research Unit, University of Toronto; Reverend Doctor Tracy Trothen; Spy Tsoukalas, research assistant, Canadian Council on Social Development; Kim Tytler, director of marketing and communications, Canadian Institute of Child Health; Susan Whermann, occupational therapist, private practitioner; Dr. Judith Wiener, professor, Department of Human Development and Applied Psychology, Ontario Institute for Studies in Education, University of Toronto; Kim Zarzour, author of *Battling the Schoolyard Bully*.

Index